This book is dedicated to you dad, as it was yc
the power of sacred numb

Front cover art by

Melanie Codling

www.melcosart.co.uk

Contents

Introduction – What is Numerology?

Numerology acknowledges and explains the power of sacred number energy in our lives. Sacred number energy is the language of the universe. Everything we see, hear, feel, smell touch in this 3D reality is fundamentally energy and number frequency. Energy waves from Radio waves to gamma rays are differentiated by their number frequency, they have different properties and purpose, just as atoms owe their purpose and properties to the number of protons, neutrons, and electrons present. Hydrogen has one proton and one electron, Carbon has six protons and six electrons, two very different elements with different purposes and properties, differentiated only by the number of protons and electrons within. Even the meanders of a river express themselves in calculatable number ratios.

It was the ancient civilisations that realised this truth as the ancient Egyptians and Babylonians used number energy to guide their lives. Later Pythagoras realised the significance and further researched the importance of sacred number in our lives... and so Pythagorean Numerology was born.

Pythagorean Numerology is based on the truth that we are all immortal spiritual beings having a 3D human experience on earth. We have multiple lives all with the purpose of our own personal spiritual evolution. We sit with our guide before each life time and discuss our ongoing issues, difficulties, and energies that we are yet to achieve that we may like to tackle in this incarnation. After consideration of these needs, we decide on our Life Path and Birthday energy to achieve in this life time. A person's Life Path number is calculated from total of their date of birth.

The numbers of your day of birth, need to be added together to achieve a single number or master number 11 or 22.

For example: if you were born on the 1st- 9th, you already have a single number. If you were born on the 11th or 22nd then you should leave these as they are to add at the end because master numbers are not reduced. If you were born on the 10th, 12th - 21st, or 23rd – 31st, then you need to add both numbers together to reach your single number, keep this figure to add at the end.

Then do the same with the month, use the single number for the month, e.g., January = 1, or add double numbers together to get the single digit

(October 10th = 1, December 12th = 3. If you were born in November (the 11th month) you should keep the 11, keep this figure to add at the end.

Finally add all the digits of your year of birth until you get a single or master number (11, 22).   Take the final digit from the year and add it to the final digits for the month and day to come to your Life Path Number.

For Example: A person born on the 29th of October 1975

Day Calculation – 2 + 9 = 11 (keep this, it's a master number)

Month Calculation - 1 + 0 = 1

Year Calculation – 1 + 9 + 7 + 5 = 22 (keep this, it's a master number)

Finally add these 3 final numbers (11 + 1 + 22 = 34/7

This person has a 34/7 Life Path with a 29/11 Birthday Number.

When we have remembered the next step in our spiritual evolution or Life Purpose (Life Path and Birthday Number) we decide which talents and motivations, that we have already accrued from other incarnations, to bring with us in our 'Tool Box.' Our 'Tool Box' contains the talents, motivations, and characteristics that we are going to bring with us to assist us in the achievement of our purpose.

I will elaborate on the 'Tool Box' energies in book 2 and 3. For now my focus for this book is the clarification of a person's 'Purpose' for this incarnation.

A bit about me

I studied Numerology in isolation from childhood but never shared my findings with others, I just sat alone in wonderment of the accuracy of the numbers when explaining the characteristics of others in my life and my own chart. For many years, my study was research based, theoretical and kept to myself until it was confirmed to me when, with the advent of compact discs or CD's, I obtained a past life regression CD and, for my birthday, a personal compact disc player. I found a quiet, comfortable space and pressed play. The guided visualisation took me on a journey through many brightly coloured tubes until I was so relaxed, I felt like a head on a pillow, no body... then I was taken to my first significant past life... I've never been good at creating crisp bright images in my head, I'm more feeling and intuitive, so when a clear crisp picture surrounded me, I had to take a moment to stare around me in wonder. The picture was as clear as the view through my eyes.

I was in a massive stable with horse riding equipment mounted all over the walls, I felt that I tended horses in this life. I looked in front of me, I saw a woman that I just knew was me. I was dressed in a long baby blue dress with a long white apron from my chest to my knees. I looked to my left and saw a man, he didn't look like anyone that I knew in my current life, but I recognised his energy, he was my dad in my current life but my husband in this experience. I knew straight away that I felt unloved by my husband in this experience and then realised that my father and I also have issues regarding love in my current lifetime. This is a perfect illustration of how we often take multiple life times to overcome issues, we don't always achieve our purpose and challenges straight away, it can take many experiences on earth for our soul to learn a lesson and we can also take unresolved trauma with us until it's resolved. This was illustrated further for me during my multiple life experience.

Remember that I said I tended horses during my experience, well when taken to the moment of my death in the experience, I saw horse hooves flying towards my face. In that moment, I realised why, in this life time, I was mortally terrified when standing near to a horse. I often visited my friend's farm as a teenager, when I first visited, I was terrified to be near the horse, and I naturally wanted to approach the horse from the side. When I got on the horse, it felt natural, and I moved naturally in rhythm with the horse. My friend was convinced that I had ridden before, but I had never ridden a horse before in my current life time. We may take issues and trauma from incarnation to incarnation, but we also take talents with us, abilities that we just naturally have, untrained natural skills, all developed and accrued in your other multiple experiences.

This experience brought my theory to life, and I really felt strongly that I should help other people with my Numerology knowledge and intuition.

Introduction - A Client's overall Life Blue Print

I have noticed that Numerology chart numbers are habitually explained in isolation. This is your Life Path Number; this is your Expression Number and so on... But very few descriptions teach a person how to blend all the numbers together to reveal a person's Life Purpose and challenges with the talents, passions, and personality that they brought with them to help them achieve and transcend their purpose and challenges, in other words the 'big picture' or the 'Blue Print.'

We all have a life purpose so that we can take the next step in our personal evolution. 'Purpose' encompasses both the Life Path and Birthday Number. These two energies are meant to be a struggle to achieve, as they are energies that a person is working towards not a talent they already possess. There should be a 90% focus on the development and the eventual achievement of the Life Path Number with a 10% focus on the Birthday Number which is a major supporting sub lesson to the Life Path.

All the other numbers in your chart are your 'Tool Box' to help you achieve your purpose.

The tools in your 'Tool Box' are

- Your Expression Number or main talents
- Your Soul Urge Number or motivations
- Your Maturity Number or developing talents
- Your Personality Number or the way others see you
- Your Focus Numbers or added abilities from using different names to your birth name.
- Karmic Intensifiers & Weaknesses

The above list are the energies that are already possessed, the number energies that a person can use to assist them in achieving their purpose.

Important note about the - Sub Lessons

Many people have just a single digit for their Life Path and/or Birthday Number but most Life Paths and Birthday numbers have sub lessons, for example, *34*/7 or *24*/6. There are five types of Life Path Number 7 (7, 16, 25, 34 & 52) and three types of Birthday Number 7 (7th,16th, & 25th). There are five types of Life Path Number 6 (6, 15, 24, 42, & 51) and three types of Birthday Number 6 (6th, 15th & 24th) and so on for all the number energies, 1 – 9. There's also 4 types of Master 11 Life Path (11, 29, 38 & 47) but only one Master 22/4 and one Master 33/6. Life Path numbers go up to 55 but Birthday numbers only go up to 31.

How to use this book

This book focuses on the individual lessons within the main Life Path and Birthday Number energies. For example, the 7 in the Life Path 34/7 and the 11 in the Birthday 29/11.

But when reading for yourself or others, it's important that you also look at, refer to, consider, and apply these sub lesson energies, as the learning and application of these less important sub lesson energies will help a person to achieve their main Life Path type and Birthday Number type.

When considering the sub lessons, you can refer to the relevant energies within this book to add the detail needed when reading for yourself and others.

When looking at the charts, you will see that a person's Life Path Number (the most important number in any chart) must be approximately 90% of a person's focus to achieve in this incarnation, the Life Path number and the sub lessons should be a person's priority. The Birthday Number and it's sub lessons are a major sub focus of a person's Life Purpose that must also be considered but with lesser priority, approximately 10% focus. The columns of the charts exist alongside each other and should both be considered.

See below 'The Blue Print' in pictorial form

The PURPOSE - The next step in a person's Spiritual Evolution

The **Life Path Number** is the most important 'Purpose Number'
The **Birthday Number** is the major sub lesson of the Life Path Number

---

The Tool Box - The Number Energies that Support 'The Purpose'

Most Importantly the Expression & Soul Urge Number

Expression Number - Your Talents	Soul Urge Number - Your Motivations

The other more minor number energies in the 'Tool Box'

Maturity Number	Personality Number
Emerging Talent	How others see you

Focus Number(s)	Intensifiers & Karmic Weakness
Added talent from name changes.	Talent & Weakness from other lives.

This book is the first of a trilogy

This first book, **'Remember Your Life Purpose', Live the life you chose** focuses solely on the comprehensive definition of a person's all important 'Life Purpose,' so I will be focusing on the Life Path & Birthday Number.

The second book, **'Remember Your Talents', Your tools to live the life you chose** focuses solely on the comprehensive definition of how a person's talents (Expression Number) can be used to help a person achieve their 'Life Purpose.'

The third book, **'Remember Your Motivations', Your drive to live the life you chose** focuses solely on the comprehensive definition of how a person's passion and motivation (Soul Urge Number) can be used to help a person achieve their 'Life Purpose.'

The next section shows you in detail, lesson by lesson, exactly what you are here to achieve, the detail of your Life Purpose, what you are here for depending on your main Life Path and Birthday number combination. Remember the charts show the detailed lessons of the main Life Path and Birthday number for you to bring together, as this is the most important description of a person's 'Life Purpose.' Don't forget to look at and dig into those sub lessons as well to add further depth and detail.

For example, a 34/7 Life Path with Birthday 29/11 should focus first and foremost on the description of the Life Path 7 with Birthday Master 11 but to dig a little deeper, the 3 and the 4 energy need to be referred to and harnessed to support the 7 Life Path and the 2 and the 9 energy need to be referred to and harnessed to support the 11 Birthday Number. This can be complicated at first, but over time you will understand the energies so well that you will understand, refer to and blend them spontaneously.

Your all-important Life Path Number

Your life path number is the most important and powerful number in your chart because it is the contract of development that you agreed with your spirit guide before this life time. Your Life Path is your purpose because it represents your chosen areas for development in this incarnation. Think of your life path as the king of your kingdom with all the other numbers in your chart existing solely to serve your king (life path). The achievement of this path is not going to be easy, it is not a talent, it has your added potential talent, but if you were not up to the task, you would not have it in your life path, it is your lesson and your chosen evolution for this incarnation. You will experience obstacles on the journey to this path but that is the whole point, your ultimate goal in this life is to overcome the difficulties and transcend them. You may just have one number for your life path, or you may have a life path that includes steps or sub lessons like this 34/7. The number furthest to the right is your ultimate life path number, 34/**7**, the two numbers to the left are your steps to help you achieve your life path. The most important of your steps or sub lessons is the number closest to the forward slash 3**4**/7. Your individual life path is made totally individual by the sub lessons and all the other numbers in your chart, they all have an influence in the flavour of you, like the choice of herbs in a meal.

The main Life Path and Birthday Number Combinations

Life Path & Birthday Number One (1)

You have chosen to incarnate to learn the lessons of the 1 life path energy because when speaking to your spirit guide before this life, you highlighted that you needed to learn the lessons of the 1 energy. You are here to develop independence and a sense of intuitive confidence which enables you to take risks, to take the road less travelled and bring positive creative energy into this world. You are here to be a catalyst for change, from new ground-breaking ideas through to art and innovation, to be comfortable with yourself if different from the norm. You must learn to see your uniqueness as a gift.

When you are successfully achieving your Life Purpose, creative ideas, projects and energy flow like a river and your confidence, not based on the approval of others, is established, and used to project unique new ideas that you manifest powerfully. You engage in self-discovery to constantly develop yourself and you have the leadership, assertiveness, and bravery to be an independent warrior with your bright and brutally honest, strong demeanour. You have a massive energy field, you are joyful, passionate, full of personal magnetism and very productive.

Your challenges are primarily in the realms of confidence and creativity, your creativity will always manifest even if it is in bad or destructive ways. You need to come to terms with your responsibility and the power of your choices, for example planning a crime may not be the best choice to manifest your creativity, so use your power responsibly. Also, your need for approval from others can cripple your confidence thus repressing your creativity until it bursts out through substance abuse, food, or sex. When you are like this, your reproductive and lower areas of your torso can cause you problems... You can see your uniqueness as a curse and feel weird, different, out of place or somehow inferior, but it's actually a gift.

The 1 energy is associated with beginnings, you are developing towards being the driving force, the first initiating masculine number. The 1 is associated with God, Source energy, the creator, and the sun. You are here to learn to be a creative, initiator and pioneer of unique new ideas that you channel directly from Source. You are here to channel innovation, to be a catalyst for positive change, always developing yourself to be better. Whether you are initiating ideas in the corporate world to benefit us as consumers or standing at an easel painting your creations onto canvas, you are here to bring that creative energy, whatever that may be, to improve things.

However, you create whatever you do, you always create, positive and negative, so you must be careful that you are not pumping your creative energy into negative pursuits, for example, you could create an app to help others or a virus to cause destruction.

You need to find and embrace your own uniqueness and be confident and proud to do things differently, even if you are seen by others as eccentric. You need to work towards your own individuality, innovate and be proud to take your ideas forward with your team behind you. You should not see any merit in doing what everyone else is doing, or following convention, you need to be original, new and do something different. You may hold yourself back by being ashamed of your uniqueness, feel that you and your ideas are not good enough or that your unique perspective is useless. You must learn to surge ahead and defeat your low self-image. When you are struggling you might seek validation for your uniqueness and let negative feedback or naysayers stop you. This is wrong, your unique individuality is yours only and it can change your life for the better when you confidently embrace and express it with gratitude.

You are here to learn to be a powerful leader, strong enough to know your will and be able to assert your will to get things done. You need to be competitive, strong and develop your potential to be a powerful cause fighter. You must be resilient, a powerful trendsetter and brave protector with the potential to be pioneering and innovative.

When you are achieving your life path, you are a successful leader, creator, productive doer, and improver. You may work and create in the classical arts, music, dance, writing to being a visionary of new ideas and innovation. All this together gives you high potential in business. You are a perfectionist who can be too critical of yourself and others which means that you may have unreachable targets for yourself and others, setting yourself and others up for failure.

You are here to learn to be determined to succeed and be willing to grasp new challenges with power. When you are confident in your creativity, you will love the spotlight and all the accolades and respect that come with it. You must always strive to be better, to develop yourself further towards personal success. Success for you will be the confident expression of new ideas, the independence, and the powerful leaderships skills to enable you to surge ahead and reach the top no matter what other people say.

Your path needs you to prefer action, to initiate, create practical solutions and get started, to feel impatience with the planning stage and be a driven, doer. You are here to start with power and learn to stay engaged to get the job done because you tend to lose interest after your initial idea. You must learn by experience rather than by theory, thought, preparation or planning, to you, only action makes the difference.

When you act on new ideas, you can challenge others comfort zone which could provoke negative reactions. So, to help you achieve your path you must be willing to take risks and be brave to surge ahead despite others fear reactions.

You need to learn to be independent, and act without reliance on others, but also realise that you are interdependent. Healthy independence should be manifested as the confidence to know that you can do it. But sometimes you can be too independent and push people away with your passionate, aggressive manner. You need to understand that you need others too because you can lose momentum after the initial idea which could hinder the achievement and expression of your ideas. For example, a person with a 2 life path can support and plan your idea, a 3 will help you express your idea and someone with the 4 energy with be the one that helps you build your idea into a business with a strong foundation, and so on. The skill for you to develop is to know when to be independent and when to be interdependent.

When you are following your 1 Life Path successfully, you are a master of personal development, a confident, independent risk taker, a noticeably confident, authoritative leader with the assertiveness and bravery to surge ahead. You may think that you do not really need people, but when you do work with others, you like to be in charge. You need to learn to bring people together in order to bring your ideas to fruition. You like to be the best; you are extremely competitive, and you put your own needs first. You can be a bit of a show-off, and sometimes come across aggressive, but that is because you are passionate, driven and results orientated. You have high expectations, and are successful, honourable, and responsible, self-motivated, self-reliant, enthusiastic, and playful.

You are full of boundless energy, bouncing around everyone like Tigger, impatient and desperate to make an impact.

When struggling with a low vibration, you can be egotistical, you may feel you are better than others and convince yourself that you do not need others help, simply because you do not trust others to do a good job, consequently, you can have problems in your leadership around delegation. Or in contrast, you may tell yourself that you are not good enough, struggle to be heard due to you own low self-worth, crave external validation, and end up standing stock still, crippled by fear. You may have been ridiculed for your uniqueness, or told that you and your ideas are weird, which makes you feel different and out of place. As a consequence, you can become overly independent, self-absorbed, and closed off from others, but it is vital that you connect with others and bring them together to help you develop your ideas.

The counter side of determination is stubbornness, you also have a fiery temper when feeling negative. You are controlling and co-dependent which will impact the way you lead. At your worst you can have a very autocratic style, sometimes even tyrannical. You can be ruthless, intimidating, and critical with suppressed guilt or anger that can be expressed in damaging ways. You can also be selfish, impatient, and intolerant, pushing others needs aside in favour of your own agenda. You have vast amounts of energy that will express positively or negatively, you need to overcome insecurity to stop you discharging energy negatively through obsession, addiction, or self-absorption.

But you can also drag your heals, become apathetic and lazy, especially if your confidence is low and you do not believe in your own abilities. Your choices have powerful consequences so you must keep this in mind and take responsibility for your choices. Relationships are not uppermost in your mind, but you are intensely loyal when in a relationship, career goals or causes are more likely to be at the forefront of your mind.

Careers that will help you to develop your life path:

Self-employment, CEO's, Management, Entrepreneur, Inventing, Administration, Teaching, Alternative therapies, Entertainment, Gardening, Art, Design, Construction.

Key attributes – Active, resolute, tenacious, confident, bright, and honest, natural innovators.

Socially – Quiet, Powerful, and Independent.

Colour – Red, the first colour and a power colour, dangerous when in the negative

Subtle body – Root Chakra, security, and the traditional element of earth

Day – Sunday

Astrology – Aries and Leo

Life Path 1 with Birthday Number 2

Life Path Number 1 (90% Focus)	Birthday Number 2 (10% Focus)
You are here to learn to connect to source energy to download / channel unique new ideas. You often hide your ideas due to low confidence. You are here to learn to be happy in the limelight expressing new ideas for an audience.	You are here to learn to be responsible to others and the team. You can be too responsible and do too much. You are irresponsible if you feel undervalued and resentful
You are here to learn to be the ideas person, but you struggle to bring your unique ideas to reality because you lose interest quickly after the initial idea.	You must learn to improve your social skills, focus on widening and deepening your relationships and make decisions subjectively. It is important that you deepen your relationships and connect 121
You are here to learn to be confident in your uniqueness because unique people have unique ground-breaking ideas. It is important that you are not craving validation from others.	You must learn not to smother your loved ones or have expectations that can never be met. OR you may back away from wanting love because it hurts too badly. You need to balance your intense need for love
You need to be a practical initiator, a doer, action orientated that learns by experience. Only action makes the difference.	You are here to learn to be intuitive and sensitive to the needs of others. You are here to be of service to others, the development of intuition will aid you in this journey
You need to learn to trust your intuitive voice within. You must achieve balanced confidence in yourself & your abilities, fed by strong connection & trust in your intuition. You bring your ideas without fear. You must not seek validation from others or base your confidence on what others say.	You are here to learn to be a cooperative team player to get the job done as part of a cohesive team. You can be a disruptive, uncooperative drama queen.
You need to bring unique, new ideas	You must develop the assertiveness

that break barriers, or challenge others comfort zones, you must learn to be brave, confident and be willing to take risks	to demand boundaries to being overworked, walked all over, taken advantage of, and/or taken for granted. You must not be a "shape shifter" who changes who you are in order to please others or keep the peace.
You are here to learn to be interdependent, not so independent that you push others away and refuse to delegate. You cannot do everything alone. Independence is an illusion; we are all interconnected	You are here to serve the leader, the team, the task and be dependable. You can always be counted upon to keep the cogs turning behind the scenes
You need to be determined to succeed. Constant self-discovery and development is key for you to develop complete trust in the skills you have learned and mastered to serve as a kind of "security blanket" for you when you are feeling insecure	You are here to be the tactful mediator of the team, helping to resolve conflicts fairly and for the good of the team. You hate conflict and often run and hide until it is over
You need to learn to be a powerful leader, be dominant and assertive. You must lead others to the fruition of your ideas, but with balanced personal power	You are here to learn to plan the next steps after the initial idea & build a team to achieve it. The energy of the two is the nurturer of ideas and a builder of teams
Your power causes ripples, both positive and negative, you must remember that great power brings great responsibility. You must ensure that your intentions are good	You must learn to give yourself your own kudos. Oftentimes you judge yourself on what everyone else says or thinks about you. You need to develop your internal compass and turn inward for validation, do what you think you should do

Life Path 1 with Birthday Number 3

Life Path Number 1 (90% Focus)	Birthday Number 3 (10% Focus)
You are here to learn to connect to source energy to download / channel unique new ideas. You often hide your ideas due to low confidence. You are here to learn to be happy in the limelight expressing new ideas for an audience.	You are here to learn to express yourself verbally to inspire, inform and delight. You may struggle in some way verbally, chronic shyness, speech delay, stutter or struggling to find the words
You are here to learn to be the ideas person, but you struggle to bring your unique ideas to reality because you lose interest quickly after the initial idea	You are here to learn to express yourself creatively to inspire, inform and delight. But you may struggle to progress, execute, and finish creative projects, due to lack of self-belief
You are here to learn to be confident in your uniqueness because unique people have unique ground-breaking ideas. It is important that you are not craving validation from others.	You must learn to be dynamic, take risks and be confident to enjoy the attention and limelight of an audience. You can be shy, under confident and feel unable to take risks.
You need to be a practical initiator, a doer, action orientated that learns by experience. Only action makes the difference	You need to develop as an entrepreneur who is able to promote, network and make money creatively. But you may procrastinate and fail to stay focused and work inconsistently.
You need to learn to trust your intuitive voice within. You must achieve balanced confidence in yourself & your abilities, fed by strong connection & trust in your intuition. You bring your ideas without fear. You must not seek validation from others or base your confidence on what others say.	You are here to learn to express your emotions positively. You can be extremely sensitive to criticism and other people's emotions, causing you to express emotions negatively

You need to bring unique, new ideas that break barriers, or challenge others comfort zones, you must learn to be brave, confident and be willing to take risks	You are here to develop the habit of acting, be a doer and executer of ideas. When low, you can struggle with apathy, laziness and lack of focus and direction
You are here to learn to be interdependent, not so independent that you push others away and refuse to delegate. You cannot do everything alone. Independence is an illusion; we are all interconnected	You are here to learn to be social, talkative, the life of the party and bringer of fun & positivity. You need to be the networker, communicating an emotional message. You can be quiet and struggle to speak
You need to be determined to succeed. Constant self-discovery and development is key for you to develop complete trust in the skills you have learned and mastered to serve as a kind of "security blanket" for you when you are feeling insecure	You must develop interdependence, life path 3's like to be looked after and can be prone to avoiding work or anything needing routine and commitment
You need to learn to be a powerful leader, be dominant and assertive. You must lead others to the fruition of your ideas, but with balanced personal power	You are here to be opportunistic, to network, make useful connections and snap up opportunities to spread the word and progress ideas and projects
Your power causes ripples, both positive and negative, you must remember that great power brings great responsibility. You must ensure that your intentions are good	You must learn to take responsibility and listen to guidance; you can be irresponsible. You must think before you act, and take full responsibility for what you do

Life Path 1 with Birthday Number 4

Life Path Number 1 (90% Focus)	Birthday Number 4 (10% Focus)
You are here to learn to connect to source energy to download / channel unique new ideas. You often hide your ideas due to low confidence. You are here to learn to be happy in the limelight expressing new ideas for an audience.	You are here to learn to commit to a person and/or place, so that you can put down roots and dig the foundations for security. You can be uncommitted and therefore unable to build stability and security
You are here to learn to be the ideas person, but you struggle to bring your unique ideas to reality because you lose interest quickly after the initial idea	You are here to learn to set and achieve goals to take you on your journey towards inner and outer stability and security. Foundations, structures, families, and business empires are built 1 goal at a time.
You are here to learn to be confident in your uniqueness because unique people have unique ground-breaking ideas. It is important that you are not craving validation from others	You are here to learn to plan, create a process and/or procedure to ensure the achievement of your goals. You can be directionless, lazy and block your own progression
You need to be a practical initiator, a doer, action orientated that learns by experience. Only action makes the difference	You are here to develop deep meticulous focus on achieving stability, like a stable home, business or income and building your inner security. You can be scattered
You need to learn to trust your intuitive voice within. You must achieve balanced confidence in yourself & your abilities, fed by strong connection & trust in your intuition. You bring your ideas without fear. You must not seek validation from others or base your confidence on what others say.	You are here to learn to be detail orientated, analytical, organised, and accurate to ensure your plans and processes are watertight. You can be disorganised and miss steps in the plan

You need to bring unique, new ideas that break barriers, or challenge others comfort zones, you must learn to be brave, confident and be willing to take risks	You are here to develop a work ethic, to work hard and develop enjoyment of routine work and tasks. When low you can be lazy and stuck in 1 place, without progression
You are here to learn to be interdependent, not so independent that you push others away and refuse to delegate. You cannot do everything alone. Independence is an illusion; we are all interconnected	You are here to develop patient perseverance, so that every step in the process towards your goals for your stable foundation are taken. You are prone to impatience and missing steps
You need to be determined to succeed. Constant self-discovery and development is key for you to develop complete trust in the skills you have learned and mastered to serve as a kind of "security blanket" for you when you are feeling insecure	You are here to learn to come to terms with limitation — both the limitations that are externally imposed on you and the limitations that you impose upon yourself.
You need to learn to be a powerful leader, be dominant and assertive. You must lead others to the fruition of your ideas, but with balanced personal power	You are here to look at your wounded or problematic relationships and work through the feelings of lack and pain they have brought to you.
Your power causes ripples, both positive and negative, you must remember that great power brings great responsibility. You must ensure that your intentions are good	You are prone to choosing social isolation, avoiding social situations due to social anxiety. It is important that you socialise regularly in familiar groups and with likeminded friends.

Life Path 1 with Birthday Number 5

Life Path Number 1 (90% Focus)	Birthday Number 5 (10% Focus)
You are here to learn to connect to source energy to download / channel unique new ideas. You often hide your ideas due to low confidence. You are here to learn to be happy in the limelight expressing new ideas for an audience.	You are easily bored and want to look at or study lots of topics. Initial varied experience is needed in order to choose a specialism, you are here to learn to be disciplined, to continue with a topic or activity beyond the boredom of the detail, towards mastery and specialism.
You are here to learn to be the ideas person, but you struggle to bring your unique ideas to reality because you lose interest quickly after the initial idea	You are here to develop the ability to balance variety, change and adventure with the stability of family and skill mastery. You can be totally spontaneous and take risks, jumping from one experience to another, but never settling or progressing
You are here to learn to be confident in your uniqueness because unique people have unique ground-breaking ideas. It is important that you are not craving validation from others	You need to learn to be extremely intuitive and access your intuitive wisdom when making decisions, assessing people and situations.
You need to be a practical initiator, a doer, action orientated that learns by experience. Only action makes the difference	You are here to develop your ability to attain inner freedom and outer freedom by doing things you might not want to do. Doing what you want is not necessarily freedom, you can become a slave to your desires. Freedom and discipline are inherently linked.
You need to learn to trust your intuitive voice within. You must achieve balanced confidence in yourself & your abilities, fed by strong connection & trust in your intuition. You bring your	You are here to learn to develop your verbal and written communication skills towards charismatic sharing of ideas and stories related to your specialism.

ideas without fear. You must not seek validation from others or base your confidence on what others say.	You have the potential to be a great communicator
You need to bring unique, new ideas that break barriers, or challenge others comfort zones, you must learn to be brave, confident and be willing to take risks	You are here to learn to be committed, dependable, to do what you say you are going to do. You often forget what you promise because you are so chaotic, scattered, and changeable, looking for the next new experience
You are here to learn to be interdependent, not so independent that you push others away and refuse to delegate. You cannot do everything alone. Independence is an illusion; we are all interconnected	You are here to develop your social skills and charisma, to have the potential to be fun loving, positive, and optimistic. You can be uptight and argumentative
You need to be determined to succeed. Constant self-discovery and development is key for you to develop complete trust in the skills you have learned and mastered to serve as a kind of "security blanket" for you when you are feeling insecure	You are here to develop consistent independence. You can swing from independence to dependence and back again. Risky behaviour and 'get rich quick' schemes can bring on dependence
You need to learn to be a powerful leader, be dominant and assertive. You must lead others to the fruition of your ideas, but with balanced personal power	You are here to learn to develop fearlessness and help others to live fearlessly. You can be fearful of many things, restriction, and boredom, to name but a few. You need to challenge yourself and others past your own comfort zone
Your power causes ripples, both positive and negative, you must remember that great power brings great responsibility. You must ensure that your intentions are good	You are here to learn to make good use of your energy and drive, if you feel restricted and under confident, you will be restless, and you may turn into a drama queen. Use your energy for experience and adventure, be courageous

Life Path 1 with Birthday Number 6

Life Path Number 1 (90% Focus)	Birthday Number 6 (10% Focus)
You are here to learn to connect to source energy to download / channel unique new ideas. You often hide your ideas due to low confidence. You are here to learn to be happy in the limelight expressing new ideas for an audience.	You are here to be a visionary of the ideal, the dreamer of a utopian world. You must act to create a better world with your ideals.
You are here to learn to be the ideas person, but you struggle to bring your unique ideas to reality because you lose interest quickly after the initial idea	You are here to learn to not use your ideals as a benchmark for your happiness. You must not base your emotional wellbeing on the achievement of your ideals. You often judge yourself and others for not hitting perfection, causing you great unhappiness
You are here to learn to be confident in your uniqueness because unique people have unique ground-breaking ideas. It is important that you are not craving validation from others	Your perfectionism can make you an over achiever due to your constant self-judgement. You never meet your own standards. You must keep your big picture in mind and not get stuck in petty detail. You can often judge small imperfections and ruin or miss your successes.
You need to be a practical initiator, a doer, action orientated that learns by experience. Only action makes the difference	You are here to learn to be a nurturer, compassionate caring and giving, especially to those that are vulnerable or struggling within your close relationships, your community, and the wider world. Your judgemental nature can make you cruel and neglectful.
You need to learn to trust your intuitive voice within. You must achieve balanced confidence in yourself & your abilities, fed by	You are here to develop boundaries to ensure your mental and physical health. You do a lot for others, sometimes too much, which can make

strong connection & trust in your intuition. You bring your ideas without fear. You must not seek validation from others or base your confidence on what others say.	you feel undervalued, unappreciated, and ill with exhaustion. You may force unsolicited advice and meddle in other people's affairs.
You need to bring unique, new ideas that break barriers, or challenge others comfort zones, you must learn to be brave, confident and be willing to take risks	You are here to develop your social skills and be a team player. You must break through low self-esteem to be talkative, fun loving and relaxed around others. You can be shy and hide in the background.
You are here to learn to be interdependent, not so independent that you push others away and refuse to delegate. You cannot do everything alone. Independence is an illusion; we are all interconnected	You are here to create a stable, nurturing, tranquil home to maintain your security and well-being. Then nurture a family in an environment of stability and love. When low you can be a selfish, neglectful drama queen.
You need to be determined to succeed. Constant self-discovery and development is key for you to develop complete trust in the skills you have learned and mastered to serve as a kind of "security blanket" for you when you are feeling insecure	You are here to learn to be responsible and do good for those you care for. People naturally put you in positions of responsibility, but you often resent always being the 'responsible one.' Have boundaries on your responsibility so that you do not do too much.
You need to learn to be a powerful leader, be dominant and assertive. You must lead others to the fruition of your ideas, but with balanced personal power	You are here to learn to develop and use your artistic and aesthetic potential. Artistic, enhancing make up, great art and home designs. You have great musical potential that you may not develop.
Your power causes ripples, both positive and negative, you must remember that great power brings great responsibility. You must ensure that your intentions are good	

Life Path 1 with Birthday Number 7

Life Path Number 1 (90% Focus)	Birthday Number 7 (10% Focus)
You are here to learn to connect to source energy to download / channel unique new ideas. You often hide your ideas due to low confidence. You are here to learn to be happy in the limelight expressing new ideas for an audience.	You are here to learn to have faith that you are an immortal soul that has experience from previous lives. You must trust the soul within you by listening to and following your intuition without over thinking and applying logic. Listen to and follow your inner voice and feel safe enough to communicate your soul wisdom to the world without fear of ridicule
You are here to learn to be the ideas person, but you struggle to bring your unique ideas to reality because you lose interest quickly after the initial idea	You are here to trust that the world is not against you. The universe is everything existing in perfect balance, it is like a cosmic library of all knowledge and experience. We must experience it all to learn and evolve
You are here to learn to be confident in your uniqueness because unique people have unique ground-breaking ideas. It is important that you are not craving validation from others	Your focus for this lifetime must be Inner development rather than outer development and success. You must develop yourself constantly with self-discovery and spiritual wisdom. Meditation and time in nature is imperative for you
You need to be a practical doer and initiator, action orientated that learns by experience. Only action makes the difference	You are here to learn to be a problem solver, thinker, a studier of the metaphysical and the big questions. You need to research, learn, and analyse theories to accrue wisdom.
You need to learn to trust your intuitive voice within. You must achieve balanced confidence in yourself & your abilities, fed by	You are here to learn to filter your research through your intuition and use your research of other people's theories for your own needs. You

strong connection & trust in your intuition. You bring your ideas without fear. You must not seek validation from others or base your confidence on what others say.	can be too analytical and ignore your intuition. Or totally spiritual and ignore other theories. You must balance the two.
You need to bring unique, new ideas that break barriers, or challenge others comfort zones, you must learn to be brave, confident and be willing to take risks	You are here to be a free thinker, to be less interested in popular culture and following norms of fashion and appearance. This can make you feel different and out of place and lonely
You are here to learn to be interdependent, not so independent that you push others away and refuse to delegate. You cannot do everything alone. Independence is an illusion; we are all interconnected	You are here to develop the ability to focus on something long enough to develop it into something useful. You can be a little scattered and struggle to focus
You need to be determined to succeed. Constant self-discovery and development is key for you to develop complete trust in the skills you have learned and mastered to serve as a kind of "security blanket" for you when you are feeling insecure	You are here to develop interdependence, self-sufficiency but also a healthy dependence on other people. You like to do things for yourself but take care not to push others away
You need to learn to be a powerful leader, be dominant and assertive. You must lead others to the fruition of your ideas, but with balanced personal power	You are here to learn to deal with and reconcile your sensitive emotions. Others often think you are aloof, but you are a well of deep emotions. You need to connect emotionally, both to yourself and to other people
Your power causes ripples, both positive and negative, you must remember that great power brings great responsibility. You must ensure that your intentions are good	You are here to learn to balance your need to be alone and work alone with social contact. You love to be alone, but you must ensure that you do not isolate yourself beyond what is healthy

Life Path 1 with Birthday Number 8

Life Path Number 1 (90% Focus)	Birthday Number 8 (10% Focus)
You are here to learn to connect to source energy to download / channel unique new ideas. You often hide your ideas due to low confidence. You are here to learn to be happy in the limelight expressing new ideas for an audience.	You are both spiritual and worldly. But you are here to learn the secrets of worldly financial success. You seek the freedom that comes from financial success. But freedom brings responsibility, your ethics will be tested multiple times
You are here to learn to be the ideas person, but you struggle to bring your unique ideas to reality because you lose interest quickly after the initial idea	You are here to learn to use your financial success as a tool to help others achieve the same financial success. You often spend your abundance on materialistic status symbols rather than helping others
You are here to learn to be confident in your uniqueness because unique people have unique ground-breaking ideas. It is important that you are not craving validation from others	You are here to develop a healthy attitude towards money. You may resent or hate wealthy people, or you may feel guilty about your own wealth. You must understand that financial wealth does not equate to poor ethics
You need to be a practical initiator, a doer, action orientated that learns by experience. Only action makes the difference	You are here to develop balanced determination for achievement but with integrity and for the good of others. You can be either obsessed with achievement or fearful of achievement from low self-esteem. It is important that you develop a positive mindset because you attract what you think about.
You need to learn to trust your intuitive voice within. You must achieve balanced confidence in yourself & your abilities, fed by	You are here to develop inner confidence and balanced personal power. You can swing from over dominance or misuse of power to

33

strong connection & trust in your intuition. You bring your ideas without fear. You must not seek validation from others or base your confidence on what others say.	hiding away or submission to others
You need to bring unique, new ideas that break barriers, or challenge others comfort zones, you must learn to be brave, confident and be willing to take risks	You are here to develop skilled leadership, which consists of subject competence coupled with excellent social skills and charisma
You are here to learn to be interdependent, not so independent that you push others away and refuse to delegate. You cannot do everything alone. Independence is an illusion; we are all interconnected	You are here to work hard as an excellent practical businessperson, but you must ensure that you do not work too hard, you need time out and time for your family
You need to be determined to ethically succeed. Constant self-discovery and development is key for you to develop complete trust in the skills you have learned and mastered to serve as a kind of "security blanket" for you when you are feeling insecure	You are here to be worldly, strong, resilient, disciplined, and realistic. To be successful you need to be strong, tough, and able to cope with The ups and downs of the world
You need to learn to be a powerful leader, be dominant and assertive. You must lead others to the fruition of your ideas, but with balanced personal power	You are here to develop bravery and the courage to take risks to progress. Success comes from having the bravery to take risks
Your power causes ripples, both positive and negative, you must remember that great power brings great responsibility. You must ensure that your intentions are good	You are here to develop organisation and management skills, resolve to making things happen and to define and meet your goals.

Life Path 1 with Birthday Number 9

Life Path Number 1 (90% Focus)	Birthday Number 9 (10% Focus)
You are here to learn to connect to source energy to download / channel unique new ideas. You often hide your ideas due to low confidence. You are here to learn to be happy in the limelight expressing new ideas for an audience.	You are here to learn to follow your intuitive wisdom and live to spiritual laws, rather than worldly laws, conventions, and ideals. You tend to follow worldly laws and prejudices as an excuse for your actions. But if you had followed your intuitive spiritual wisdom, you would not have acted that way. Focus on faith over logic
You are here to learn to be the ideas person, but you struggle to bring your unique ideas to reality because you lose interest quickly after the initial idea	You are here to learn to act with integrity for the benefit of others. You are powerful and you must use your power for the benefit of others. You can act for selfish or nefarious reasons
You are here to learn to be confident in your uniqueness because unique people have unique ground-breaking ideas. It is important that you are not craving validation from others	You are here to learn to lead by example, do you practise what you preach? You can be quite domineering, an adviser with all the answers. But you must let others make their own mistakes
You need to be a practical initiator, a doer, action orientated that learns by experience. Only action makes the difference	You are here to make your life your teaching, you need to counsel with wisdom. You are a developed soul, the totality of all the numbers, full of cellular experience and higher knowledge
You need to learn to trust your intuitive voice within. You must achieve balanced confidence in yourself & your abilities, fed by strong connection & trust in your intuition. You bring your ideas without fear. You must not seek	You are here to develop broad mindedness, meet and accept diverse people. You must learn to be a humanitarian and make the world a better place. You need a global consciousness, as you can be narrow minded, judgemental, and

validation from others or base your confidence on what others say.	even bigoted.
You need to bring unique, new ideas that break barriers, or challenge others comfort zones, you must learn to be brave, confident and be willing to take risks	You are here to learn to take responsibility for your powerful choices. You sometimes run away from the consequences of your actions
You are here to learn to be interdependent, not so independent that you push others away and refuse to delegate. You cannot do everything alone. Independence is an illusion; we are all interconnected	You need to develop towards being a successful entrepreneur or businessperson if it is with something you feel passionate about. You must choose work that has meaning for you. You are a powerful force for change
You need to be determined to succeed. Constant self-discovery and development is key for you to develop complete trust in the skills you have learned and mastered to serve as a kind of "security blanket" for you when you are feeling insecure	You are here to develop excellent social skills and charisma. You could develop the skills of a powerful speaker and influencer of others. People will hang on your every word
You need to learn to be a powerful leader, be dominant and assertive. You must lead others to the fruition of your ideas, but with balanced personal power	You are here to look after the wellbeing of others. But when you are in trouble or need support, people do not notice. You must ask for what you need, you must ask for help
Your power causes ripples, both positive and negative, you must remember that great power brings great responsibility. You must ensure that your intentions are good	You are here to wrap things up, let go and surrender. You can have a victim mentality, holding onto feelings that no longer serve you, unable to move on from perceived injustice, normally rooted in family issues.

Life Path 1 with Birthday Master 11

Life Path Number 1 (90% Focus)	Birthday Master 11 (10% Focus)
You are here to learn to connect to source energy to download / channel unique new ideas. You often hide your ideas due to low confidence. You are here to learn to be happy in the limelight expressing new ideas for an audience.	You are an old soul, with higher potential and higher responsibility to improve the world. You are here to learn to connect to source energy to channel unique new ideas and messages to change the world. You are here to learn to be happy in the limelight expressing new ideas for an audience. You need to develop and trust your massive intuitive potential. You often hide your ideas due to low confidence
You are here to learn to be the ideas person, but you struggle to bring your unique ideas to reality because you lose interest quickly after the initial idea	You are here to learn to be the ideas person, but you struggle to bring your unique ideas to reality because you lose interest quickly after the initial idea of sabotage yourself due to crippling low confidence. You are an idealistic dreamer whose ideas are often not grounded in reality
You are here to learn to be confident in your uniqueness because unique people have unique ground-breaking ideas. It is important that you are not craving validation from others	You are here to learn to be confident in your uniqueness because unique people have unique ground-breaking ideas. It is important that you are not craving validation from others. Your validation should come from your intuition.
You need to be a practical initiator, a doer, action orientated that learns by experience. Only action makes the difference	You need to bring unique, new ideas that break barriers, or challenge others comfort zone. You must learn to be brave, confident and be willing to take risks
You need to learn to trust your intuitive voice within. You must achieve balanced confidence in	You need to be a practical initiator, a doer, action orientated that learns by experience. Ideas will stay

yourself & your abilities, fed by strong connection & trust in your intuition. You bring your ideas without fear. You must not seek validation from others or base your confidence on what others say.	unmanifested until you act! Only action brings change
You need to bring unique, new ideas that break barriers, or challenge others comfort zones, you must learn to be brave, confident and be willing to take risks	You need to set intentions then use spiritual practice and visualisation to channel your advanced, intense master energy into initiation and action. Unchanneled or mismanaged energy can cause intense nervous energy and anxiety. You may medicate these with unhealthy substances.
You are here to learn to be interdependent, not so independent that you push others away and refuse to delegate. You cannot do everything alone. Independence is an illusion; we are all interconnected	You are here to learn to be interdependent, not so independent that you push others away and refuse to delegate. You cannot do everything alone. Independence is an illusion; we are all interconnected
You need to be determined to succeed. Constant self-discovery and development is key for you to develop complete trust in the skills you have learned and mastered to serve as a kind of "security blanket" for you when you are feeling insecure	You need to be determined to succeed. Constant self-discovery and intuitive spiritual development is key for you to develop complete trust in the skills you have learned and mastered to serve as a kind of "security blanket" for you when you are feeling insecure
You need to learn to be a powerful leader, be dominant and assertive. You must lead others to the fruition of your ideas, but with balanced personal power	You need to learn to be a supportive, nurturing leader, be firm and assertive but also empathic and supportive. You must lead others to the fruition of your ideas, but with balanced personal power
Your power causes ripples, both positive and negative, you must	Your power causes ripples, both positive and negative, you must

remember that great power brings great responsibility. You must ensure that your intentions are good	remember that great power brings great responsibility. You must ensure that your intentions are good
	You are here to learn to be responsible to others, your family, team, or group but in a balanced way. You can be too responsible and do too much. You are irresponsible if you feel undervalued, resentful, and exhausted.
	You must develop and improve your social skills, focus on widening and deepening your relationships and make decisions subjectively. It is important that you deepen your relationships and connect 121 You may struggle to maintain long term close and romantic relationships.
	You must learn not to smother your loved ones or have expectations that can never be met. OR back away from wanting love because it hurts too badly. You need to balance your intense need for love for healthy relationships.
	You are here to learn to be intuitive and sensitive to the needs of others. You are here to be of service to others, the development of intuition will aid you in this journey
	You are here to learn to be a cooperative team player to get the job done as part of a cohesive team. You can be a disruptive, uncooperative drama queen.

	You must develop the assertiveness to demand boundaries to being overworked, walked all over, taken advantage of, and/or taken for granted. You must not be a "shape shifter" who changes who you are in order to please others or keep the peace. Be you and consider yourself too.
	You are here to serve the world, help the team, the task and be dependable. You can always be relied upon to keep the cogs turning behind the scenes
	You are here to be the tactful mediator of the team/group/family, helping to resolve conflicts fairly and for the good of everyone involved. You hate conflict and often run and hide until it is over
	You are here to learn to plan the next steps after channelling your message or idea & build a team to achieve it. The energy of the 11/2 needs to be the nurturer of ideas and a builder of teams
	You must learn to give yourself your own kudos. Oftentimes you judge yourself on what everyone else says or thinks about you. You need to develop your internal compass and turn inward for validation, do what YOU think you should do

Life Path 1 with Birthday Master 22/4

Life Path Number 1 (90% Focus)	Birthday Master 22/4 (10% Focus)
You are here to learn to connect to source energy to download / channel unique new ideas. You often hide your ideas due to low confidence. You are here to learn to be happy in the limelight expressing new ideas for an audience.	You are an old soul, as spiritual as you are practical, here to channel and then manifest ideas in reality to build world safety, stability, and security. You must learn to handle the master builder energy and focus it to manifestation. You have a big responsibility to the team and the world to build structures (buildings, concepts, body, mind, spirit, businesses, organisations, even an empire for the purpose of world stability and security
You are here to learn to be the ideas person, but you struggle to bring your unique ideas to reality because you lose interest quickly after the initial idea	You must develop and improve your social skills, focus on widening and deepening your relationships to assist you to manifest your big ideas. It is important that you learn to deepen your relationships and connect 121, you cannot do this alone!
You are here to learn to be confident in your uniqueness because unique people have unique ground-breaking ideas. It is important that you are not craving validation from others	You must learn to have balanced, healthy relationships with others that are part of your sense of security. You must learn not to smother your loved ones and your team or have expectations that can never be met. OR Your big task in this lifetime may disrupt your love relationships. You may back away from wanting love because it hurts too badly or attacks your sense of security
You need to be a practical initiator, a doer, action orientated that learns by experience. Only action makes	You are here to learn to listen to and follow your intuition.

the difference	Intuition is needed for you to be sensitive to the needs of others. You are here to be of service to change the world, the development of intuition will aid you in this journey
You need to learn to trust your intuitive voice within. You must achieve balanced confidence in yourself & your abilities, fed by strong connection & trust in your intuition. You bring your ideas without fear. You must not seek validation from others or base your confidence on what others say.	You are here to learn to be a cooperative team player to get the job done as part of a cohesive team. You may fail to communicate effectively with others. You can be a hard-headed and high handed at times.
You need to bring unique, new ideas that break barriers, or challenge others comfort zones, you must learn to be brave, confident and be willing to take risks	You must develop the assertiveness to demand boundaries to being overworked, walked all over, taken advantage of, and/or taken for granted. You must also develop your ability to respect other people's boundaries and not be high handed.
You are here to learn to be interdependent, not so independent that you push others away and refuse to delegate. You cannot do everything alone. Independence is an illusion; we are all interconnected.	You are here to be of service to the world, the leader, the team, the task and be dependable. You can always be counted upon to keep the cogs turning behind the scenes
You need to be determined to succeed. Constant self-discovery and development is key for you to develop complete trust in the skills you have learned and mastered to serve as a kind of "security blanket" for you when you are feeling insecure	You are extremely sensitive, and you hate and run away from conflict. But you are here to learn to be a tactful mediator, helping to resolve conflicts fairly and for the good of the team/family/group
You need to learn to be a powerful	You are here to learn to stay focused

leader, be dominant and assertive. You must lead others to the fruition of your ideas, but with balanced personal power	and plan the next steps after you have channelled a new idea & build a team to achieve it. The energy of the 22 needs to be the nurturer, the builder of ideas and teams.
Your power causes ripples, both positive and negative, you must remember that great power brings great responsibility. You must ensure that your intentions are good	You must learn to give yourself your own kudos. Oftentimes you judge yourself on what everyone else says or thinks about you. You need to develop your internal compass and turn inward for validation, do what you think you should do
	You are here to learn to commit to a person and/or place, so that you can put down roots and dig the foundations for security. You can be uncommitted and therefore unable to build stability and security
	You are here to learn to set and achieve goals to take you on your journey towards inner and outer stability and security. Foundations, structures, families, and business empires are built 1 goal at a time.
	You are here to learn to plan, create a process and/or procedure to ensure the achievement of your goals and bring strength and stability to dynamic ideas. You can be directionless, lazy and block your own progression.
	You are here to develop deep meticulous focus on achieving stability, like a stable home, business or income and building your inner security. You can be scattered and

	miss steps in your impatience.
	You are here to learn to be detail orientated, analytical, organised, and accurate to ensure your plans and processes are watertight. You can be disorganised, flaky and miss steps in your plan
	Your master 22/4 Birthday means that you are an old soul and you have agreed to bring safety, stability, and security to the world. You innovate and build empires, organisations, and businesses. This involves hard work, detail focus, routine work, and tasks. You are here to develop a work ethic, to work hard and develop enjoyment of routine work and tasks
	You are here to develop patient perseverance, so that every step in the process towards your goals for your stable foundation are taken. You are prone to impatience and corner cutting.
	You are here to develop determination and the perseverance to keep going past obstacles to achieve your goals. You are prone to giving up at the first hurdle.
	You are here to learn to come to terms with limitation — both the limitations that are externally imposed on you and the limitations that you impose upon yourself.
	You are here to look at your wounded or problematic relationships and work through the feelings of lack and pain they have brought to you. All

	experiences have lessons embedded within them
	Avoid social isolation by socialising regularly in familiar groups and with likeminded friends.

Your Life Path & Birthday Number Two (2)

You have chosen to incarnate to learn the lessons of the 2 life path energy because when speaking to your spirit guide before this life, you highlighted that you needed to learn the lessons of the 2 energy. You are here to make a difference in the world through service, an unsung hero, driven to serve and help others. You need to clarify the boundaries of your responsibility and learn to work with others in a spirit of harmony, balance, and mutual support.

At your highest vibration, you stand for unity, cooperation, caring, nurturing, and parental protection. You take complete responsibility for your life, balancing yours and others needs equally. You assure the success of great undertakings and achievements with your drive to serve, help, instruct, guide, assist and support. You are a big hearted person who can be counted on for anything for the common good. But you are not conscious of this ability because you have transcended cooperation and see others as part of your larger self, you have become a source of loving service to all.

Your challenges are that wanting to be so helpful can cause you to subordinate your own needs and enter servitude, ignoring your own feelings and doing what you 'should' do. You can feel responsible for others happiness, have trouble saying no, over commit and ignore your limits, causing you to feel resentment. You must act on what you truly feel, or you will swing from give give give to stubborn unhelpfulness, resistance, and conflict. When in resentful stubborn resistance, you can be the opposite of parental, prone to co-dependent substance abuse, disruptive and fearful.

The 2 energy is the first of the feminine numbers, passive with a willingness to follow. You need to learn to work as a responsible member of a team, you have the potential to be dependable, cooperative, gentle, charming, supportive, intuitive, and diplomatic and to love working with others, especially one-two-one. You need to learn to value being in relationships and give your relationships top priority, relationships should be the most important thing in your life. As you develop, you will learn to prefer quality in your relationships over quantity, so you are more likely to have few, deep relationships rather than many shallow ones.

You must learn to cooperate and network with everyone around you which suggests that you may have difficulty with cooperation and developing close emotional connections. Without boundaries to how much you will do for others, you may sink into servitude, resentment, anger, and aggression. Early in life, you may have struggled to play nice and work as part of a team.

You are here to learn to be of service to the idea, of service to the leader and of service to the team, group, and family. You must learn to nurture ideas past the point of initial expression, plan the next steps and build the team ready for execution. The team/group/family needs to be able to depend on you to keep the cogs turning behind the scenes. But with this service comes the need to set boundaries for how much you will do and tolerate. Boundaries are important for your physical, mental, and emotional health and they will stop you from burning out with exhaustion.

You are working towards an energy of support and relationship building, this needs you to collaborate, but you must ensure that your input and opinions are not disregarded. Other people may confuse your gentle, shy nature with weakness, but you are powerful and capable in your own right. You must ensure that you value your own abilities so that others value them too.

To maintain your self-esteem, develop your own intuitive inner compass and make decisions internally without always relying on others to make your decisions for you. When you make your own intuitive decisions and act, you will show your strength, but you must also develop the ability to take responsibility for the consequences for your decisions and actions. You must always act responsibly for the good of the team but take care not to lose yourself in the crowd.

Struggles with your love relationships may reveal that you have an unbalanced attitude to love. You may smother your loved ones and impose expectations that can never be met. Or on the opposite of the polarity, you might hide from love completely and maintain distance because you think love is too painful. You must learn to balance your need for love, to care deeply but not be too smothering, investing too much interest in other people's lives. Or not to be totally rejecting of love entirely and depriving yourself of all deep connections.

Your life path 2 needs you to develop and improve your interpersonal skills and know how to deal with all kinds of people. You are extremely intuitive and sensitive to energy, you must learn to use your intuitive sensitivity to your advantage, pick up on the smallest nuances of another's feelings and emotions, to assess other people's needs.

Your sensitivity means that you are painfully shy when you meet people, especially at first, and this can negatively affect how you communicate with others. Additionally, you struggle to deal with conflict, you tend to run away and refuse to deal with difficult situations. But you must learn how to manage your sensitivity to help you to communicate skilfully, face conflict head on and speak with tact and diplomacy.

You must develop the ability to skilfully widen and deepen your relationships, to work harmoniously and responsibly within a team and make relationships your top priority. You can be a humorous conversationalist, the life of the party, a great listener, dependable, kind, empathetic, cooperative, and a great friend but these skills must be worked on and developed. Developing your social skills will make you more persuasive, influential, charismatic, and powerful, turning you into an excellent adviser, counsellor, and Businessperson, especially when it comes to schmoozing clients and building lucrative relationships. You may like or have an interest in things like astrology, numerology, tarot, and other New Age practices, but you must protect yourself from negativity from others.

Alongside this, you have to learn to manage your sensitivity for service and develop patience, gentleness, forgiveness and always be worthy of trust and respect. You should definitely be the one to be counted on in sensitive situations. You are a deep thinker, who needs to learn to understand others well and develop your artistic and musical abilities.

Your two energy has excellent musical potential, with practise you could understand the vibrational nature of music. You notice subtle differences in tone, making you an accurate, very perfectionistic musician or a music critic.

However, you have the potential to communicate without thought or filter, to not have clear personal boundaries or have any idea where your responsibilities stop, leading to conflict, exhaustion, and burnout. You need boundaries regarding how you behave and how you are willing to be treated and you need to be sure that you are not over giving to your own detriment. You rely on others too much and you forget to consider your own needs, making the balance between yours and others needs a major issue in your life. Your need to serve can cause you to help far too much and put others needs above your own, leading you to go beyond healthy altruism into servitude.

When you give too much or are timid and lacking in personal power, others step on you like a door mat and even take the credit for your hard work with you playing second fiddle. After lengthy periods of over work for others, you start to blame those you are serving, fostering resentment, mood swings, conflict, and blame. It is okay to be in avid service but if you do not act on how, you really feel and listen to your own needs just as avidly, you will tip into resentment, swing from give give to stubborn refusal, and irresponsibility, inevitably causing conflict.

Careers that will help you to develop your life path:

Negotiators, Mediators, Teachers, Care givers, Counsellors, Sales and being in business partnership, Nursing, Hospitality and Art therapy.

Key attributes – Diplomatic, Creative, Intuitive, and emotional
Socially – Outgoing, Friendly, and Supportive.

Colour – Orange, a mixture of the dominating red and the more cerebral, strong minded yellow

Subtle body – Sacral Chakra, calmness or turbulence, the traditional element of water

Astrology – The Moon, zodiac signs of Cancer and Pisces

Life Path 2 with Birthday Number 1

Life Path Number 2 (90% Focus)	Birthday Number 1 (10% Focus)
You are here to learn to be responsible to others and the team. You can be too responsible and do too much. You are irresponsible if you feel undervalued and resentful	You are here to learn to connect to source energy to download / channel unique new ideas. You often hide your ideas due to low confidence. You are here to learn to be happy in the limelight expressing new ideas for an audience.
You must learn to improve your social skills, focus on widening and deepening your relationships and make decisions subjectively. It is important that you deepen your relationships and connect 121	You are here to learn to be the ideas person, but you struggle to bring your unique ideas to reality because you lose interest quickly after the initial idea.
You must learn not to smother your loved ones or have expectations that can never be met. OR you may back away from wanting love because it hurts too badly. You need to balance your intense need for love	You are here to learn to be confident in your uniqueness because unique people have unique ground-breaking ideas. It is important that you are not craving validation from others.
You are here to learn to be intuitive and sensitive to the needs of others. You are here to be of service to others, the development of intuition will aid you in this journey	You need to be a practical initiator, a doer, action orientated that learns by experience. Only action makes the difference.
You are here to learn to be a cooperative team player to get the job done as part of a cohesive team. You can be a disruptive, uncooperative drama queen.	You need to learn to trust your intuitive voice within. You must achieve balanced confidence in yourself & your abilities, fed by strong connection & trust in your intuition. You bring your ideas without fear. You must not seek validation from others or base your confidence on what others say.
You must develop the assertiveness	You need to bring unique, new ideas

to demand boundaries to being overworked, walked all over, taken advantage of, and/or taken for granted. You must not be a "shape shifter" who changes who you are in order to please others or keep the peace.	that break barriers, or challenge others comfort zones, you must learn to be brave, confident and be willing to take risks
You are here to serve the leader, the team, the task and be dependable. You can always be counted upon to keep the cogs turning behind the scenes	You are here to learn to be interdependent, not so independent that you push others away and refuse to delegate. You cannot do everything alone. Independence is an illusion; we are all interconnected
You are here to be the tactful mediator of the team, helping to resolve conflicts fairly and for the good of the team. You hate conflict and often run and hide until it is over	You need to be determined to succeed. Constant self-discovery and development is key for you to develop complete trust in the skills you have learned and mastered to serve as a kind of "security blanket" for you when you are feeling insecure
You are here to learn to plan the next steps after the initial idea & build a team to achieve it. The energy of the two is the nurturer of ideas and a builder of teams	You need to learn to be a powerful leader, be dominant and assertive. You must lead others to the fruition of your ideas, but with balanced personal power
You must learn to give yourself your own kudos. Oftentimes you judge yourself on what everyone else says or thinks about you. You need to develop your internal compass and turn inward for validation, do what you think you should do	Your power causes ripples, both positive and negative, you must remember that great power brings great responsibility. You must ensure that your intentions are good.

Life Path 2 with Birthday Number 3

Life Path Number 2 (90% Focus)	Birthday Number 3 (10% Focus)
You are here to learn to be responsible to others and the team. You can be too responsible and do too much. You are irresponsible if you feel undervalued and resentful.	You are here to learn to express yourself verbally to inspire, inform and delight. You may struggle in some way verbally, chronic shyness, speech delay, stutter or struggling to find the words.
You must learn to improve your social skills, focus on widening and deepening your relationships and make decisions subjectively. It is important that you deepen your relationships and connect 121	You are here to learn to express yourself creatively to inspire, inform and delight. But you may struggle to progress, execute, and finish creative projects, due to lack of self-belief
You must learn not to smother your loved ones or have expectations that can never be met. OR you may back away from wanting love because it hurts too badly. You need to balance your intense need for love	You must learn to be dynamic, take risks and be confident to enjoy the attention and limelight of an audience. You can be shy, under confident and feel unable to take risks.
You are here to learn to be intuitive and sensitive to the needs of others. You are here to be of service to others, the development of intuition will aid you in this journey	You need to develop as an entrepreneur who is able to promote, network and make money creatively. But you may procrastinate and fail to stay focused and work inconsistently.
You are here to learn to be a cooperative team player to get the job done as part of a cohesive team. You can be a disruptive, uncooperative drama queen.	You are here to learn to express your emotions positively. You can be extremely sensitive to criticism and other people's emotions, causing you to express emotions negatively
You must develop the assertiveness to demand boundaries to being overworked, walked all over, taken advantage of, and/or taken for	You are here to develop the habit of acting, be a doer and executer of ideas. When low, you can struggle with apathy, laziness and lack of

granted. You must not be a "shape shifter" who changes who you are in order to please others or keep the peace.	focus and direction
You are here to serve the leader, the team, the task and be dependable. You can always be counted upon to keep the cogs turning behind the scenes	You are here to learn to be social, talkative, the life of the party and bringer of fun & positivity. You need to be the networker, communicating an emotional message. You can be quiet and struggle to speak
You are here to be the tactful mediator of the team, helping to resolve conflicts fairly and for the good of the team. You hate conflict and often run and hide until it is over	You must develop interdependence, life path 3's like to be looked after and can be prone to avoiding work or anything needing routine and commitment
You are here to learn to plan the next steps after the initial idea & build a team to achieve it. The energy of the two is the nurturer of ideas and a builder of teams	You are here to be opportunistic, to network, make useful connections and snap up opportunities to spread the word and progress ideas and projects
You must learn to give yourself your own kudos. Oftentimes you judge yourself on what everyone else says or thinks about you. You need to develop your internal compass and turn inward for validation, do what you think you should do	You must learn to take responsibility and listen to guidance; you can be irresponsible. You must think before you act, and take full responsibility for what you do

Life Path 2 with Birthday Number 4

Life Path Number 2 (90% Focus)	Birthday Number 4 (10% Focus)
You are here to learn to be responsible to others and the team. You can be too responsible and do too much. You are irresponsible if you feel undervalued and resentful	You are here to learn to commit to a person and/or place, so that you can put down roots and dig the foundations for security. You can be uncommitted and therefore unable to build stability and security
You must learn to improve your social skills, focus on widening and deepening your relationships and make decisions subjectively. It is important that you deepen your relationships and connect 121	You are here to learn to set and achieve goals to take you on your journey towards inner and outer stability and security. Foundations, structures, families, and business empires are built 1 goal at a time.
You must learn not to smother your loved ones or have expectations that can never be met. OR you may back away from wanting love because it hurts too badly. You need to balance your intense need for love	You are here to learn to plan, create a process and/or procedure to ensure the achievement of your goals. You can be directionless, lazy and block your own progression
You are here to learn to be intuitive and sensitive to the needs of others. You are here to be of service to others, the development of intuition will aid you in this journey	You are here to develop deep meticulous focus on achieving stability, like a stable home, business or income and building your inner security. You can be scattered
You are here to learn to be a cooperative team player to get the job done as part of a cohesive team. You can be a disruptive, uncooperative drama queen.	You are here to learn to be detail orientated, analytical, organised, and accurate to ensure your plans and processes are watertight. You can be disorganised and miss steps in the plan
You must develop the assertiveness to demand boundaries to being overworked,	You are here to develop a work ethic, to work hard and develop enjoyment of routine work and

walked all over, taken advantage of, and/or taken for granted. You must not be a "shape shifter" who changes who you are in order to please others or keep the peace.

tasks. When low you can be lazy and stuck in 1 place, without progression

You are here to serve the leader, the team, the task and be dependable. You can always be counted upon to keep the cogs turning behind the scenes

You are here to develop patient perseverance, so that every step in the process towards your goals for your stable foundation are taken. You are prone to impatience and missing steps

You are here to be the tactful mediator of the team, helping to resolve conflicts fairly and for the good of the team. You hate conflict and often run and hide until it is over

You are here to learn to come to terms with limitation — both the limitations that are externally imposed on you and the limitations that you impose upon yourself.

You are here to learn to plan the next steps after the initial idea & build a team to achieve it. The energy of the two is the nurturer of ideas and a builder of teams

You are here to look at your wounded or problematic relationships and work through the feelings of lack and pain they have brought to you.

You must learn to give yourself your own kudos. Oftentimes you judge yourself on what everyone else says or thinks about you. You need to develop your internal compass and turn inward for validation, do what you think you should do

You are prone to choosing social isolation, avoiding social situations due to social anxiety. It is important that you socialise regularly in familiar groups and with likeminded friends.

Life Path 2 with Birthday Number 5

Life Path Number 2 (90% Focus)	Birthday Number 5 (10% Focus)
You are here to learn to be responsible to others and the team. You can be too responsible and do too much. You are irresponsible if you feel undervalued and resentful	You are easily bored and want to look at or study lots of topics. Initial varied experience is needed in order to choose a specialism, you are here to learn to be disciplined, to continue with a topic or activity beyond the boredom of the detail, towards mastery and specialism.
You must learn to improve your social skills, focus on widening and deepening your relationships and make decisions subjectively. It is important that you deepen your relationships and connect 121	You are here to develop the ability to balance variety, change and adventure with the stability of family and skill mastery. You can be totally spontaneous and take risks, jumping from one experience to another, but never settling or progressing
You must learn not to smother your loved ones or have expectations that can never be met. OR you may back away from wanting love because it hurts too badly. You need to balance your intense need for love	You need to learn to be extremely intuitive and access your intuitive wisdom when making decisions, assessing people and situations.
You are here to learn to be intuitive and sensitive to the needs of others. You are here to be of service to others, the development of intuition will aid you in this journey	You are here to develop your ability to attain inner freedom and outer freedom by doing things you might not want to do. Doing what you want is not necessarily freedom, you can become a slave to your desires. Freedom and discipline are inherently linked.
You are here to learn to be a cooperative team player to get the job done as part of a cohesive team. You can be a disruptive,	You are here to learn to develop your verbal and written communication skills towards charismatic sharing of ideas and

uncooperative drama queen.

stories related to your specialism. You have the potential to be a great communicator

You must develop the assertiveness to demand boundaries to being overworked, walked all over, taken advantage of, and/or taken for granted. You must not be a "shape shifter" who changes who you are in order to please others or keep the peace.

You are here to learn to be committed, dependable, to do what you say you are going to do. You often forget what you promise because you are so chaotic, scattered, and changeable, looking for the next new experience

You are here to serve the leader, the team, the task and be dependable. You can always be counted upon to keep the cogs turning behind the scenes

You are here to develop your social skills and charisma, to have the potential to be fun loving, positive, and optimistic. You can be uptight and argumentative

You are here to be the tactful mediator of the team, helping to resolve conflicts fairly and for the good of the team. You hate conflict and often run and hide until it is over

You are here to develop consistent independence. You can swing from independence to dependence and back again. Risky behaviour and 'get rich quick' schemes can bring on dependence

You are here to learn to plan the next steps after the initial idea & build a team to achieve it. The energy of the two is the nurturer of ideas and a builder of teams

You are here to learn to develop fearlessness and help others to live fearlessly. You can be fearful of many things, restriction, and boredom, to name but a few. You need to challenge yourself and others past your own comfort zone

You must learn to give yourself your own kudos. Oftentimes you judge yourself on what everyone else says or thinks about you. You need to develop your internal compass and turn inward for validation, do what YOU think you should do

You are here to learn to make good use of your energy and drive, if you feel restricted and under confident, you will be restless, and you may turn into a drama queen. Use your energy for experience and adventure, be courageous

Life Path 2 with Birthday Number 6

Life Path Number 2 (90% Focus)	Birthday Number 6 (10% Focus)
You are here to learn to be responsible to others and the team. You can be too responsible and do too much. You are irresponsible if you feel undervalued and resentful	You are here to be a visionary of the ideal, the dreamer of a utopian world. You must act to create a better world with your ideals.
You must learn to improve your social skills, focus on widening and deepening your relationships and make decisions subjectively. It is important that you deepen your relationships and connect 121	You are here to learn to not use your ideals as a benchmark for your happiness. You must not base your emotional wellbeing on the achievement of your ideals. You often judge yourself and others for not hitting perfection, causing you great unhappiness
You must learn not to smother your loved ones or have expectations that can never be met. OR you may back away from wanting love because it hurts too badly. You need to balance your intense need for love	Your perfectionism can make you an over achiever due to your constant self-judgement. You never meet your own standards. You must keep your big picture in mind and not get stuck in petty detail. You can often judge small imperfections and ruin or miss your successes.
You are here to learn to be intuitive and sensitive to the needs of others. You are here to be of service to others, the development of intuition will aid you in this journey	You are here to learn to be a nurturer, compassionate caring and giving, especially to those that are vulnerable or struggling within your close relationships, your community, and the wider world. Your judgemental nature can make you cruel and neglectful.
You are here to learn to be a cooperative team player to get the job done as part of a cohesive team. You can be a disruptive, uncooperative drama queen.	You are here to develop boundaries to ensure your mental and physical health. You do a lot for others, sometimes too much, which can make you feel undervalued, unappreciated, and ill with exhaustion. You may force

You must develop the assertiveness to demand boundaries to being overworked, walked all over, taken advantage of, and/or taken for granted. You must not be a "shape shifter" who changes who you are in order to please others or keep the peace.

unsolicited advice and meddle in other people's affairs.

You are here to develop your social skills and be a team player. You must break through low self-esteem to be talkative, fun loving and relaxed around others. You can be shy and hide in the background.

You are here to serve the leader, the team, the task and be dependable. You can always be counted upon to keep the cogs turning behind the scenes

You are here to create a stable, nurturing, tranquil home to maintain your security and well-being. Then nurture a family in an environment of stability and love. When low you can be a selfish, neglectful drama queen.

You are here to be the tactful mediator of the team, helping to resolve conflicts fairly and for the good of the team. You hate conflict and often run and hide until it is over

You are here to learn to be responsible and do good for those you care for. People naturally put you in positions of responsibility, but you often resent always being the 'responsible one.' Have boundaries on your responsibility so that you do not do too much.

You are here to learn to plan the next steps after the initial idea & build a team to achieve it. The energy of the two is the nurturer of ideas and a builder of teams

You are here to learn to develop and use your artistic and aesthetic potential. Artistic, enhancing make up, great art and home designs. You have great musical potential that you may not develop.

You must learn to give yourself your own kudos. Oftentimes you judge yourself on what everyone else says or thinks about you. You need to develop your internal compass and turn inward for validation, do what you think you should do

Life Path 2 with Birthday Number 7

Life Path Number 2 (90% Focus)	Birthday Number 7 (10% Focus)
You are here to learn to be responsible to others and the team. You can be too responsible and do too much. You are irresponsible if you feel undervalued and resentful	You are here to learn to have faith that you are an immortal soul that has experience from previous lives. You must trust the soul within you by listening to and following your intuition without over thinking and applying logic. Listen to and follow your inner voice and feel safe enough to communicate your soul wisdom to the world without fear of ridicule.
You must learn to improve your social skills, focus on widening and deepening your relationships and make decisions subjectively. It is important that you deepen your relationships and connect 121	You are here to trust that the world is not against you. The universe is everything existing in perfect balance, it is like a cosmic library of all knowledge and experience. We must experience it all to learn and evolve
You must learn not to smother your loved ones or have expectations that can never be met. OR you may back away from wanting love because it hurts too badly. You need to balance your intense need for love	Your focus for this lifetime must be Inner development rather than outer development and success. You must develop yourself constantly with self-discovery and spiritual wisdom. Meditation and time in nature is imperative for you
You are here to learn to be intuitive and sensitive to the needs of others. You are here to be of service to others, the development of intuition will aid you in this journey	You are here to learn to be a problem solver, thinker, a studier of the metaphysical and the big questions. You need to research, learn, and analyse theories to accrue wisdom.
You are here to learn to be a cooperative team player to get the job done as part of a cohesive team. You can be a disruptive,	You are here to learn to filter your research through your intuition and use your research of other people's theories for your own needs. You

uncooperative drama queen.	can be too analytical and ignore your intuition. Or totally spiritual and ignore other theories. You must balance the two.
You must develop the assertiveness to demand boundaries to being overworked, walked all over, taken advantage of, and/or taken for granted. You must not be a "shape shifter" who changes who you are in order to please others or keep the peace.	You are here to be a free thinker, to be less interested in popular culture and following norms of fashion and appearance. This can make you feel different and out of place and lonely
You are here to serve the leader, the team, the task and be dependable. You can always be counted upon to keep the cogs turning behind the scenes	You are here to develop the ability to focus on something long enough to develop it into something useful. You can be a little scattered and struggle to focus
You are here to be the tactful mediator of the team, helping to resolve conflicts fairly and for the good of the team. You hate conflict and often run and hide until it is over	You are here to develop interdependence, self-sufficiency but also a healthy dependence on other people. You like to do things for yourself but take care not to push others away
You are here to learn to plan the next steps after the initial idea & build a team to achieve it. The energy of the two is the nurturer of ideas and a builder of teams	You are here to learn to deal with and reconcile your sensitive emotions. Others often think you are aloof, but you are a well of deep emotions. You need to connect emotionally, both to yourself and to other people
You must learn to give yourself your own kudos. Oftentimes you judge yourself on what everyone else says or thinks about you. You need to develop your internal compass and turn inward for validation, do what you think you should do	You are here to learn to balance your need to be alone and work alone with social contact. You love to be alone, but you must ensure that you do not isolate yourself beyond what is healthy

Life Path 2 with Birthday Number 8

Life Path Number 2 (90% Focus)	Birthday Number 8 (10% Focus)
You are here to learn to be responsible to others and the team. You can be too responsible and do too much. You are irresponsible if you feel undervalued and resentful	You are both spiritual and worldly. But you are here to learn the secrets of worldly financial success. You seek the freedom that comes from financial success. But freedom brings responsibility, your ethics will be tested multiple times
You must learn to improve your social skills, focus on widening and deepening your relationships and make decisions subjectively. It is important that you deepen your relationships and connect 121	You are here to learn to use your financial success as a tool to help others achieve the same financial success. You often spend your abundance on materialistic status symbols rather than helping others
You must learn not to smother your loved ones or have expectations that can never be met. OR you may back away from wanting love because it hurts too badly. You need to balance your intense need for love	You are here to develop a healthy attitude towards money. You may resent or hate wealthy people, or you may feel guilty about your own wealth. You must understand that financial wealth does not equate to poor ethics
You are here to learn to be intuitive and sensitive to the needs of others. You are here to be of service to others, the development of intuition will aid you in this journey	You are here to develop balanced determination for achievement but with integrity and for the good of others. You can be either obsessed with achievement or fearful of achievement from low self-esteem. It is important that you develop a positive mindset because you attract what you think about.
You are here to learn to be a cooperative team player to get the job done as part of a cohesive team. You can be a disruptive, uncooperative drama queen.	You are here to develop inner confidence and balanced personal power. You can swing from over dominance or misuse of power to hiding away or submission to others

You must develop the assertiveness to demand boundaries to being overworked, walked all over, taken advantage of, and/or taken for granted. You must not be a "shape shifter" who changes who you are in order to please others or keep the peace.

You are here to develop skilled leadership, which consists of subject competence coupled with excellent social skills and charisma

You are here to serve the leader, the team, the task and be dependable. You can always be counted upon to keep the cogs turning behind the scenes

You are here to work hard as an excellent practical businessperson, but you must ensure that you do not work too hard, you need time out and time for your family

You are here to be the tactful mediator of the team, helping to resolve conflicts fairly and for the good of the team. You hate conflict and often run and hide until it is over

You are here to be worldly, strong, resilient, disciplined, and realistic. To be successful you need to be strong, tough, and able to cope with

The ups and downs of the world

You are here to learn to plan the next steps after the initial idea & build a team to achieve it. The energy of the two is the nurturer of ideas and a builder of teams

You are here to develop bravery and the courage to take risks to progress. Success comes from having the bravery to take risks

You must learn to give yourself your own kudos. Oftentimes you judge yourself on what everyone else says or thinks about you. You need to develop your internal compass and turn inward for validation, do what you think you should do

You are here to develop organisation and management skills, resolve to making things happen and to define and meet your goals.

Life Path 2 with Birthday Number 9

Life Path Number 2 (90% Focus)	Birthday Number 9 (10% Focus)
You are here to learn to be responsible to others and the team. You can be too responsible and do too much. You are irresponsible if you feel undervalued and resentful.	You are here to learn to follow your intuitive wisdom and live to spiritual laws, rather than worldly laws, conventions, and ideals. You tend to follow worldly laws and prejudices as an excuse for your actions. But if you had followed your intuitive spiritual wisdom, you would not have acted that way. Focus on faith over logic
You must learn to improve your social skills, focus on widening and deepening your relationships and make decisions subjectively. It is important that you deepen your relationships and connect 121	You are here to learn to act with integrity for the benefit of others. You are powerful and you must use your power for the benefit of others. You can act for selfish or nefarious reasons
You must learn not to smother your loved ones or have expectations that can never be met. OR you may back away from wanting love because it hurts too badly. You need to balance your intense need for love	You are here to learn to lead by example, do you practise what you preach? You can be quite domineering, an adviser with all the answers. But you must let others make their own mistakes
You are here to learn to be intuitive and sensitive to the needs of others. You are here to be of service to others, the development of intuition will aid you in this journey	You are here to make your life your teaching, you need to counsel with wisdom. You are a developed soul, the totality of all the numbers, full of cellular experience and higher knowledge
You are here to learn to be a cooperative team player to get the job done as part of a cohesive team. You can be a disruptive, uncooperative drama queen.	You are here to develop broad mindedness, meet and accept diverse people. You must learn to be a humanitarian and make the world a better place. You need a global consciousness, as you can be narrow minded, judgemental, and even

bigoted.

You must develop the assertiveness to demand boundaries to being overworked, walked all over, taken advantage of, and/or taken for granted. You must not be a "shape shifter" who changes who you are in order to please others or keep the peace.

You are here to learn to take responsibility for your powerful choices. You sometimes run away from the consequences of your actions

You are here to serve the leader, the team, the task and be dependable. You can always be counted upon to keep the cogs turning behind the scenes

You need to develop towards being a successful entrepreneur or businessperson if it is with something you feel passionate about. You must choose work that has meaning for you. You are a powerful force for change

You are here to be the tactful mediator of the team, helping to resolve conflicts fairly and for the good of the team. You hate conflict and often run and hide until it is over

You are here to develop excellent social skills and charisma. You could develop the skills of a powerful speaker and influencer of others. People will hang on your every word

You are here to learn to plan the next steps after the initial idea & build a team to achieve it. The energy of the two is the nurturer of ideas and a builder of teams

You are here to look after the wellbeing of others. But when you are in trouble or need support, people do not notice. You must ask for what you need, you must ask for help

You must learn to give yourself your own kudos. Oftentimes you judge yourself on what everyone else says or thinks about you. You need to develop your internal compass and turn inward for validation, do what you think you should do

You are here to wrap things up, let go and surrender. You can have a victim mentality, holding onto feelings that no longer serve you, unable to move on from perceived injustice, normally rooted in family issues.

Life Path 2 with Birthday Master 11

Life Path Number 2 (90% Focus)	Birthday Master 11 (10% Focus)
You are here to learn to be responsible to others and the team. You can be too responsible and do too much. You are irresponsible if you feel undervalued and resentful	You are an old soul, with higher potential and higher responsibility to improve the world. You are here to learn to connect to source energy to channel unique new ideas and messages to change the world. You are here to learn to be happy in the limelight expressing new ideas for an audience. You need to develop and trust your massive intuitive potential. You often hide your ideas due to low confidence
You must learn to improve your social skills, focus on widening and deepening your relationships and make decisions subjectively. It is important that you deepen your relationships and connect 121	You are here to learn to be the ideas person, but you struggle to bring your unique ideas to reality because you lose interest quickly after the initial idea of sabotage yourself due to crippling low confidence. You are an idealistic dreamer whose ideas are often not grounded in reality
You must learn not to smother your loved ones or have expectations that can never be met. OR you may back away from wanting love because it hurts too badly. You need to balance your intense need for love	You are here to learn to be confident in your uniqueness because unique people have unique ground-breaking ideas. It is important that you are not craving validation from others. Your validation should come from your intuition.
You are here to learn to be intuitive and sensitive to the needs of others. You are here to be of service to others, the development of intuition will aid you in this journey	You need to bring unique, new ideas that break barriers, or challenge others comfort zone. You must learn to be brave, confident and be willing to take risks
You are here to learn to be a cooperative team player to get the job done as part of a cohesive team.	You need to be a practical initiator, a doer, action orientated that learns by experience. Ideas will stay

You can be a disruptive, uncooperative drama queen.

unmanifested until you act!

Only action brings change

You must develop the assertiveness to demand boundaries to being overworked, walked all over, taken advantage of, and/or taken for granted. You must not be a "shape shifter" who changes who you are in order to please others or keep the peace.

You need to set intentions then use spiritual practice and visualisation to channel your advanced, intense master energy into initiation and action. Unchanneled or mismanaged energy can cause intense nervous energy and anxiety. You may medicate these with unhealthy substances.

You are here to serve the leader, the team, the task and be dependable. You can always be counted upon to keep the cogs turning behind the scenes

You are here to learn to be interdependent, not so independent that you push others away and refuse to delegate. You cannot do everything alone. Independence is an illusion; we are all interconnected

You are here to be the tactful mediator of the team, helping to resolve conflicts fairly and for the good of the team. You hate conflict and often run and hide until it is over

You need to be determined to succeed. Constant self-discovery and intuitive spiritual development is key for you to develop complete trust in the skills you have learned and mastered to serve as a kind of "security blanket" for you when you are feeling insecure

You are here to learn to plan the next steps after the initial idea & build a team to achieve it. The energy of the two is the nurturer of ideas and a builder of teams

You need to learn to be a supportive, nurturing leader, be firm and assertive but also empathic and supportive. You must lead others to the fruition of your ideas, but with balanced personal power

You must learn to give yourself your own kudos. Oftentimes you judge yourself on what everyone else says or thinks about you. You need to develop your internal compass and turn inward for validation, do what

Your power causes ripples, both positive and negative, you must remember that great power brings great responsibility. You must ensure that your intentions are good

you think you should do		
		You are here to learn to be responsible to others, your family, team, or group but in a balanced way. You can be too responsible and do too much. You are irresponsible if you feel undervalued, resentful, and exhausted.
		You must develop and improve your social skills, focus on widening and deepening your relationships and make decisions subjectively. It is important that you deepen your relationships and connect 121
		You may struggle to maintain long term close and romantic relationships.
		You must learn not to smother your loved ones or have expectations that can never be met. OR back away from wanting love because it hurts too badly. You need to balance your intense need for love for healthy relationships.
		You are here to learn to be intuitive and sensitive to the needs of others. You are here to be of service to others, the development of intuition will aid you in this journey
		You are here to learn to be a cooperative team player to get the job done as part of a cohesive team. You can be a disruptive, uncooperative drama queen.
		You must develop the assertiveness to demand boundaries to being overworked, walked all over, taken

	advantage of, and/or taken for granted. You must not be a "shape shifter" who changes who you are in order to please others or keep the peace. Be you and consider yourself too.
	You are here to serve the world, help the team, the task and be dependable. You can always be relied upon to keep the cogs turning behind the scenes
	You are here to be the tactful mediator of the team/group/family, helping to resolve conflicts fairly and for the good of everyone involved. You hate conflict and often run and hide until it is over
	You are here to learn to plan the next steps after channelling your message or idea & build a team to achieve it. The energy of the 11/2 needs to be the nurturer of ideas and a builder of teams
	You must learn to give yourself your own kudos. Oftentimes you judge yourself on what everyone else says or thinks about you. You need to develop your internal compass and turn inward for validation, do what YOU think you should do

Life Path 2 with Birthday Master 22/4

Life Path Number 2 (90% Focus)	Birthday Master 22/4 (10% Focus)
You are here to learn to be responsible to others and the team. You can be too responsible and do too much. You are irresponsible if you feel undervalued and resentful	You are an old soul, as spiritual as you are practical, here to channel and then manifest ideas in reality to build world safety, stability, and security. You must learn to handle the master builder energy and focus it to manifestation. You have a big responsibility to the team and the world to build structures (buildings, concepts, body, mind, spirit, businesses, organisations, even an empire for the purpose of world stability and security
You must learn to improve your social skills, focus on widening and deepening your relationships and make decisions subjectively. It is important that you deepen your relationships and connect 121	You must develop and improve your social skills, focus on widening and deepening your relationships to assist you to manifest your big ideas. It is important that you learn to deepen your relationships and connect 121, you cannot do this alone!
You must learn not to smother your loved ones or have expectations that can never be met. OR you may back away from wanting love because it hurts too badly. You need to balance your intense need for love	You must learn to have balanced, healthy relationships with others that are part of your sense of security. You must learn not to smother your loved ones and your team or have expectations that can never be met. OR Your big task in this lifetime may disrupt your love relationships. You may back away from wanting love because it hurts too badly or attacks

	your sense of security
You are here to learn to be intuitive and sensitive to the needs of others. You are here to be of service to others, the development of intuition will aid you in this journey	You are here to learn to listen to and follow your intuition. Intuition is needed for you to be sensitive to the needs of others. You are here to be of service to change the world, the development of intuition will aid you in this journey
You are here to learn to be a cooperative team player to get the job done as part of a cohesive team. You can be a disruptive, uncooperative drama queen.	You are here to learn to be a cooperative team player to get the job done as part of a cohesive team. You may fail to communicate effectively with others. You can be a hard-headed and high handed at times.
You must develop the assertiveness to demand boundaries to being overworked, walked all over, taken advantage of, and/or taken for granted. You must not be a "shape shifter" who changes who you are in order to please others or keep the peace.	You must develop the assertiveness to demand boundaries to being overworked, walked all over, taken advantage of, and/or taken for granted. You must also develop your ability to respect other people's boundaries and not be high handed.
You are here to serve the leader, the team, the task and be dependable. You can always be counted upon to keep the cogs turning behind the scenes	You are here to be of service to the world, the leader, the team, the task and be dependable. You can always be counted upon to keep the cogs turning behind the scenes
You are here to be the tactful mediator of the team, helping to resolve conflicts fairly and for the good of the team. You hate conflict and often run and hide until it is over	You are extremely sensitive, and you hate and run away from conflict. But you are here to learn to be a tactful mediator, helping to resolve conflicts fairly and for the good of the team/family/group

You are here to learn to plan the next steps after the initial idea & build a team to achieve it. The energy of the two is the nurturer of ideas and a builder of teams	You are here to learn to stay focused and plan the next steps after you have channelled a new idea & build a team to achieve it. The energy of the 22 needs to be the nurturer, the builder of ideas and teams.
You must learn to give yourself your own kudos. Oftentimes you judge yourself on what everyone else says or thinks about you. You need to develop your internal compass and turn inward for validation, do what you think you should do	You must learn to give yourself your own kudos. Oftentimes you judge yourself on what everyone else says or thinks about you. You need to develop your internal compass and turn inward for validation, do what you think you should do
	You are here to learn to commit to a person and/or place, so that you can put down roots and dig the foundations for security. You can be uncommitted and therefore unable to build stability and security
	You are here to learn to set and achieve goals to take you on your journey towards inner and outer stability and security. Foundations, structures, families, and business empires are built 1 goal at a time.
	You are here to learn to plan, create a process and/or procedure to ensure the achievement of your goals and bring strength and stability to dynamic ideas. You can be directionless, lazy and block your own progression.
	You are here to develop deep meticulous focus on achieving stability, like a stable home, business or income and building your inner

	security. You can be scattered and miss steps in your impatience.
	You are here to learn to be detail orientated, analytical, organised, and accurate to ensure your plans and processes are watertight. You can be disorganised, flaky and miss steps in your plan
	Your master 22/4 Birthday means that you are an old soul and you have agreed to bring safety, stability, and security to the world. You innovate and build empires, organisations, and businesses. This involves hard work, detail focus, routine work, and tasks. You are here to develop a work ethic, to work hard and develop enjoyment of routine work and tasks
	You are here to develop patient perseverance, so that every step in the process towards your goals for your stable foundation are taken. You are prone to impatience and corner cutting.
	You are here to develop determination and the perseverance to keep going past obstacles to achieve your goals. You are prone to giving up at the first hurdle.
	You are here to learn to come to terms with limitation — both the limitations that are externally imposed on you and the limitations that you impose upon yourself.
	You are here to look at your wounded or problematic

	relationships and work through the feelings of lack and pain they have brought to you. All experiences have lessons embedded within them
	Avoid social isolation by socialising regularly in familiar groups and with likeminded friends.

Your Life Path & Birthday Number Three (3)

You have chosen to incarnate to learn the lesson of the 3 life path energy because when speaking to your spirit guide before this life, you highlighted that you needed to learn the lessons of the 3 energy. You are here to learn to use your emotional sensitivity to bring positive self-expression to the world. You need to confront issues of blocked, distorted expression, as well as emotional over sensitivity. This will not be an easy task for you but that is okay, we are all a work in progress.

When you are walking your Life Path at your highest vibration, you will be filled with child like fun, a thrill seeker who loves scary movies and excitement. You may get involved with extreme sports or other exciting, activities.

At your best you can be highly creative, energetic, dynamic, independent, talkative, sure of yourself, optimistic and determined. Your potential for creative, emotional verbal expression gives you the opportunity to develop as an entertainer, teacher, or motivational speaker.

You must work toward confident, authentic emotional expression that makes you able to speak publicly. Use carefully chosen words, spoken from the heart with the power to move people to tears or laughter and inspire action that can change the world in big or small ways. You have potential power of expression combined with compassion and sensitivity, filled with passion and love, moving others to joy and inspiration. You must express your feelings and needs directly, explore self-expression like art, dance, acting or physical activity and confront and move through self-doubt.

Your early challenges are that you may struggle with self-expression, especially with your speech, this can express as a speech delay or a stutter or in some cases selective mutism. You may encounter difficulties expressing yourself, from speech impediments to chronic shyness. You can struggle to find the right words to express what you mean and feel. You can also express yourself negatively by whining, complaining, bad mouthing or criticizing, be careful not to become an emotional sponge for others.

You need to work on and develop the way you express yourself towards others. You may have had speech difficulties in your early life or have verbally abused others but that's part of the difficulty of this life path, to overcome difficulties relating to self-expression.

When you are travelling your path at a high vibration, you have the potential for sensitive, positive verbal enthusiasm that inspires tears or laughter or inspires action to change the community and the world.

You are fearful of public speaking and may find the idea of public speaking or expressing your emotions uncomfortable or even frightening.

The energy of the 3 is a forceful, intellectual number, you have the potential to be talented, communicative, and attractive. Your skill that you need to develop in this lifetime is inspired emotional verbal and artistic expression, as communication and analysis are your chief areas of potential, development, and evolution. You would help yourself with self-development, Martial Arts, Dance and/or athletic or adrenaline sport. You have the potential to be an inspiring communicator, you could do this better by putting yourself in situations where your message can be spread, in the media, on television and film or on 'you tube.'

You need to develop the confidence to express to, and connect with, an audience and control your audience's emotional state from thrills to tears to laughter and back again. Some 3's write, others speak, act and perform music, create art, embark on dangerous stunts and even physical skill performances like athletics or dangerous sports. You will always be expressing; you just need to ensure that you are expressing positively. You are here to acquire an audience, in order to deliver an important message to inspire, inform and delight. Your 3 energy has the potential to be the joker, you love to tell jokes and you can be and should, work towards being, an excellent communicator or excel in another forms of self-expression.

You have the potential to be popular, charismatic and have lots of friends, that you make easily. You will develop to prefer to be working as part of a team. When you are developing well, your fun loving personality will cheer everyone up, you will smile a lot and have boundless enthusiasm. You have the potential to be charming and witty, a friendly party animal who lives in the moment.

You hate authority, routine, and schedule, you want a relaxed schedule, working to your own time.

You are here to manage your emotional sensitivity because you are prone to emotional outbursts both positive and negative. You are an emotional sponge to others, and you are always absorbing and projecting your emotions. You can express to support and entertain, or you can express your emotions very negatively, through tears, sadness, anger, aggression, and abusive behaviour.

Your 3 life path energy needs you to be social and highly interactive. To develop, you need to be involved, to laugh and have fun, be charming and witty. You need to develop the confidence to be in the limelight, the centre of attention when with others, let loose and be the entertainer.

You may have struggled with depression, acute shyness, seriousness, and negativity at low times in your life, but as you evolve, you will become much more confident and communicative. You would develop and thrive with a flexible work schedule, so that you can live freely to look after your own needs, discover yourself and be free to express feelings, ideas, visions, and creativity.

However, you are an emotional sponge who is hypersensitive to criticism, this gives you the potential to harbour speech impediments, shyness, and self-doubt. Your emotional 3 energy can cause you to be abusive, disruptive, melodramatic, easily bored, flighty, and hard to focus on one thing. You can also be changeable, scattered, directionless and, at times, irresponsible, often needing guidance and improvements in your self-discipline. You can be inconsistent with work, hop from job to job or not work at all.

You block your own self-expression because of low self-esteem and perfectionism, causing fear of expression because you feel inferior to others. This can make you fearful about entering the working world as you feel you are not up to the task, so you channel yourself into lesser past times than your talents allow. Your low self-worth only serves to block your creative, expressive energy and has the potential to bring on depression and anxiety.

You can be lazy and irresponsible when you are low, but you are here to be a doer and an executer of action and expression in the world. You can also be unbelievably selfish, and inconsistent, taking advantage of those around you and using them for what they can give you. This puts you at risk of becoming dependent and constantly in need of guidance.

Your 3 energy urges you to be opportunistic, to see opportunities but most importantly, to act on those opportunities. When you act with good intention, you will swing away from irresponsible action towards responsible action. Taking responsibility is another important learning point for you in this life time.

Careers that would help you achieve your Life Path:

Verbal arts, acting, Comedian, Holiday rep, Event planning, Singing, Dancing, Media production, Teaching, Counselling, Adviser, Managing people, Social Services, Entrepreneurship, Law, Business and Sales.

Key Attributes – Energetic, successful, and talented.

Socially – Fun, Talkative and Enthusiastic.

Colour – Yellow, the colour of the flame

Subtle body – Solar Plexus Chakra, the motivator, fire in your belly, associated with the fire element

Day – Wednesday

Astrology – Mercury, zodiac signs Gemini and Virgo

Life Path 3 with Birthday Number 1

Life Path Number 3 (90% Focus)	Birthday Number 1 (10% Focus)
You are here to learn to express yourself verbally to inspire, inform and delight. You may struggle in some way verbally, chronic shyness, speech delay, stutter or struggling to find the words	You are here to learn to connect to source energy to download / channel unique new ideas. You often hide your ideas due to low confidence. You are here to learn to be happy in the limelight expressing new ideas for an audience.
You are here to learn to express yourself creatively to inspire, inform and delight. But you may struggle to progress, execute, and finish creative projects, due to lack of self-belief	You are here to learn to be the ideas person, but you struggle to bring your unique ideas to reality because you lose interest quickly after the initial idea.
You must learn to be dynamic, take risks and be confident to enjoy the attention and limelight of an audience. You can be shy, under confident and feel unable to take risks.	You are here to learn to be confident in your uniqueness because unique people have unique ground-breaking ideas. It is important that you are not craving validation from others.
You need to develop as an entrepreneur who is able to promote, network and make money creatively. But you may procrastinate and fail to stay focused and work inconsistently.	You need to be a practical initiator, a doer, action orientated that learns by experience. Only action makes the difference.
You are here to learn to express your emotions positively. You can be extremely sensitive to criticism and other people's emotions, causing you to express emotions negatively	You need to learn to trust your intuitive voice within. You must achieve balanced confidence in yourself & your abilities, fed by strong connection & trust in your intuition. You bring your ideas without fear. You must not seek validation from others or base your confidence on what others say.

You are here to develop the habit of acting, be a doer and executer of ideas. When low, you can struggle with apathy, laziness and lack of focus and direction	You need to bring unique, new ideas that break barriers, or challenge others comfort zones, you must learn to be brave, confident and be willing to take risks
You are here to learn to be social, talkative, the life of the party and bringer of fun & positivity. You need to be the networker, communicating an emotional message. You can be quiet and struggle to speak	You are here to learn to be interdependent, not so independent that you push others away and refuse to delegate. You cannot do everything alone. Independence is an illusion; we are all interconnected
You must develop interdependence, life path 3's like to be looked after and can be prone to avoiding work or anything needing routine and commitment	You need to be determined to succeed. Constant self-discovery and development is key for you to develop complete trust in the skills you have learned and mastered to serve as a kind of "security blanket" for you when you are feeling insecure
You are here to be opportunistic, to network, make useful connections and snap up opportunities to spread the word and progress ideas and projects	You need to learn to be a powerful leader, be dominant and assertive. You must lead others to the fruition of your ideas, but with balanced personal power
You must learn to take responsibility and listen to guidance; you can be irresponsible. You must think before you act, and take full responsibility for what you do	Your power causes ripples, both positive and negative, you must remember that great power brings great responsibility. You must ensure that your intentions are good

Life Path 3 with Birthday Number 2

Life Path Number 3 (90% Focus)	Birthday Number 2 (10% Focus)
You are here to learn to express yourself verbally to inspire, inform and delight. You may struggle in some way verbally, chronic shyness, speech delay, stutter or struggling to find the words	You are here to learn to be responsible to others and the team. You can be too responsible and do too much. You are irresponsible if you feel undervalued and resentful
You are here to learn to express yourself creatively to inspire, inform and delight. But you may struggle to progress, execute, and finish creative projects, due to lack of self-belief	You must learn to improve your social skills, focus on widening and deepening your relationships and make decisions subjectively. It is important that you deepen your relationships and connect 121
You must learn to be dynamic, take risks and be confident to enjoy the attention and limelight of an audience. You can be shy, under confident and feel unable to take risks.	You must learn not to smother your loved ones or have expectations that can never be met. OR you may back away from wanting love because it hurts too badly. You need to balance your intense need for love
You need to develop as an entrepreneur who is able to promote, network and make money creatively. But you may procrastinate and fail to stay focused and work inconsistently.	You are here to learn to be intuitive and sensitive to the needs of others. You are here to be of service to others, the development of intuition will aid you in this journey
You are here to learn to express your emotions positively. You can be extremely sensitive to criticism and other people's emotions, causing you to express emotions negatively	You are here to learn to be a cooperative team player to get the job done as part of a cohesive team. You can be a disruptive, uncooperative drama queen.
You are here to develop the habit of acting, be a doer and executer of ideas. When low, you can struggle with apathy, laziness and lack of	You must develop the assertiveness to demand boundaries to being overworked, walked all over, taken advantage

focus and direction	of, and/or taken for granted. You must not be a "shape shifter" who changes who you are in order to please others or keep the peace.
You are here to learn to be social, talkative, the life of the party and bringer of fun & positivity. You need to be the networker, communicating an emotional message. You can be quiet and struggle to speak	You are here to serve the leader, the team, the task and be dependable. You can always be counted upon to keep the cogs turning behind the scenes
You must develop interdependence, life path 3's like to be looked after and can be prone to avoiding work or anything needing routine and commitment	You are here to be the tactful mediator of the team, helping to resolve conflicts fairly and for the good of the team. You hate conflict and often run and hide until it is over
You are here to be opportunistic, to network, make useful connections and snap up opportunities to spread the word and progress ideas and projects	You are here to learn to plan the next steps after the initial idea & build a team to achieve it. The energy of the two is the nurturer of ideas and a builder of teams
You must learn to take responsibility and listen to guidance; you can be irresponsible. You must think before you act, and take full responsibility for what you do	You must learn to give yourself your own kudos. Oftentimes you judge yourself on what everyone else says or thinks about you. You need to develop your internal compass and turn inward for validation, do what you think you should do

Life Path 3 with Birthday Number 4

Life Path Number 3 (90% Focus)	Birthday Number 4 (10% Focus)
You are here to learn to express yourself verbally to inspire, inform and delight. You may struggle in some way verbally, chronic shyness, speech delay, stutter or struggling to find the words	You are here to learn to commit to a person and/or place, so that you can put down roots and dig the foundations for security. You can be uncommitted and therefore unable to build stability and security
You are here to learn to express yourself creatively to inspire, inform and delight. But you may struggle to progress, execute, and finish creative projects, due to lack of self-belief	You are here to learn to set and achieve goals to take you on your journey towards inner and outer stability and security. Foundations, structures, families, and business empires are built 1 goal at a time.
You must learn to be dynamic, take risks and be confident to enjoy the attention and limelight of an audience. You can be shy, under confident and feel unable to take risks.	You are here to learn to plan, create a process and/or procedure to ensure the achievement of your goals. You can be directionless, lazy and block your own progression
You need to develop as an entrepreneur who is able to promote, network and make money creatively. But you may procrastinate and fail to stay focused and work inconsistently.	You are here to develop deep meticulous focus on achieving stability, like a stable home, business or income and building your inner security. You can be scattered
You are here to learn to express your emotions positively. You can be extremely sensitive to criticism and other people's emotions, causing you to express emotions negatively	You are here to learn to be detail orientated, analytical, organised, and accurate to ensure your plans and processes are watertight. You can be disorganised and miss steps in the plan
You are here to develop the habit of acting, be a doer and executer of ideas. When low, you can struggle with apathy, laziness and lack of	You are here to develop a work ethic, to work hard and develop enjoyment of routine work and tasks. When low you can be lazy and stuck in 1 place,

focus and direction	without progression
You are here to learn to be social, talkative, the life of the party and bringer of fun & positivity. You need to be the networker, communicating an emotional message. You can be quiet and struggle to speak	You are here to develop patient perseverance, so that every step in the process towards your goals for your stable foundation are taken. You are prone to impatience and missing steps
You must develop interdependence, life path 3's like to be looked after and can be prone to avoiding work or anything needing routine and commitment	You are here to learn to come to terms with limitation — both the limitations that are externally imposed on you and the limitations that you impose upon yourself.
You are here to be opportunistic, to network, make useful connections and snap up opportunities to spread the word and progress ideas and projects	You are here to look at your wounded or problematic relationships and work through the feelings of lack and pain they have brought to you.
You must learn to take responsibility and listen to guidance; you can be irresponsible. You must think before you act, and take full responsibility for what you do	You are prone to choosing social isolation, avoiding social situations due to social anxiety. It is important that you socialise regularly in familiar groups and with likeminded friends.

Life Path 3 with Birthday Number 5

Life Path Number 3 (90% Focus)	Birthday Number 5 (10% Focus)
You are here to learn to express yourself verbally to inspire, inform and delight. You may struggle in some way verbally, chronic shyness, speech delay, stutter or struggling to find the words	You are easily bored and want to look at or study lots of topics. Initial varied experience is needed in order to choose a specialism, you are here to learn to be disciplined, to continue with a topic or activity beyond the boredom of the detail, towards mastery and specialism.
You are here to learn to express yourself creatively to inspire, inform and delight. But you may struggle to progress, execute, and finish creative projects, due to lack of self-belief	You are here to develop the ability to balance variety, change and adventure with the stability of family and skill mastery. You can be totally spontaneous and take risks, jumping from one experience to another, but never settling or progressing
You must learn to be dynamic, take risks and be confident to enjoy the attention and limelight of an audience. You can be shy, under confident and feel unable to take risks.	You need to learn to be extremely intuitive and access your intuitive wisdom when making decisions, assessing people and situations.
You need to develop as an entrepreneur who is able to promote, network and make money creatively. But you may procrastinate and fail to stay focused and work inconsistently.	You are here to develop your ability to attain inner freedom and outer freedom by doing things you might not want to do. Doing what you want is not necessarily freedom, you can become a slave to your desires. Freedom and discipline are inherently linked.
You are here to learn to express your emotions positively. You can be extremely sensitive to criticism and other people's emotions, causing you to express emotions negatively	You are here to learn to develop your verbal and written communication skills towards charismatic sharing of ideas and stories related to your specialism. You have the potential to be a great

	communicator
You are here to develop the habit of acting, be a doer and executer of ideas. When low, you can struggle with apathy, laziness and lack of focus and direction	You are here to learn to be committed, dependable, to do what you say you are going to do. You often forget what you promise because you are so chaotic, scattered, and changeable, looking for the next new experience
You are here to learn to be social, talkative, the life of the party and bringer of fun & positivity. You need to be the networker, communicating an emotional message. You can be quiet and struggle to speak	You are here to develop your social skills and charisma, to have the potential to be fun loving, positive, and optimistic. You can be uptight and argumentative
You must develop interdependence, life path 3's like to be looked after and can be prone to avoiding work or anything needing routine and commitment	You are here to develop consistent independence. You can swing from independence to dependence and back again. Risky behaviour and 'get rich quick' schemes can bring on dependence
You are here to be opportunistic, to network, make useful connections and snap up opportunities to spread the word and progress ideas and projects	You are here to learn to develop fearlessness and help others to live fearlessly. You can be fearful of many things, restriction, and boredom, to name but a few. You need to challenge yourself and others past your own comfort zone
You must learn to take responsibility and listen to guidance; you can be irresponsible. You must think before you act, and take full responsibility for what you do	You are here to learn to make good use of your energy and drive, if you feel restricted and under confident, you will be restless, and you may turn into a drama queen. Use your energy for experience and adventure, be courageous

Life Path 3 with Birthday Number 6

Life Path Number 3 (90% Focus)	Birthday Number 6 (10% Focus)
You are here to learn to express yourself verbally to inspire, inform and delight. You may struggle in some way verbally, chronic shyness, speech delay, stutter or struggling to find the words	You are here to be a visionary of the ideal, the dreamer of a utopian world. You must act to create a better world with your ideals.
You are here to learn to express yourself creatively to inspire, inform and delight. But you may struggle to progress, execute, and finish creative projects, due to lack of self-belief	You are here to learn to not use your ideals as a benchmark for your happiness. You must not base your emotional wellbeing on the achievement of your ideals. You often judge yourself and others for not hitting perfection, causing you great unhappiness
You must learn to be dynamic, take risks and be confident to enjoy the attention and limelight of an audience. You can be shy, under confident and feel unable to take risks.	Your perfectionism can make you an over achiever due to your constant self-judgement. You never meet your own standards. You must keep your big picture in mind and not get stuck in petty detail. You can often judge small imperfections and ruin or miss your successes.
You need to develop as an entrepreneur who is able to promote, network and make money creatively. But you may procrastinate and fail to stay focused and work inconsistently.	You are here to learn to be a nurturer, compassionate caring and giving, especially to those that are vulnerable or struggling within your close relationships, your community, and the wider world. Your judgemental nature can make you cruel and neglectful.
You are here to learn to express your emotions positively. You can be extremely sensitive to criticism and other people's emotions, causing you to express emotions negatively	You are here to develop boundaries to ensure your mental and physical health. You do a lot for others, sometimes too much, which can make you feel undervalued,

	unappreciated, and ill with exhaustion. You may force unsolicited advice and meddle in other people's affairs.
You are here to develop the habit of acting, be a doer and executer of ideas. When low, you can struggle with apathy, laziness and lack of focus and direction	You are here to develop your social skills and be a team player. You must break through low self-esteem to be talkative, fun loving and relaxed around others. You can be shy and hide in the background.
You are here to learn to be social, talkative, the life of the party and bringer of fun & positivity. You need to be the networker, communicating an emotional message. You can be quiet and struggle to speak	You are here to create a stable, nurturing, tranquil home to maintain your security and well-being. Then nurture a family in an environment of stability and love. When low you can be a selfish, neglectful drama queen.
You must develop interdependence, life path 3's like to be looked after and can be prone to avoiding work or anything needing routine and commitment	You are here to learn to be responsible and do good for those you care for. People naturally put you in positions of responsibility, but you often resent always being the 'responsible one.' Have boundaries on your responsibility so that you do not do too much.
You are here to learn to be opportunistic, to network, make useful connections and snap up opportunities to spread the word and progress ideas and projects	You are here to learn to develop and use your artistic and aesthetic potential. Artistic, enhancing make up, great art and home designs. You have great musical potential that you may not develop.
You must learn to take responsibility and listen to guidance; you can be irresponsible. You must think before you act, and take full responsibility for what you do	

Life Path 3 with Birthday Number 7

Life Path Number 3 (90% Focus)	Birthday Number 7 (10% Focus)
You are here to learn to express yourself verbally to inspire, inform and delight. You may struggle in some way verbally, chronic shyness, speech delay, stutter or struggling to find the words	You are here to learn to have faith that you are an immortal soul that has experience from previous lives. You must trust the soul within you by listening to and following your intuition without over thinking and applying logic. Listen to and follow your inner voice and feel safe enough to communicate your soul wisdom to the world without fear of ridicule
You are here to learn to express yourself creatively to inspire, inform and delight. But you may struggle to progress, execute, and finish creative projects, due to lack of self-belief	You are here to trust that the world is not against you. The universe is everything existing in perfect balance, it is like a cosmic library of all knowledge and experience. We must experience it all to learn and evolve
You must learn to be dynamic, take risks and be confident to enjoy the attention and limelight of an audience. You can be shy, under confident and feel unable to take risks.	Your focus for this lifetime must be Inner development rather than outer development and success. You must develop yourself constantly with self-discovery and spiritual wisdom. Meditation and time in nature is imperative for you
You need to develop as an entrepreneur who is able to promote, network and make money creatively. But you may procrastinate and fail to stay focused and work inconsistently.	You are here to learn to be a problem solver, thinker, a studier of the metaphysical and the big questions. You need to research, learn, and analyse theories to accrue wisdom.
You are here to learn to express your emotions positively. You can be extremely sensitive to criticism and other people's emotions, causing	You are here to learn to filter your research through your intuition and use your research of other people's theories for your own

you to express emotions negatively	needs. You can be too analytical and ignore your intuition. Or totally spiritual and ignore other theories. You must balance the two.
You are here to develop the habit of acting, be a doer and executer of ideas. When low, you can struggle with apathy, laziness and lack of focus and direction	You are here to be a free thinker, to be less interested in popular culture and following norms of fashion and appearance. This can make you feel different and out of place and lonely
You are here to learn to be social, talkative, the life of the party and bringer of fun & positivity. You need to be the networker, communicating an emotional message. You can be quiet and struggle to speak	You are here to develop the ability to focus on something long enough to develop it into something useful. You can be a little scattered and struggle to focus
You must develop interdependence, life path 3's like to be looked after and can be prone to avoiding work or anything needing routine and commitment	You are here to develop interdependence, self-sufficiency but also a healthy dependence on other people. You like to do things for yourself but take care not to push others away
You are here to be opportunistic, to network, make useful connections and snap up opportunities to spread the word and progress ideas and projects	You are here to learn to deal with and reconcile your sensitive emotions. Others often think you are aloof, but you are a well of deep emotions. You need to connect emotionally, both to yourself and to other people
You must learn to take responsibility and listen to guidance; you can be irresponsible. You must think before you act, and take full responsibility for what you do	You are here to learn to balance your need to be alone and work alone with social contact. You love to be alone, but you must ensure that you do not isolate yourself beyond what is healthy

Life Path 3 with Birthday Number 8

Life Path Number 3 (90% Focus)	Birthday Number 8 (10% Focus)
You are here to learn to express yourself verbally to inspire, inform and delight. You may struggle in some way verbally, chronic shyness, speech delay, stutter or struggling to find the words	You are both spiritual and worldly. But you are here to learn the secrets of worldly financial success. You seek the freedom that comes from financial success. But freedom brings responsibility, your ethics will be tested multiple times
You are here to learn to express yourself creatively to inspire, inform and delight. But you may struggle to progress, execute, and finish creative projects, due to lack of self-belief	You are here to learn to use your financial success as a tool to help others achieve the same financial success. You often spend your abundance on materialistic status symbols rather than helping others
You must learn to be dynamic, take risks and be confident to enjoy the attention and limelight of an audience. You can be shy, under confident and feel unable to take risks.	You are here to develop a healthy attitude towards money. You may resent or hate wealthy people, or you may feel guilty about your own wealth. You must understand that financial wealth does not equate to poor ethics
You need to develop as an entrepreneur who is able to promote, network and make money creatively. But you may procrastinate and fail to stay focused and work inconsistently.	You are here to develop balanced determination for achievement but with integrity and for the good of others. You can be either obsessed with achievement or fearful of achievement from low self-esteem. It is important that you develop a positive mindset because you attract what you think about.
You are here to learn to express your emotions positively. You can be extremely sensitive to criticism and other people's emotions, causing you to express emotions negatively	You are here to develop inner confidence and balanced personal power. You can swing from over dominance or misuse of power to hiding away or submission to others

You are here to develop the habit of acting, be a doer and executer of ideas. When low, you can struggle with apathy, laziness and lack of focus and direction	You are here to develop skilled leadership, which consists of subject competence coupled with excellent social skills and charisma
You are here to learn to be social, talkative, the life of the party and bringer of fun & positivity. You need to be the networker, communicating an emotional message. You can be quiet and struggle to speak	You are here to work hard as an excellent practical businessperson, but you must ensure that you do not work too hard, you need time out and time for your family
You must develop interdependence, life path 3's like to be looked after and can be prone to avoiding work or anything needing routine and commitment	You are here to be worldly, strong, resilient, disciplined, and realistic. To be successful you need to be strong, tough, and able to cope with The ups and downs of the world
You are here to be opportunistic, to network, make useful connections and snap up opportunities to spread the word and progress ideas and projects	You are here to develop bravery and the courage to take risks to progress. Success comes from having the bravery to take risks
You must learn to take responsibility and listen to guidance; you can be irresponsible. You must think before you act, and take full responsibility for what you do	You are here to develop organisation and management skills, resolve to making things happen and to define and meet your goals.

Life Path 3 with Birthday Number 9

Life Path Number 3 (90% Focus)	Birthday Number 9 (10% Focus)
You are here to learn to express yourself verbally to inspire, inform and delight. You may struggle in some way verbally, chronic shyness, speech delay, stutter or struggling to find the words	You are here to learn to follow your intuitive wisdom and live to spiritual laws, rather than worldly laws, conventions, and ideals. You tend to follow worldly laws and prejudices as an excuse for your actions. But if you had followed your intuitive spiritual wisdom, you would not have acted that way. Focus on faith over logic
You are here to learn to express yourself creatively to inspire, inform and delight. But you may struggle to progress, execute, and finish creative projects, due to lack of self-belief	You are here to learn to act with integrity for the benefit of others. You are powerful and you must use your power for the benefit of others. You can act for selfish or nefarious reasons
You must learn to be dynamic, take risks and be confident to enjoy the attention and limelight of an audience. You can be shy, under confident and feel unable to take risks.	You are here to learn to lead by example, do you practise what you preach? You can be quite domineering, an adviser with all the answers. But you must let others make their own mistakes
You need to develop as an entrepreneur who is able to promote, network and make money creatively. But you may procrastinate and fail to stay focused and work inconsistently.	You are here to make your life your teaching, you need to counsel with wisdom. You are a developed soul, the totality of all the numbers, full of cellular experience and higher knowledge
You are here to learn to express your emotions positively. You can be extremely sensitive to criticism and other people's emotions, causing you to express emotions negatively	You are here to develop broad mindedness, meet and accept diverse people. You must learn to be a humanitarian and make the world a better place. You need a global consciousness, as you can be narrow minded, judgemental, and even

	bigoted.
You are here to develop the habit of acting, be a doer and executer of ideas. When low, you can struggle with apathy, laziness and lack of focus and direction	You are here to learn to take responsibility for your powerful choices. You sometimes run away from the consequences of your actions
You are here to learn to be social, talkative, the life of the party and bringer of fun & positivity. You need to be the networker, communicating an emotional message. You can be quiet and struggle to speak	You need to develop towards being a successful entrepreneur or businessperson if it is with something you feel passionate about. You must choose work that has meaning for you. You are a powerful force for change
You must develop interdependence, life path 3's like to be looked after and can be prone to avoiding work or anything needing routine and commitment	You are here to develop excellent social skills and charisma. You could develop the skills of a powerful speaker and influencer of others. People will hang on your every word
You are here to be opportunistic, to network, make useful connections and snap up opportunities to spread the word and progress ideas and projects	You are here to look after the wellbeing of others. But when you are in trouble or need support, people do not notice. You must ask for what you need, you must ask for help
You must learn to take responsibility and listen to guidance; you can be irresponsible. You must think before you act, and take full responsibility for what you do	You are here to wrap things up, let go and surrender. You can have a victim mentality, holding onto feelings that no longer serve you, unable to move on from perceived injustice, normally rooted in family issues.

Life Path 3 with Birthday Master 11

Life Path Number 3 (90% Focus)	Birthday Master 11 (10% Focus)
You are here to learn to express yourself verbally to inspire, inform and delight. You may struggle in some way verbally, chronic shyness, speech delay, stutter or struggling to find the words	You are an old soul, with higher potential and higher responsibility to improve the world. You are here to learn to connect to source energy to channel unique new ideas and messages to change the world. You are here to learn to be happy in the limelight expressing new ideas for an audience. You need to develop and trust your massive intuitive potential. You often hide your ideas due to low confidence
You are here to learn to express yourself creatively to inspire, inform and delight. But you may struggle to progress, execute, and finish creative projects, due to lack of self-belief	You are here to learn to be the ideas person, but you struggle to bring your unique ideas to reality because you lose interest quickly after the initial idea of sabotage yourself due to crippling low confidence. You are an idealistic dreamer whose ideas are often not grounded in reality
You must learn to be dynamic, take risks and be confident to enjoy the attention and limelight of an audience. You can be shy, under confident and feel unable to take risks.	You are here to learn to be confident in your uniqueness because unique people have unique ground-breaking ideas. It is important that you are not craving validation from others. Your validation should come from your intuition.
You need to develop as an entrepreneur who is able to promote, network and make money creatively. But you may procrastinate and fail to stay focused and work inconsistently.	You need to bring unique, new ideas that break barriers, or challenge others comfort zone. You must learn to be brave, confident and be willing to take risks
You are here to learn to express your emotions positively. You can be	You need to be a practical initiator, a doer, action orientated that learns

extremely sensitive to criticism and other people's emotions, causing you to express emotions negatively	by experience. Ideas will stay unmanifested until you act! Only action brings change
You are here to develop the habit of acting, be a doer and executer of ideas. When low, you can struggle with apathy, laziness and lack of focus and direction	You need to set intentions then use spiritual practice and visualisation to channel your advanced, intense master energy into initiation and action. Unchanneled or mismanaged energy can cause intense nervous energy and anxiety. You may medicate these with unhealthy substances.
You are here to learn to be social, talkative, the life of the party and bringer of fun & positivity. You need to be the networker, communicating an emotional message. You can be quiet and struggle to speak	You are here to learn to be interdependent, not so independent that you push others away and refuse to delegate. You cannot do everything alone. Independence is an illusion; we are all interconnected
You must develop interdependence, life path 3's like to be looked after and can be prone to avoiding work or anything needing routine and commitment	You need to be determined to succeed. Constant self-discovery and intuitive spiritual development is key for you to develop complete trust in the skills you have learned and mastered to serve as a kind of "security blanket" for you when you are feeling insecure
You are here to be opportunistic, to network, make useful connections and snap up opportunities to spread the word and progress ideas and projects	You need to learn to be a supportive, nurturing leader, be firm and assertive but also empathic and supportive. You must lead others to the fruition of your ideas, but with balanced personal power
You must learn to take responsibility and listen to guidance; you can be irresponsible. You must think before you act, and take full responsibility for what you do	Your power causes ripples, both positive and negative, you must remember that great power brings great responsibility. You must ensure that your intentions are good

	You are here to learn to be responsible to others, your family, team, or group but in a balanced way. You can be too responsible and do too much. You are irresponsible if you feel undervalued, resentful, and exhausted.
	You must develop and improve your social skills, focus on widening and deepening your relationships and make decisions subjectively. It is important that you deepen your relationships and connect 121
	You may struggle to maintain long term close and romantic relationships.
	You must learn not to smother your loved ones or have expectations that can never be met. OR back away from wanting love because it hurts too badly. You need to balance your intense need for love for healthy relationships.
	You are here to learn to be intuitive and sensitive to the needs of others. You are here to be of service to others, the development of intuition will aid you in this journey
	You are here to learn to be a cooperative team player to get the job done as part of a cohesive team. You can be a disruptive, uncooperative drama queen.
	You must develop the assertiveness to demand boundaries to being overworked, walked all over, taken advantage of, and/or taken for

	granted. You must not be a "shape shifter" who changes who you are in order to please others or keep the peace. Be you and consider yourself too.
	You are here to serve the world, help the team, the task and be dependable. You can always be relied upon to keep the cogs turning behind the scenes
	You are here to be the tactful mediator of the team/group/family, helping to resolve conflicts fairly and for the good of everyone involved. You hate conflict and often run and hide until it is over
	You are here to learn to plan the next steps after channelling your message or idea & build a team to achieve it. The energy of the 11/2 needs to be the nurturer of ideas and a builder of teams
	You must learn to give yourself your own kudos. Oftentimes you judge yourself on what everyone else says or thinks about you. You need to develop your internal compass and turn inward for validation, do what YOU think you should do

Life Path 3 with Birthday Master 22/4

Life Path Number 3 (90% Focus)	Birthday Master 22/4 (10% Focus)
You are here to learn to express yourself verbally to inspire, inform and delight. You may struggle in some way verbally, chronic shyness, speech delay, stutter or struggling to find the words	You are an old soul, as spiritual as you are practical, here to channel and then manifest ideas in reality to build world safety, stability, and security. You must learn to handle the master builder energy and focus it to manifestation. You have a big responsibility to the team and the world to build structures (buildings, concepts, body, mind, spirit, businesses, organisations, even an empire for the purpose of world stability and security
You are here to learn to express yourself creatively to inspire, inform and delight. But you may struggle to progress, execute, and finish creative projects, due to lack of self-belief	You must develop and improve your social skills, focus on widening and deepening your relationships to assist you to manifest your big ideas. It is important that you learn to deepen your relationships and connect 121, you cannot do this alone!
You must learn to be dynamic, take risks and be confident to enjoy the attention and limelight of an audience. You can be shy, under confident and feel unable to take risks.	You must learn to have balanced, healthy relationships with others that are part of your sense of security. You must learn not to smother your loved ones and your team or have expectations that can never be met. OR Your big task in this lifetime may disrupt your love relationships. You may back away from wanting love because it hurts too badly or attacks your sense of security

You need to develop as an entrepreneur who is able to promote, network and make money creatively. But you may procrastinate and fail to stay focused and work inconsistently.	You are here to learn to listen to and follow your intuition. Intuition is needed for you to be sensitive to the needs of others. You are here to be of service to change the world, the development of intuition will aid you in this journey
You are here to learn to express your emotions positively. You can be extremely sensitive to criticism and other people's emotions, causing you to express emotions negatively	You are here to learn to be a cooperative team player to get the job done as part of a cohesive team. You may fail to communicate effectively with others. You can be a hard-headed and high handed at times.
You are here to develop the habit of acting, be a doer and executer of ideas. When low, you can struggle with apathy, laziness and lack of focus and direction	You must develop the assertiveness to demand boundaries to being overworked, walked all over, taken advantage of, and/or taken for granted. You must also develop your ability to respect other people's boundaries and not be high handed.
You are here to learn to be social, talkative, the life of the party and bringer of fun & positivity. You need to be the networker, communicating an emotional message. You can be quiet and struggle to speak	You are here to be of service to the world, the leader, the team, the task and be dependable. You can always be counted upon to keep the cogs turning behind the scenes
You must develop a healthy sense of interdependence. Life path 3's like to be looked after and can be prone to avoiding work or anything needing routine and commitment	You are extremely sensitive, and you hate and run away from conflict. But you are here to learn to be a tactful mediator, helping to resolve conflicts fairly and for the good of the team/family/group
You are here to be opportunistic, to network, make useful connections	You are here to learn to stay focused and plan the next steps after you

and snap up opportunities to spread the word and progress ideas and projects	have channelled a new idea & build a team to achieve it. The energy of the 22 needs to be the nurturer, the builder of ideas and teams.
You must learn to take responsibility and listen to guidance; you can be irresponsible. You must think before you act, and take full responsibility for what you do	You must learn to give yourself your own kudos. Oftentimes you judge yourself on what everyone else says or thinks about you. You need to develop your internal compass and turn inward for validation, do what you think you should do
	You are here to learn to commit to a person and/or place, so that you can put down roots and dig the foundations for security. You can be uncommitted and therefore unable to build stability and security
	You are here to learn to set and achieve goals to take you on your journey towards inner and outer stability and security. Foundations, structures, families, and business empires are built 1 goal at a time.
	You are here to learn to plan, create a process and/or procedure to ensure the achievement of your goals and bring strength and stability to dynamic ideas. You can be directionless, lazy and block your own progression.
	You are here to develop deep meticulous focus on achieving stability, like a stable home, business or income and building your inner security. You can be scattered and miss steps in your impatience.

	You are here to learn to be detail orientated, analytical, organised, and accurate to ensure your plans and processes are watertight. You can be disorganised, flaky and miss steps in your plan
	Your master 22/4 Birthday means that you are an old soul and you have agreed to bring safety, stability, and security to the world. You innovate and build empires, organisations, and businesses. This involves hard work, detail focus, routine work, and tasks. You are here to develop a work ethic, to work hard and develop enjoyment of routine work and tasks
	You are here to develop patient perseverance, so that every step in the process towards your goals for your stable foundation are taken. You are prone to impatience and corner cutting.
	You are here to develop determination and the perseverance to keep going past obstacles to achieve your goals. You are prone to giving up at the first hurdle.
	You are here to learn to come to terms with limitation — both the limitations that are externally imposed on you and the limitations that you impose upon yourself.
	You are here to look at your wounded or problematic relationships and work through the feelings of lack and pain they have brought to you. All experiences have

	lessons embedded within them
	Avoid social isolation by socialising regularly in familiar groups and with likeminded friends.

Your Life Path & Birthday Number Four (4)

You have chosen to incarnate to learn the lessons of the 4 life path energy because when speaking to your spirit guide before this life, you highlighted that you needed to learn the lessons of the 4 energy. You are here to learn lessons around perseverance and staying power, to be organised and structured, to persevere and overcome and to create your own secure foundation. You are here to teach while also being a student, to achieve stability and security by patiently following a gradual process towards selected goals.

When you are achieving your Life Path successfully, you are a builder of strength, safety and security creating a solid foundation to any business or undertaking. You are organised, honest, and appreciative of structure and stability. You take responsibility, make clear plans, broken into steps and you commit to a step by step process which achieves any goal. You do this with strength, ambition, and perseverance. You have the potential to analyse the path from where you are to your goal, break it down into steps and act, you can also teach others to do the same. You always prepare well, commit, and follow through step by step.

Your challenges are that you can be competitive yet insecure about the validity of your beliefs and ideas or on the flipside, you can be rigid and opinionated. You may experience difficult trials and experiences that test your stability and security. For example, your worries surrounding not having enough resources can turn you into a workaholic missing out on quality time with the family you are trying to make secure.

You may experience psychological rigidity, manifesting as stubborn self-deception or tunnel vision. You may not listen to others advice and just hope that things will just work themselves out without you going through the steps to make sure. You have difficulties with process, and you need to learn the necessity of preparation and not skipping steps. But when you do formulate a sound process, you can use that process elsewhere in your life.

You are here to learn to build security, steadiness, practicality, and routine, by committing to a person or place, planting roots, and building foundations so that you can grow. You must set goals, develop a work ethic & be hard working to progress, achieve and attain security.

When you have set your goals, you must plan and create a process for your goal achievement and take each step with perseverance and without missing steps through impatience. You have the potential to excel in the business world as a builder, founder of a corporation or empire, but you want it all now. You work in bursts of enthusiasm to get things started and quickly get it done. You could be at risk in business of being seduced by 'get rich quick' schemes in your impatience to just get it all now.

To achieve the stability that you are here to achieve, you need to develop your skills as a planner and a builder of process through analysing the detail. You need to find out how things, ideas, and concepts work, learn to analyse ideas and structure, stripping it down to its component parts to look at it in detail.

You need to solve puzzles and overcome challenges to build a business empire, home, and family for your emotional, financial, and physical stability. But you tend to be directionless and lazy. You need to bring in some structure, set goals and work towards them step by step, to create a strong stable foundation on which to build your life and work.

Your path is to develop towards being the stable cornerstone of any society or enterprise. You have lots of internal strength, vigour and fortitude, great problem solving skills and a sharp business mind who needs to be committed to your goals. But you tend to be lazy and directionless, wasting your keen intelligence or a workaholic who is obsessively tied to your career or business and neglecting your family. You must find your work life balance.

To succeed you need to commit to putting your theories into practical application, with logic, good accuracy, and attention to detail. You need to take advantage of your intellect and put your skills to good use, by setting a direction for your life, planning, and achieving your goals methodically, step by step with no cutting corners in your impatience to get it done.

You are here to learn to be an exceptional decision maker, always very honest, 'fair and square,' a realist with a pragmatic approach to everything you do. When you have perfected your rational decision making skills, you could develop towards being an adviser, and practical business person, especially in property and finance. This is because you have the potential to be very grounded, practical, and logical. You must learn to analyse and organise detailed information effectively, as it is the detail that is the strength in any structure or organisation. However, you can be impatient and fail to spend enough time on the detail, your lack of patience could impact your determination to persevere. The impact of rushed inaccurate work on your foundations is collapse!

You need to develop loyalty, reliability, be dependable, committed, and compliant, which will bode very well for building an empire, family, and home. But your path to security could cause anxiety for you in business because you never know for sure what might happen in the future, even with good forecasting. Nevertheless, you need to be determined to succeed past obstacles. You need to be hardworking and completely focused on your goals, not lazy, scattered, and directionless.

Socially, you can be a little serious and awkward, so you keep yourself to yourself and prefer a small group of friends with similar interests. You can also be aggressively opinionated and rigid to your beliefs, even when given good evidence to the contrary.

Building a home and family would be good for your development towards stability and security, as it appeals to your sense of security. You can and must be very parental and guide your children well, with responsibility and with good intentions.

You must battle laziness and apathy with a strong work ethic and learn to happily take on and execute routine tasks for your business, career, and family.

However, you are prone to holding onto issues from your early life, like perceived wounded relationships from your past that you are holding onto thus inhibiting your own emotional development. Limitations and difficult relationships are the best way for you to learn and develop your soul in this incarnation. You must look for the lesson within your adversity and learn it rather than developing a victim mentality that stops you from progressing.

You have issues with dependency and independence, either being overly independent and insisting on doing everything yourself, all the way to being totally dependent, with others taking care of your needs. You need to use your initiative and take on some of the workload and responsibility. You must learn to have the attitude of interdependence, sometimes you can do things alone and other times you need the help and assistance of others. You must develop beyond being unhealthily independent and isolated or unhealthily dependent and hidden away from reality.

You have the potential to skip steps to your goal because you do not have the patience to follow a slow arduous process. This can bring short term relief but be bad in the long term, you must live by the quote, 'Proper preparation prevents poor performance.'

You can lack direction without a practical application to your goals, making you change jobs and goals a lot. You need to see things through to the end and put down roots. Take care not to rush the process or get stuck in one bit of the process, never moving forward.

Achieving the 4 energy is all about having a direction, goals, a plan, and a step by step method. It's about working hard on each step and moving forwards slowly and accurately towards the achievement of your goals.

You have the potential to stay firmly rooted in your comfort zone, with a tendency to be lazy and apathetic. You can be rigid, stubborn, and opinionated about your beliefs or unsure of the validity of your beliefs, but you will still fight to win the argument, even if unsure! However, you can give up easily when things get difficult, you could do with more perseverance, or you can become directionless and prone to depression. It is important that you ground yourself, put down roots and commit to something that will bring you stability and security.

You can also be irresponsible or overly responsible, a champion of emotional hysterics or stoic and emotionally distant. Your habit is to bottle up your feelings until the situation explodes. You need to notice your emotional responses and triggers as they occur to help you to channel your emotions more authentically and consistently.

Careers that would help you achieve your life path:

Mathematicians, Auditors, Bookkeepers, Accountants, Banking and Finance, Analysts, Editors, Builders, Surveyors, Architects, Estate Agents, Engineers, Scientists, Planners, Law Enforcement, Research and Managers/CEOs.

Key Attributes – Dependable, Trustworthy, High endurance and Stamina

Socially – Quiet, Awkward and Exclusive.

Colours – Green and Pink

Subtle body – Heart Chakra, freedom, and the element of air

Day – Thursdays and Saturdays

Astrologically – Mars, zodiac signs Scorpio and Capricorn

Life Path 4 with Birthday Number 1

Life Path Number 4 (90% Focus)	Birthday Number 1 (10% Focus)
You are here to learn to commit to a person and/or place, so that you can put down roots and dig the foundations for security. You can be uncommitted and therefore unable to build stability and security	You are here to learn to connect to source energy to download / channel unique new ideas. You often hide your ideas due to low confidence. You are here to learn to be happy in the limelight expressing new ideas for an audience.
You are here to learn to set and achieve goals to take you on your journey towards inner and outer stability and security. Foundations, structures, families, and business empires are built 1 goal at a time.	You are here to learn to be the ideas person, but you struggle to bring your unique ideas to reality because you lose interest quickly after the initial idea.
You are here to learn to plan, create a process and/or procedure to ensure the achievement of your goals. You can be directionless, lazy and block your own progression	You are here to learn to be confident in your uniqueness because unique people have unique ground-breaking ideas. It is important that you are not craving validation from others.
You are here to develop deep meticulous focus on achieving stability, like a stable home, business or income and building your inner security. You can be scattered	You need to be a practical initiator, a doer, action orientated that learns by experience. Only action makes the difference.
You are here to learn to be detail orientated, analytical, organised, and accurate to ensure your plans and processes are watertight. You can be disorganised and miss steps in the plan	You need to learn to trust your intuitive voice within. You must achieve balanced confidence in yourself & your abilities, fed by strong connection & trust in your intuition. You bring your ideas without fear. You must not seek validation from others or base your confidence on what others say.
You are here to develop a work ethic, to work hard and develop	You need to bring unique, new ideas that break barriers, or challenge

enjoyment of routine work and tasks. When low you can be lazy and stuck in one place, without progression	others comfort zones, you must learn to be brave, confident and be willing to take risks
You are here to develop patient perseverance, so that every step in the process towards your goals for your stable foundation are taken. You are prone to impatience and missing steps	You are here to learn to be interdependent, not so independent that you push others away and refuse to delegate. You cannot do everything alone. Independence is an illusion; we are all interconnected
You are here to learn to come to terms with limitation — both the limitations that are externally imposed on you and the limitations that you impose upon yourself.	You need to be determined to succeed. Constant self-discovery and development is key for you to develop complete trust in the skills you have learned and mastered to serve as a kind of "security blanket" for you when you are feeling insecure
You are here to look at your wounded or problematic relationships and work through the feelings of lack and pain they have brought to you.	You need to learn to be a powerful leader, be dominant and assertive. You must lead others to the fruition of your ideas, but with balanced personal power
You are prone to choosing social isolation, avoiding social situations due to social anxiety. It is important that you socialise regularly in familiar groups and with likeminded friends.	Your power causes ripples, both positive and negative, you must remember that great power brings great responsibility. You must ensure that your intentions are good

Life Path 4 with Birthday Number 2

Life Path Number 4 (90% Focus)	Birthday Number 2 (10% Focus)
You are here to learn to commit to a person and/or place, so that you can put down roots and dig the foundations for security. You can be uncommitted and therefore unable to build stability and security	You are here to learn to be responsible to others and the team. You can be too responsible and do too much. You are irresponsible if you feel undervalued and resentful
You are here to learn to set and achieve goals to take you on your journey towards inner and outer stability and security. Foundations, structures, families, and business empires are built 1 goal at a time.	You must learn to improve your social skills, focus on widening and deepening your relationships and make decisions subjectively. It is important that you deepen your relationships and connect 121
You are here to learn to plan, create a process and/or procedure to ensure the achievement of your goals. You can be directionless, lazy and block your own progression	You must learn not to smother your loved ones or have expectations that can never be met. OR you may back away from wanting love because it hurts too badly. You need to balance your intense need for love
You are here to develop deep meticulous focus on achieving stability, like a stable home, business or income and building your inner security. You can be scattered	You are here to learn to be intuitive and sensitive to the needs of others. You are here to be of service to others, the development of intuition will aid you in this journey
You are here to learn to be detail orientated, analytical, organised, and accurate to ensure your plans and processes are watertight. You can be disorganised and miss steps in the plan	You are here to learn to be a cooperative team player to get the job done as part of a cohesive team. You can be a disruptive, uncooperative drama queen.
You are here to develop a work ethic, to work hard and develop enjoyment of routine work and tasks. When low you can be lazy and stuck in 1 place, without progression	You must develop the assertiveness to demand boundaries to being overworked, walked all over, taken advantage of, and/or taken for granted. You must not be a "shape

	shifter" who changes who you are in order to please others or keep the peace.
You are here to develop patient perseverance, so that every step in the process towards your goals for your stable foundation are taken. You are prone to impatience and missing steps	You are here to serve the leader, the team, the task and be dependable. You can always be counted upon to keep the cogs turning behind the scenes
You are here to learn to come to terms with limitation — both the limitations that are externally imposed on you and the limitations that you impose upon yourself.	You are here to be the tactful mediator of the team, helping to resolve conflicts fairly and for the good of the team. You hate conflict and often run and hide until it is over
You are here to look at your wounded or problematic relationships and work through the feelings of lack and pain they have brought to you.	You are here to learn to plan the next steps after the initial idea & build a team to achieve it. The energy of the two is the nurturer of ideas and a builder of teams
You are prone to choosing social isolation, avoiding social situations due to social anxiety. It is important that you socialise regularly in familiar groups and with likeminded friends.	You must learn to give yourself your own kudos. Oftentimes you judge yourself on what everyone else says or thinks about you. You need to develop your internal compass and turn inward for validation, do what you think you should do

Life Path 4 with Birthday Number 3

Life Path Number 4 (90% Focus)	Birthday Number 3 (10% Focus)
You are here to learn to commit to a person and/or place, so that you can put down roots and dig the foundations for security. You can be uncommitted and therefore unable to build stability and security.	You are here to learn to express yourself verbally to inspire, inform and delight. You may struggle in some way verbally, chronic shyness, speech delay, stutter or struggling to find the words.
You are here to learn to set and achieve goals to take you on your journey towards inner and outer stability and security. Foundations, structures, families, and business empires are built 1 goal at a time.	You are here to learn to express yourself creatively to inspire, inform and delight. But you may struggle to progress, execute, and finish creative projects, due to lack of self-belief
You are here to learn to plan, create a process and/or procedure to ensure the achievement of your goals. You can be directionless, lazy and block your own progression	You must learn to be dynamic, take risks and be confident to enjoy the attention and limelight of an audience. You can be shy, under confident and feel unable to take risks.
You are here to develop deep meticulous focus on achieving stability, like a stable home, business or income and building your inner security. You can be scattered	You need to develop as an entrepreneur who is able to promote, network and make money creatively. But you may procrastinate and fail to stay focused and work inconsistently.
You are here to learn to be detail orientated, analytical, organised, and accurate to ensure your plans and processes are watertight. You can be disorganised and miss steps in the plan	You are here to learn to express your emotions positively. You can be extremely sensitive to criticism and other people's emotions, causing you to express emotions negatively
You are here to develop a work ethic, to work hard and develop enjoyment of routine work and tasks. When low you can be lazy and	You are here to develop the habit of acting, be a doer and executer of ideas. When low, you can struggle with apathy, laziness and lack of

113

stuck in 1 place, without progression	focus and direction
You are here to develop patient perseverance, so that every step in the process towards your goals for your stable foundation are taken. You are prone to impatience and missing steps	You are here to learn to be social, talkative, the life of the party and bringer of fun & positivity. You need to be the networker, communicating an emotional message. You can be quiet and struggle to speak
You are here to learn to come to terms with limitation — both the limitations that are externally imposed on you and the limitations that you impose upon yourself.	You must develop interdependence, life path 3's like to be looked after and can be prone to avoiding work or anything needing routine and commitment
You are here to look at your wounded or problematic relationships and work through the feelings of lack and pain they have brought to you.	You are here to be opportunistic, to network, make useful connections and snap up opportunities to spread the word and progress ideas and projects
You are prone to choosing social isolation, avoiding social situations due to social anxiety. It is important that you socialise regularly in familiar groups and with likeminded friends.	You must learn to take responsibility and listen to guidance; you can be irresponsible. You must think before you act, and take full responsibility for what you do

Life Path 4 with Birthday Number 5

Life Path Number 4 (90% Focus)	Birthday Number 5 (10% Focus)
You are here to learn to commit to a person and/or place, so that you can put down roots and dig the foundations for security. You can be uncommitted and therefore unable to build stability and security	You are easily bored and want to look at or study lots of topics. Initial varied experience is needed in order to choose a specialism, you are here to learn to be disciplined, to continue with a topic or activity beyond the boredom of the detail, towards mastery and specialism.
You are here to learn to set and achieve goals to take you on your journey towards inner and outer stability and security. Foundations, structures, families, and business empires are built 1 goal at a time.	You are here to develop the ability to balance variety, change and adventure with the stability of family and skill mastery. You can be totally spontaneous and take risks, jumping from one experience to another, but never settling or progressing
You are here to learn to plan, create a process and/or procedure to ensure the achievement of your goals. You can be directionless, lazy and block your own progression	You need to learn to be extremely intuitive and access your intuitive wisdom when making decisions, assessing people and situations.
You are here to develop deep meticulous focus on achieving stability, like a stable home, business or income and building your inner security. You can be scattered	You are here to develop your ability to attain inner freedom and outer freedom by doing things you might not want to do. Doing what you want is not necessarily freedom, you can become a slave to your desires. Freedom and discipline are inherently linked.
You are here to learn to be detail orientated, analytical, organised, and accurate to ensure your plans and processes are watertight. You can be disorganised and miss steps in the plan	You are here to learn to develop your verbal and written communication skills towards charismatic sharing of ideas and stories related to your specialism. You have the potential to be a great communicator

You are here to develop a work ethic, to work hard and develop enjoyment of routine work and tasks. When low you can be lazy and stuck in 1 place, without progression	You are here to learn to be committed, dependable, to do what you say you are going to do. You often forget what you promise because you are so chaotic, scattered, and changeable, looking for the next new experience
You are here to develop patient perseverance, so that every step in the process towards your goals for your stable foundation are taken. You are prone to impatience and missing steps	You are here to develop your social skills and charisma, to have the potential to be fun loving, positive, and optimistic. You can be uptight and argumentative
You are here to learn to come to terms with limitation — both the limitations that are externally imposed on you and the limitations that you impose upon yourself.	You are here to develop consistent independence. You can swing from independence to dependence and back again. Risky behaviour and 'get rich quick' schemes can bring on dependence
You are here to look at your wounded or problematic relationships and work through the feelings of lack and pain they have brought to you.	You are here to learn to develop fearlessness and help others to live fearlessly. You can be fearful of many things, restriction, and boredom, to name but a few. You need to challenge yourself and others past your own comfort zone
You are prone to choosing social isolation, avoiding social situations due to social anxiety. It is important that you socialise regularly in familiar groups and with likeminded friends.	You are here to learn to make good use of your energy and drive, if you feel restricted and under confident, you will be restless, and you may turn into a drama queen. Use your energy for experience and adventure, be courageous

Life Path 4 with Birthday Number 6

Life Path Number 4 (90% Focus)	Birthday Number 6 (10% Focus)
You are here to learn to commit to a person and/or place, so that you can put down roots and dig the foundations for security. You can be uncommitted and therefore unable to build stability and security	You are here to be a visionary of the ideal, the dreamer of a utopian world. You must act to create a better world with your ideals.
You are here to learn to set and achieve goals to take you on your journey towards inner and outer stability and security. Foundations, structures, families, and business empires are built 1 goal at a time.	You are here to learn to not use your ideals as a benchmark for your happiness. You must not base your emotional wellbeing on the achievement of your ideals. You often judge yourself and others for not hitting perfection, causing you great unhappiness
You are here to learn to plan, create a process and/or procedure to ensure the achievement of your goals. You can be directionless, lazy and block your own progression	Your perfectionism can make you an over achiever due to your constant self-judgement. You never meet your own standards. You must keep your big picture in mind and not get stuck in petty detail. You can often judge small imperfections and ruin or miss your successes.
You are here to develop deep meticulous focus on achieving stability, like a stable home, business or income and building your inner security. You can be scattered	You are here to learn to be a nurturer, compassionate caring and giving, especially to those that are vulnerable or struggling within your close relationships, your community, and the wider world. Your judgemental nature can make you cruel and neglectful.
You are here to learn to be detail orientated, analytical, organised, and accurate to ensure your plans and processes are watertight. You can be disorganised and miss steps	You are here to develop boundaries to ensure your mental and physical health. You do a lot for others, sometimes too much, which can make you feel undervalued,

in the plan	unappreciated, and ill with exhaustion. You may force unsolicited advice and meddle in other people's affairs.
You are here to develop a work ethic, to work hard and develop enjoyment of routine work and tasks. When low you can be lazy and stuck in 1 place, without progression	You are here to develop your social skills and be a team player. You must break through low self-esteem to be talkative, fun loving and relaxed around others. You can be shy and hide in the background.
You are here to develop patient perseverance, so that every step in the process towards your goals for your stable foundation are taken. You are prone to impatience and missing steps	You are here to create a stable, nurturing, tranquil home to maintain your security and well-being. Then nurture a family in an environment of stability and love. When low you can be a selfish, neglectful drama queen.
You are here to learn to come to terms with limitation — both the limitations that are externally imposed on you and the limitations that you impose upon yourself.	You are here to learn to be responsible and do good for those you care for. People naturally put you in positions of responsibility, but you often resent always being the 'responsible one.' Have boundaries on your responsibility so that you do not do too much.
You are here to look at your wounded or problematic relationships and work through the feelings of lack and pain they have brought to you.	You are here to learn to develop and use your artistic and aesthetic potential. Artistic, enhancing make up, great art and home designs. You have great musical potential that you may not develop.
You are prone to choosing social isolation, avoiding social situations due to social anxiety. It is important that you socialise regularly in familiar groups and with likeminded friends.	

Life Path 4 with Birthday Number 7

Life Path Number 4 (90% Focus)	Birthday Number 7 (10% Focus)
You are here to learn to commit to a person and/or place, so that you can put down roots and dig the foundations for security. You can be uncommitted and therefore unable to build stability and security	You are here to learn to have faith that you are an immortal soul that has experience from previous lives. You must trust the soul within you by listening to and following your intuition without over thinking and applying logic. Listen to and follow your inner voice and feel safe enough to communicate your soul wisdom to the world without fear of ridicule
You are here to learn to set and achieve goals to take you on your journey towards inner and outer stability and security. Foundations, structures, families, and business empires are built 1 goal at a time.	You are here to trust that the world is not against you. The universe is everything existing in perfect balance, it is like a cosmic library of all knowledge and experience. We must experience it all to learn and evolve
You are here to learn to plan, create a process and/or procedure to ensure the achievement of your goals. You can be directionless, lazy and block your own progression	Your focus for this lifetime must be Inner development rather than outer development and success. You must develop yourself constantly with self-discovery and spiritual wisdom. Meditation and time in nature is imperative for you
You are here to develop deep meticulous focus on achieving stability, like a stable home, business or income and building your inner security. You can be scattered	You are here to learn to be a problem solver, thinker, a studier of the metaphysical and the big questions. You need to research, learn, and analyse theories to accrue wisdom.
You are here to learn to be detail orientated, analytical, organised, and accurate to ensure your plans and processes are watertight. You	You are here to learn to filter your research through your intuition and use your research of other people's theories for your own needs. You

can be disorganised and miss steps in the plan	can be too analytical and ignore your intuition. Or totally spiritual and ignore other theories. You must balance the two.
You are here to develop a work ethic, to work hard and develop enjoyment of routine work and tasks. When low you can be lazy and stuck in 1 place, without progression	You are here to be a free thinker, to be less interested in popular culture and following norms of fashion and appearance. This can make you feel different and out of place and lonely
You are here to develop patient perseverance, so that every step in the process towards your goals for your stable foundation are taken. You are prone to impatience and missing steps	You are here to develop the ability to focus on something long enough to develop it into something useful. You can be a little scattered and struggle to focus
You are here to learn to come to terms with limitation — both the limitations that are externally imposed on you and the limitations that you impose upon yourself.	You are here to develop interdependence, self-sufficiency but also a healthy dependence on other people. You like to do things for yourself but take care not to push others away
You are here to look at your wounded or problematic relationships and work through the feelings of lack and pain they have brought to you.	You are here to learn to deal with and reconcile your sensitive emotions. Others often think you are aloof, but you are a well of deep emotions. You need to connect emotionally, both to yourself and to other people
You are prone to choosing social isolation, avoiding social situations due to social anxiety. It is important that you socialise regularly in familiar groups and with likeminded friends.	You are here to learn to balance your need to be alone and work alone with social contact. You love to be alone, but you must ensure that you do not isolate yourself beyond what is healthy

Life Path 4 with Birthday Number 8

Life Path Number 4 (90% Focus)	Birthday Number 8 (10% Focus)
You are here to learn to commit to a person and/or place, so that you can put down roots and dig the foundations for security. You can be uncommitted and therefore unable to build stability and security	You are both spiritual and worldly. But you are here to learn the secrets of worldly financial success. You seek the freedom that comes from financial success. But freedom brings responsibility, your ethics will be tested multiple times
You are here to learn to set and achieve goals to take you on your journey towards inner and outer stability and security. Foundations, structures, families, and business empires are built 1 goal at a time.	You are here to learn to use your financial success as a tool to help others achieve the same financial success. You often spend your abundance on materialistic status symbols rather than helping others
You are here to learn to plan, create a process and/or procedure to ensure the achievement of your goals. You can be directionless, lazy and block your own progression	You are here to develop a healthy attitude towards money. You may resent or hate wealthy people, or you may feel guilty about your own wealth. You must understand that financial wealth does not equate to poor ethics
You are here to develop deep meticulous focus on achieving stability, like a stable home, business or income and building your inner security. You can be scattered	You are here to develop balanced determination for achievement but with integrity and for the good of others. You can be either obsessed with achievement or fearful of achievement from low self-esteem. It is important that you develop a positive mindset because you attract what you think about.
You are here to learn to be detail orientated, analytical, organised, and accurate to ensure your plans and processes are watertight. You can be disorganised and miss steps in the plan	You are here to develop inner confidence and balanced personal power. You can swing from over dominance or misuse of power to hiding away or submission to others

You are here to develop a work ethic, to work hard and develop enjoyment of routine work and tasks. When low you can be lazy and stuck in 1 place, without progression	You are here to develop skilled leadership, which consists of subject competence coupled with excellent social skills and charisma
You are here to develop patient perseverance, so that every step in the process towards your goals for your stable foundation are taken. You are prone to impatience and missing steps	You are here to work hard as an excellent practical businessperson, but you must ensure that you do not work too hard, you need time out and time for your family
You are here to learn to come to terms with limitation — both the limitations that are externally imposed on you and the limitations that you impose upon yourself.	You are here to be worldly, strong, resilient, disciplined, and realistic. To be successful you need to be strong, tough, and able to cope with The ups and downs of the world
You are here to look at your wounded or problematic relationships and work through the feelings of lack and pain they have brought to you.	You are here to develop bravery and the courage to take risks to progress. Success comes from having the bravery to take risks
You are prone to choosing social isolation, avoiding social situations due to social anxiety. It is important that you socialise regularly in familiar groups and with likeminded friends.	You are here to develop organisation and management skills, resolve to making things happen and to define and meet your goals.

Life Path 4 with Birthday Number 9

Life Path Number 4 (90% focus)	Birthday Number 9 (10% Focus)
You are here to learn to commit to a person and/or place, so that you can put down roots and dig the foundations for security. You can be uncommitted and therefore unable to build stability and security	You are here to learn to follow your intuitive wisdom and live to spiritual laws, rather than worldly laws, conventions, and ideals. You tend to follow worldly laws and prejudices as an excuse for your actions. But if you had followed your intuitive spiritual wisdom, you would not have acted that way. Focus on faith over logic
You are here to learn to set and achieve goals to take you on your journey towards inner and outer stability and security. Foundations, structures, families, and business empires are built 1 goal at a time.	You are here to learn to act with integrity for the benefit of others. You are powerful and you must use your power for the benefit of others. You can act for selfish or nefarious reasons
You are here to learn to plan, create a process and/or procedure to ensure the achievement of your goals. You can be directionless, lazy and block your own progression	You are here to learn to lead by example, do you practise what you preach? You can be quite domineering, an adviser with all the answers. But you must let others make their own mistakes
You are here to develop deep meticulous focus on achieving stability, like a stable home, business or income and building your inner security. You can be scattered	You are here to make your life your teaching, you need to counsel with wisdom. You are a developed soul, the totality of all the numbers, full of cellular experience and higher knowledge
You are here to learn to be detail orientated, analytical, organised, and accurate to ensure your plans and processes are watertight. You can be disorganised and miss steps in the plan	You are here to develop broad mindedness, meet and accept diverse people. You must learn to be a humanitarian and make the world a better place. You need a global consciousness, as you can be narrow minded, judgemental, and

	even bigoted.
You are here to develop a work ethic, to work hard and develop enjoyment of routine work and tasks. When low you can be lazy and stuck in 1 place, without progression	You are here to learn to take responsibility for your powerful choices. You sometimes run away from the consequences of your actions
You are here to develop patient perseverance, so that every step in the process towards your goals for your stable foundation are taken. You are prone to impatience and missing steps	You need to develop towards being a successful entrepreneur or businessperson if it is with something you feel passionate about. You must choose work that has meaning for you. You are a powerful force for change
You are here to learn to come to terms with limitation — both the limitations that are externally imposed on you and the limitations that you impose upon yourself	You are here to develop excellent social skills and charisma. You could develop the skills of a powerful speaker and influencer of others. People will hang on your every word
You are here to look at your wounded or problematic relationships and work through the feelings of lack and pain they have brought to you.	You are here to look after the wellbeing of others. But when you are in trouble or need support, people do not notice. You must ask for what you need, you must ask for help
You are prone to choosing social isolation, avoiding social situations due to social anxiety. It is important that you socialise regularly in familiar groups and with likeminded friends.	You are here to wrap things up, let go and surrender. You can have a victim mentality, holding onto feelings that no longer serve you, unable to move on from perceived injustice, normally rooted in family issues.

Life Path 4 with Birthday Master 11

Life Path Number 4 (90% Focus)	Birthday Master 11 (10% Focus)
You are here to learn to commit to a person and/or place, so that you can put down roots and dig the foundations for security. You can be uncommitted and therefore unable to build stability and security	You are an old soul, with higher potential and higher responsibility to improve the world. You are here to learn to connect to source energy to channel unique new ideas and messages to change the world. You are here to learn to be happy in the limelight expressing new ideas for an audience. You need to develop and trust your massive intuitive potential. You often hide your ideas due to low confidence
You are here to learn to set and achieve goals to take you on your journey towards inner and outer stability and security. Foundations, structures, families, and business empires are built 1 goal at a time.	You are here to learn to be the ideas person, but you struggle to bring your unique ideas to reality because you lose interest quickly after the initial idea of sabotage yourself due to crippling low confidence. You are an idealistic dreamer whose ideas are often not grounded in reality
You are here to learn to plan, create a process and/or procedure to ensure the achievement of your goals. You can be directionless, lazy and block your own progression	You are here to learn to be confident in your uniqueness because unique people have unique ground-breaking ideas. It is important that you are not craving validation from others. Your validation should come from your intuition.
You are here to develop deep meticulous focus on achieving stability, like a stable home, business or income and building your inner security. You can be scattered	You need to bring unique, new ideas that break barriers, or challenge others comfort zone. You must learn to be brave, confident and be willing to take risks
You are here to learn to be detail orientated, analytical, organised, and accurate to ensure your plans	You need to be a practical initiator, a doer, action orientated that learns by experience. Ideas will stay

and processes are watertight. You can be disorganised and miss steps in the plan	unmanifested until you act! Only action brings change
You are here to develop a work ethic, to work hard and develop enjoyment of routine work and tasks. When low you can be lazy and stuck in 1 place, without progression	You need to set intentions then use spiritual practice and visualisation to channel your advanced, intense master energy into initiation and action. Unchanneled or mismanaged energy can cause intense nervous energy and anxiety. You may medicate these with unhealthy substances.
You are here to develop patient perseverance, so that every step in the process towards your goals for your stable foundation are taken. You are prone to impatience and missing steps	You are here to learn to be interdependent, not so independent that you push others away and refuse to delegate. You cannot do everything alone. Independence is an illusion; we are all interconnected
You are here to learn to come to terms with limitation — both the limitations that are externally imposed on you and the limitations that you impose upon yourself.	You need to be determined to succeed. Constant self-discovery and intuitive spiritual development is key for you to develop complete trust in the skills you have learned and mastered to serve as a kind of "security blanket" for you when you are feeling insecure
You are here to look at your wounded or problematic relationships and work through the feelings of lack and pain they have brought to you.	You need to learn to be a supportive, nurturing leader, be firm and assertive but also empathic and supportive. You must lead others to the fruition of your ideas, but with balanced personal power
You are prone to choosing social isolation, avoiding social situations due to social anxiety. It is important that you socialise regularly in familiar groups and with likeminded	Your power causes ripples, both positive and negative, you must remember that great power brings great responsibility. You must ensure that your intentions are good

friends.	
	You are here to learn to be responsible to others, your family, team, or group but in a balanced way. You can be too responsible and do too much. You are irresponsible if you feel undervalued, resentful, and exhausted.
	You must develop and improve your social skills, focus on widening and deepening your relationships and make decisions subjectively. It is important that you deepen your relationships and connect 121
	You may struggle to maintain long term close and romantic relationships.
	You must learn not to smother your loved ones or have expectations that can never be met. OR back away from wanting love because it hurts too badly. You need to balance your intense need for love for healthy relationships.
	You are here to learn to be intuitive and sensitive to the needs of others. You are here to be of service to others, the development of intuition will aid you in this journey
	You are here to learn to be a cooperative team player to get the job done as part of a cohesive team. You can be a disruptive, uncooperative drama queen.
	You must develop the assertiveness to demand boundaries to being overworked, walked all over, taken

	advantage of, and/or taken for granted. You must not be a "shape shifter" who changes who you are in order to please others or keep the peace. Be you and consider yourself too.
	You are here to serve the world, help the team, the task and be dependable. You can always be relied upon to keep the cogs turning behind the scenes
	You are here to be the tactful mediator of the team/group/family, helping to resolve conflicts fairly and for the good of everyone involved. You hate conflict and often run and hide until it is over
	You are here to learn to plan the next steps after channelling your message or idea & build a team to achieve it. The energy of the 11/2 needs to be the nurturer of ideas and a builder of teams
	You must learn to give yourself your own kudos. Oftentimes you judge yourself on what everyone else says or thinks about you. You need to develop your internal compass and turn inward for validation, do what YOU think you should do

Life Path 4 with Birthday Master 22/4

Life Path Number 4 (90% Focus)	Birthday Master 22/4 (10% Focus)
You are here to learn to commit to a person and/or place, so that you can put down roots and dig the foundations for security. You can be uncommitted and therefore unable to build stability and security	You are an old soul, as spiritual as you are practical, here to channel and then manifest ideas in reality to build world safety, stability, and security. You must learn to handle the master builder energy and focus it to manifestation. You have a big responsibility to the team and the world to build structures (buildings, concepts, body, mind, spirit, businesses, organisations, even an empire for the purpose of world stability and security
You are here to learn to set and achieve goals to take you on your journey towards inner and outer stability and security. Foundations, structures, families, and business empires are built 1 goal at a time.	You must develop and improve your social skills, focus on widening and deepening your relationships to assist you to manifest your big ideas. It is important that you learn to deepen your relationships and connect 121, you cannot do this alone!
You are here to learn to plan, create a process and/or procedure to ensure the achievement of your goals. You can be directionless, lazy and block your own progression	You must learn to have balanced, healthy relationships with others that are part of your sense of security. You must learn not to smother your loved ones and your team or have expectations that can never be met. OR Your big task in this lifetime may disrupt your love relationships. You may back away from wanting love because it hurts too badly or attacks your sense of security

You are here to develop deep meticulous focus on achieving stability, like a stable home, business or income and building your inner security. You can be scattered	You are here to learn to listen to and follow your intuition. Intuition is needed for you to be sensitive to the needs of others. You are here to be of service to change the world, the development of intuition will aid you in this journey
You are here to learn to be detail orientated, analytical, organised, and accurate to ensure your plans and processes are watertight. You can be disorganised and miss steps in the plan	You are here to learn to be a cooperative team player to get the job done as part of a cohesive team. You may fail to communicate effectively with others. You can be a hard-headed and high handed at times.
You are here to develop a work ethic, to work hard and develop enjoyment of routine work and tasks. When low you can be lazy and stuck in 1 place, without progression	You must develop the assertiveness to demand boundaries to being overworked, walked all over, taken advantage of, and/or taken for granted. You must also develop your ability to respect other people's boundaries and not be high handed.
You are here to develop patient perseverance, so that every step in the process towards your goals for your stable foundation are taken. You are prone to impatience and missing steps	You are here to be of service to the world, the leader, the team, the task and be dependable. You can always be counted upon to keep the cogs turning behind the scenes
You are here to learn to come to terms with limitation — both the limitations that are externally imposed on you and the limitations that you impose upon yourself.	You are extremely sensitive, and you hate and run away from conflict. But you are here to learn to be a tactful mediator, helping to resolve conflicts fairly and for the good of the team/family/group
You are here to look at your wounded or problematic	You are here to learn to stay focused and plan the next steps after you

relationships and work through the feelings of lack and pain they have brought to you.

have channelled a new idea & build a team to achieve it. The energy of the 22 needs to be the nurturer, the builder of ideas and teams.

You are prone to choosing social isolation, avoiding social situations due to social anxiety. It is important that you socialise regularly in familiar groups and with likeminded friends.

You must learn to give yourself your own kudos. Oftentimes you judge yourself on what everyone else says or thinks about you. You need to develop your internal compass and turn inward for validation, do what you think you should do

You are here to learn to commit to a person and/or place, so that you can put down roots and dig the foundations for security. You can be uncommitted and therefore unable to build stability and security

You are here to learn to set and achieve goals to take you on your journey towards inner and outer stability and security.

Foundations, structures, families, and business empires are built 1 goal at a time.

You are here to learn to plan, create a process and/or procedure to ensure the achievement of your goals and bring strength and stability to dynamic ideas. You can be directionless, lazy and block your own progression.

You are here to develop deep meticulous focus on achieving stability, like a stable home, business or income and building your inner security. You can be scattered and miss steps in your impatience.

	You are here to learn to be detail orientated, analytical, organised, and accurate to ensure your plans and processes are watertight. You can be disorganised, flaky and miss steps in your plan
	Your master 22/4 Birthday means that you are an old soul and you have agreed to bring safety, stability, and security to the world. You innovate and build empires, organisations, and businesses. This involves hard work, detail focus, routine work, and tasks. You are here to develop a work ethic, to work hard and develop enjoyment of routine work and tasks
	You are here to develop patient perseverance, so that every step in the process towards your goals for your stable foundation are taken. You are prone to impatience and corner cutting.
	You are here to develop determination and the perseverance to keep going past obstacles to achieve your goals. You are prone to giving up at the first hurdle.
	You are here to learn to come to terms with limitation — both the limitations that are externally imposed on you and the limitations that you impose upon yourself.
	You are here to look at your wounded or problematic relationships and work through the feelings of lack and pain they have brought to you. All experiences have

	lessons embedded within them
	Avoid social isolation by socialising regularly in familiar groups and with likeminded friends.

Your Life Path & Birthday Number Five (5)

You have chosen to incarnate to learn the lessons of the 5 life path energy because when speaking to your spirit guide before this life, you highlighted that you needed to learn the lessons of the 5 energy. You are here to learn and discover through, depth of experience, discipline, and focus, which is setting priorities and having the discipline to achieve them, brings mastery and ultimate freedom. You must work against swinging between dependence and independence and work on balance between self-reliance and family.

When you are walking your Life Path successfully, you have a thirst for knowledge on human sciences, philosophy, and esoteric matters. At your highest vibration, you are always learning, full of happiness of spirit with a zest for life. You love change, challenge and courage like an explorer, traveller, and an adventurer, here to discover what true freedom represents.

When struggling, you can be fearful of many things, fearful of action, restriction, even fearful of boredom. You must learn to be fearless and inspire other people to be fearless and find their own freedom. You must be aware of the restrictions of society but know that your sense of inner freedom cannot be compromised.

You must learn to reconcile and integrate discipline and freedom, using the first to achieve the second. This means that to achieve real freedom you need to focus with discipline on one activity in more depth rather than scratching the surface of many activities and topics. You are here to find your focus, your specialism, your mastery, then use this mastery to achieve freedom.

Your life path 5 puts you on a quest for freedom and independence, leading you to seek a wide variety of experiences that can make you scattered and spread too thin thus achieving no progression. If you work on focusing on one thing or at least one thing at a time with discipline and focus. Thus, progressing towards specialism, you can then expand and communicate charismatically, to gain further progression and inner freedom. It is important for you to start looking for depth of experience rather than breadth by focusing on one thing rather than scattering your energy over too many things. By choosing to focus on one thing deeply, you will realise that all of your varied topics of interest are linked.

Your 5 energy provides you with the potential to be a multi-talented and a resourceful 'Jack of all trades' which can further scatter your energy and reduce your attention span. You are easily bored and full of energy and drive which, pointed in negative directions, could be very damaging for you and those around you.

You tend to be unfocused, changeable, and impulsive, thriving in fast paced environments like accident and emergency or search and rescue, just ensure that you take intuitive and calculated risks. But as a 5 Life Path, you do need more focus and commitment. You learn many topics and experience a lot, but you must focus your energy rather than scattering it. Find your passion and study it so deeply that you break into the space where all your varied topics of interest connect.

Your life path 5 means that you are here to experience a lot and learn from those experiences so that you can assess your passions for areas of focus. You must experience variety, develop fearlessness, and adapt to change. You could travel, be adventurous, and experience new people, new ideas and new technology. This exploration and learning must serve to help you find your passion, a passion that you focus on totally. Your sense of adventure must never leave you, it's more about finding balance, balancing your need for variation with the stability of family and focused discipline. This balance is important for your progression and freedom.

You may be fearful of exploring new lands, languages, cultures, and new innovations but this is your path. You must find the courage and bravery to get out there and do it. You must be a fearless free thinker, not adhering to any clubs or ideologies. Ideally, you need work that offers a flexible schedule and freedom of thought without predictability or repetition.

Your life path 5 suggests that you struggle to take responsibility for your own life and the consequences of your spontaneous choices. Once again, the key is to balance your need for change, adventure and varied experience with discipline, focus, security, & family needs.

Your 5 purpose energy needs you to develop your potential to be highly creative and communicate your creativity charismatically. You could communicate verbally, in writing, and/or through your creative artistry. You have a very vivid imagination, providing you with the potential to be an excellent storyteller. Practical experience and full trust in your intuition will improve your confidence and charisma.

You must also work on your social skills and refine and develop your intuitive and clairvoyant potential. You may struggle at first with your social communication and networking skills. You must learn to intuitively read others to understand where they are coming from and get them on board. You can be a wired, tense, argumentative drama queen with an addiction to drama.

Your life path 5 needs you to be fearless and willing to speak your truth like a freedom fighter. You may limit yourself and shut yourself away because of your fears and anxieties but you must be braver, throw caution to the wind and go for it. You need to confidently live your own intuitive truth which can make you a rebel as you will not be swayed by popular opinion. You will refuse to subscribe to ideologies or to listen to guidance from others that doesn't resonate with your intuition.

Your 'I'll do what I want' attitude may feel like freedom but eventually you will realise you have actually become a slave to your desires through ill health or incarceration. You can indeed do what you want but will eating anything you want bring you freedom? Often what we think of as freedom can actually take our freedom away. Your only route to tangible and intangible freedom is discipline. The development of your mastery for improvements in your emotional health and financial freedom.

You can be uptight, wired, argumentative and judgemental, but you need to be more laid back, friendly and peace loving. You need to develop more of a 'live and let live' attitude, making you more tolerant and non-judgemental.

You need to be the director and writer of your own movie, you will not be told what to do or think, you are rebellious and a free thinker. But you can be flaky, unreliable, undisciplined, a procrastinator, easily bored and restless. You struggle with routine and commitment which can make family life a difficult proposition until you find balance. You can be a bit of a job hopper too, never having the self-discipline to see things through. This is because you have not yet found your mastery, when you do, you will be better able to commit. You make promises to help people with the sincere intention of following through, then you get side-tracked and forget to do what you promised. You do not do this deliberately; it is all part of your struggle to find focus and discipline.

You tend to be rebelliously and hedonistically addictive, overindulgent, melodramatic, and inconsistent. Freedom is not about indulging in whatever you want to excess, that is not real freedom, in fact sometimes your 'free choice' can consequently enslave you. The freedom that you are striving for will require discipline, and focused study on one task or field of study, it's the key to your success.

Your challenges are that you can be inconsistent because you are juggling too many thoughts, being pulled in too many directions making you forget your original promises.

Sometimes your 'freedom' degenerates into self-indulgence, without external restrictions. Doing what you want when you want has little to do with your purpose and it just makes you uncommitted, undependable, and irresponsible. You need focus and exercise discipline to lead you towards inner freedom.

You may fear being tied down and you may hate to commit because you prefer to be free and independent. But you can give away your independence through fear, or become over independent, down to cutting your own hair and avoiding relationships for fear of becoming too dependent. You need to balance discipline, stability and family with your own passion and self-reliance.

You are prone to high anxiety and fiery outbursts of temper because of your constant mind chatter and your constant need for stimulation, Meditation would be great to quieten your mind.

Careers that will help you achieve your life path:

Author, speaker, teacher and entrepreneur, PR, Advertising, Acting, Journalism, Management, Hospitality, Emergency Services.

Social Attributes – Sensuous, Changeable, Impulsive

Socially – Fun loving, Charming and Enthusiastic.

Colour – Light Blue

Subtle body – Throat Chakra, communication

Days – Fridays and Saturdays

Astrologically – Saturn, zodiac signs Libra and Sagittarius

Life Path 5 with Birthday Number 1

Life Path Number 5 (90% Focus)	Birthday Number 1 (10% Focus)
You are easily bored and want to look at or study lots of topics. Initial varied experience is needed in order to choose a specialism, you are here to learn to be disciplined, to continue with a topic or activity beyond the boredom of the detail, towards mastery and specialism	You are here to learn to connect to source energy to download / channel unique new ideas. You often hide your ideas due to low confidence. You are here to learn to be happy in the limelight expressing new ideas for an audience.
You are here to develop the ability to balance variety, change and adventure with the stability of family and skill mastery. You can be totally spontaneous and take risks, jumping from one experience to another, but never settling or progressing	You are here to learn to be the ideas person, but you struggle to bring your unique ideas to reality because you lose interest quickly after the initial idea.
You need to learn to be extremely intuitive and access your intuitive wisdom when making decisions, assessing people and situations.	You are here to learn to be confident in your uniqueness because unique people have unique ground-breaking ideas. It is important that you are not craving validation from others.
You are here to develop your ability to attain inner and outer freedom by doing things you might not want to do. Doing what you want is not necessarily freedom, you can become a slave to your desires. Freedom and discipline are inherently linked	You need to be a practical initiator, a doer, action orientated that learns by experience. Only action makes the difference.
You are here to learn to develop your verbal and written communication skills towards charismatic sharing of ideas and stories related to your specialism. You have the potential to be a great communicator	You need to learn to trust your intuitive voice within. You must achieve balanced confidence in yourself & your abilities, fed by strong connection & trust in your intuition. You bring your ideas without fear. You must not seek

	validation from others or base your confidence on what others say.
You are here to learn to be committed, dependable, to do what you say you are going to do. You often forget what you promise because you are so chaotic, scattered, and changeable, looking for the next new experience	You need to bring unique, new ideas that break barriers, or challenge others comfort zones, you must learn to be brave, confident and be willing to take risks
You are here to develop your social skills and charisma, to have the potential to be fun loving, positive, and optimistic. You can be uptight and argumentative	You are here to learn to be interdependent, not so independent that you push others away and refuse to delegate. You cannot do everything alone. Independence is an illusion; we are all interconnected
You are here to develop consistent independence. You can swing from independence to dependence and back again. Risky behaviour and 'get rich quick' schemes can bring on dependence	You need to be determined to succeed. Constant self-discovery and development is key for you to develop complete trust in the skills you have learned and mastered to serve as a kind of "security blanket" for you when you are feeling insecure
You are here to learn to develop fearlessness and help others to live fearlessly too. You can be fearful of many things, restriction, and boredom, to name but a few. You need to challenge yourself and others past your own comfort zone.	You need to learn to be a powerful leader, be dominant and assertive. You must lead others to the fruition of your ideas, but with balanced personal power
You are here to learn to make good use of your energy and drive, if you feel restricted and under confident, you will be restless, and you may turn into a drama queen. Use your energy for experience and adventure, be courageous	Your power causes ripples, both positive and negative, you must remember that great power brings great responsibility. You must ensure that your intentions are good

Life Path 5 with Birthday Number 2

Life Path Number 5 (90% Focus)	Birthday Number 2 (10% Focus)
You are easily bored and want to look at or study lots of topics. Initial varied experience is needed in order to choose a specialism, you are here to learn to be disciplined, to continue with a topic or activity beyond the boredom of the detail, towards mastery and specialism	You are here to learn to be responsible to others and the team. You can be too responsible and do too much. You are irresponsible if you feel undervalued and resentful
You are here to develop the ability to balance variety, change and adventure with the stability of family and skill mastery. You can be totally spontaneous and take risks, jumping from one experience to another, but never settling or progressing	You must learn to improve your social skills, focus on widening and deepening your relationships and make decisions subjectively. It is important that you deepen your relationships and connect 121
You need to learn to be extremely intuitive and access your intuitive wisdom when making decisions, assessing people and situations.	You must learn not to smother your loved ones or have expectations that can never be met. OR you may back away from wanting love because it hurts too badly. You need to balance your intense need for love
You are here to develop your ability to attain inner and outer freedom by doing things you might not want to do. Doing what you want is not necessarily freedom, you can become a slave to your desires. Freedom and discipline are inherently linked	You are here to learn to be intuitive and sensitive to the needs of others. You are here to be of service to others, the development of intuition will aid you in this journey
You are here to learn to develop your verbal and written communication skills towards charismatic sharing of ideas and stories related to your specialism. You have the potential to be a great	You are here to learn to be a cooperative team player to get the job done as part of a cohesive team. You can be a disruptive, uncooperative drama queen.

communicator

You are here to learn to be committed, dependable, to do what you say you are going to do. You often forget what you promise because you are so chaotic, scattered, and changeable, looking for the next new experience	You must develop the assertiveness to demand boundaries to being overworked, walked all over, taken advantage of, and/or taken for granted. You must not be a "shape shifter" who changes who you are in order to please others or keep the peace.
You are here to develop your social skills and charisma, to have the potential to be fun loving, positive, and optimistic. You can be uptight and argumentative	You are here to serve the leader, the team, the task and be dependable. You can always be counted upon to keep the cogs turning behind the scenes
You are here to develop consistent independence. You can swing from independence to dependence and back again. Risky behaviour and 'get rich quick' schemes can bring on dependence	You are here to be the tactful mediator of the team, helping to resolve conflicts fairly and for the good of the team. You hate conflict and often run and hide until it is over
You are here to learn to develop fearlessness and help others to live fearlessly too. You can be fearful of many things, restriction, and boredom, to name but a few. You need to challenge yourself and others past your own comfort zone.	You are here to learn to plan the next steps after the initial idea & build a team to achieve it. The energy of the two is the nurturer of ideas and a builder of teams
You are here to learn to make good use of your energy and drive, if you feel restricted and under confident, you will be restless, and you may turn into a drama queen. Use your energy for experience and adventure, be courageous	You must learn to give yourself your own kudos. Oftentimes you judge yourself on what everyone else says or thinks about you. You need to develop your internal compass and turn inward for validation, do what you think you should do

Life Path 5 with Birthday Number 3

Life Path Number 5 (90% Focus)	Birthday Number 3 (10% Focus)
You are easily bored and want to look at or study lots of topics. Initial varied experience is needed in order to choose a specialism, you are here to learn to be disciplined, to continue with a topic or activity beyond the boredom of the detail, towards mastery and specialism	You are here to learn to express yourself verbally to inspire, inform and delight. You may struggle in some way verbally, chronic shyness, speech delay, stutter or struggling to find the words.
You are here to develop the ability to balance variety, change and adventure with the stability of family and skill mastery. You can be totally spontaneous and take risks, jumping from one experience to another, but never settling or progressing	You are here to learn to express yourself creatively to inspire, inform and delight. But you may struggle to progress, execute, and finish creative projects, due to lack of self-belief
You need to learn to be extremely intuitive and access your intuitive wisdom when making decisions, assessing people and situations.	You must learn to be dynamic, take risks and be confident to enjoy the attention and limelight of an audience. You can be shy, under confident and feel unable to take risks.
You are here to develop your ability to attain inner and outer freedom by doing things you might not want to do. Doing what you want is not necessarily freedom, you can become a slave to your desires. Freedom and discipline are inherently linked	You need to develop as an entrepreneur who is able to promote, network and make money creatively. But you may procrastinate and fail to stay focused and work inconsistently.
You are here to learn to develop your verbal and written communication skills towards charismatic sharing of ideas and stories related to your specialism. You have the potential to be a great	You are here to learn to express your emotions positively. You can be extremely sensitive to criticism and other people's emotions, causing you to express emotions negatively

communicator

You are here to learn to be committed, dependable, to do what you say you are going to do. You often forget what you promise because you are so chaotic, scattered, and changeable, looking for the next new experience	You are here to develop the habit of acting, be a doer and executer of ideas. When low, you can struggle with apathy, laziness and lack of focus and direction
You are here to develop your social skills and charisma, to have the potential to be fun loving, positive, and optimistic. You can be uptight and argumentative	You are here to learn to be social, talkative, the life of the party and bringer of fun & positivity. You need to be the networker, communicating an emotional message. You can be quiet and struggle to speak
You are here to develop consistent independence. You can swing from independence to dependence and back again. Risky behaviour and 'get rich quick' schemes can bring on dependence	You must develop interdependence, life path 3's like to be looked after and can be prone to avoiding work or anything needing routine and commitment
You are here to learn to develop fearlessness and help others to live fearlessly too. You can be fearful of many things, restriction, and boredom, to name but a few. You need to challenge yourself and others past your own comfort zone.	You are here to be opportunistic, to network, make useful connections and snap up opportunities to spread the word and progress ideas and projects
You are here to learn to make good use of your energy and drive, if you feel restricted and under confident, you will be restless, and you may turn into a drama queen. Use your energy for experience and adventure, be courageous	You must learn to take responsibility and listen to guidance; you can be irresponsible. You must think before you act, and take full responsibility for what you do

Life Path 5 with Birthday Number 4

Life Path Number 5 (90% Focus)	Birthday Number 4 (10% Focus)
You are easily bored and want to look at or study lots of topics. Initial varied experience is needed in order to choose a specialism, you are here to learn to be disciplined, to continue with a topic or activity beyond the boredom of the detail, towards mastery and specialism	You are here to learn to commit to a person and/or place, so that you can put down roots and dig the foundations for security. You can be uncommitted and therefore unable to build stability and security.
You are here to develop the ability to balance variety, change and adventure with the stability of family and skill mastery. You can be totally spontaneous and take risks, jumping from one experience to another, but never settling or progressing	You are here to learn to set and achieve goals to take you on your journey towards inner and outer stability and security. Foundations, structures, families, and business empires are built 1 goal at a time.
You need to learn to be extremely intuitive and access your intuitive wisdom when making decisions, assessing people and situations.	You are here to learn to plan, create a process and/or procedure to ensure the achievement of your goals. You can be directionless, lazy and block your own progression
You are here to develop your ability to attain inner and outer freedom by doing things you might not want to do. Doing what you want is not necessarily freedom, you can become a slave to your desires. Freedom and discipline are inherently linked	You are here to develop deep meticulous focus on achieving stability, like a stable home, business or income and building your inner security. You can be scattered
You are here to learn to develop your verbal and written communication skills towards charismatic sharing of ideas and stories related to your specialism. You have the potential to be a great communicator	You are here to learn to be detail orientated, analytical, organised, and accurate to ensure your plans and processes are watertight. You can be disorganised and miss steps in the plan

You are here to learn to be committed, dependable, to do what you say you are going to do. You often forget what you promise because you are so chaotic, scattered, and changeable, looking for the next new experience

You are here to develop a work ethic, to work hard and develop enjoyment of routine work and tasks. When low you can be lazy and stuck in 1 place, without progression

You are here to develop your social skills and charisma, to have the potential to be fun loving, positive, and optimistic. You can be uptight and argumentative

You are here to develop patient perseverance, so that every step in the process towards your goals for your stable foundation are taken. You are prone to impatience and missing steps

You are here to develop consistent independence. You can swing from independence to dependence and back again. Risky behaviour and 'get rich quick' schemes can bring on dependence

You are here to learn to come to terms with limitation — both the limitations that are externally imposed on you and the limitations that you impose upon yourself.

You are here to learn to develop fearlessness and help others to live fearlessly too. You can be fearful of many things, restriction, and boredom, to name but a few. You need to challenge yourself and others past your own comfort zone.

You are here to look at your wounded or problematic relationships and work through the feelings of lack and pain they have brought to you.

You are here to learn to make good use of your energy and drive, if you feel restricted and under confident, you will be restless, and you may turn into a drama queen. Use your energy for experience and adventure, be courageous

You are prone to choosing social isolation, avoiding social situations due to social anxiety. It is important that you socialise regularly in familiar groups and with likeminded friends.

Life Path 5 with Birthday Number 6

Life Path Number 5 (90% Focus)	Birthday Number 6 (10% Focus)
You are easily bored and want to look at or study lots of topics. Initial varied experience is needed in order to choose a specialism, you are here to learn to be disciplined, to continue with a topic or activity beyond the boredom of the detail, towards mastery and specialism	You are here to be a visionary of the ideal, the dreamer of a utopian world. You must act to create a better world with your ideals.
You are here to develop the ability to balance variety, change and adventure with the stability of family and skill mastery. You can be totally spontaneous and take risks, jumping from one experience to another, but never settling or progressing	You are here to learn to not use your ideals as a benchmark for your happiness. You must not base your emotional wellbeing on the achievement of your ideals. You often judge yourself and others for not hitting perfection, causing you great unhappiness
You need to learn to be extremely intuitive and access your intuitive wisdom when making decisions, assessing people and situations.	Your perfectionism can make you an over achiever due to your constant self-judgement. You never meet your own standards. You must keep your big picture in mind and not get stuck in petty detail. You can often judge small imperfections and ruin or miss your successes.
You are here to develop your ability to attain inner and outer freedom by doing things you might not want to do. Doing what you want is not necessarily freedom, you can become a slave to your desires. Freedom and discipline are inherently linked	You are here to learn to be a nurturer, compassionate caring and giving, especially to those that are vulnerable or struggling within your close relationships, your community, and the wider world. Your judgemental nature can make you cruel and neglectful.
You are here to learn to develop your verbal and written communication skills towards	You are here to develop boundaries to ensure your mental and physical health. You do a lot for others,

charismatic sharing of ideas and stories related to your specialism. You have the potential to be a great communicator

sometimes too much, which can make you feel undervalued, unappreciated, and ill with exhaustion. You may force unsolicited advice and meddle in other people's affairs.

You are here to learn to be committed, dependable, to do what you say you are going to do. You often forget what you promise because you are so chaotic, scattered, and changeable, looking for the next new experience

You are here to develop your social skills and be a team player. You must break through low self-esteem to be talkative, fun loving and relaxed around others. You can be shy and hide in the background.

You are here to develop your social skills and charisma, to have the potential to be fun loving, positive, and optimistic. You can be uptight and argumentative

You are here to create a stable, nurturing, tranquil home to maintain your security and well-being. Then nurture a family in an environment of stability and love. When low you can be a selfish, neglectful drama queen.

You are here to develop consistent independence. You can swing from independence to dependence and back again. Risky behaviour and 'get rich quick' schemes can bring on dependence

You are here to learn to be responsible and do good for those you care for. People naturally put you in positions of responsibility, but you often resent always being the 'responsible one.' Have boundaries on your responsibility so that you do not do too much.

You are here to learn to develop fearlessness and help others to live fearlessly too. You can be fearful of many things, restriction, and boredom, to name but a few. You need to challenge yourself and others past your own comfort zone.

You are here to learn to develop and use your artistic and aesthetic potential. Artistic, enhancing make up, great art and home designs. You have great musical potential that you may not develop.

You are here to learn to make good use of your energy and drive, if you feel restricted and under confident,

you will be restless, and you may turn into a drama queen. Use your energy for experience and adventure, be courageous	

Life Path 5 with Birthday Number 7

Life Path Number 5 (90% Focus)	Birthday Number 7 (10% Focus)
You are easily bored and want to look at or study lots of topics. Initial varied experience is needed in order to choose a specialism, you are here to learn to be disciplined, to continue with a topic or activity beyond the boredom of the detail, towards mastery and specialism	You are here to learn to have faith that you are an immortal soul that has experience from previous lives. You must trust the soul within you by listening to and following your intuition without over thinking and applying logic. Listen to and follow your inner voice and feel safe enough to communicate your soul wisdom to the world without fear of ridicule
You are here to develop the ability to balance variety, change and adventure with the stability of family and skill mastery. You can be totally spontaneous and take risks, jumping from one experience to another, but never settling or progressing	You are here to trust that the world is not against you. The universe is everything existing in perfect balance, it is like a cosmic library of all knowledge and experience. We must experience it all to learn and evolve
You need to learn to be extremely intuitive and access your intuitive wisdom when making decisions, assessing people and situations.	Your focus for this lifetime must be Inner development rather than outer development and success. You must develop yourself constantly with self-discovery and spiritual wisdom. Meditation and time in nature is imperative for you
You are here to develop your ability to attain inner and outer freedom by doing things you might not want to do. Doing what you want is not necessarily freedom, you can become a slave to your desires. Freedom and discipline are inherently linked	You are here to learn to be a problem solver, thinker, a studier of the metaphysical and the big questions. You need to research, learn, and analyse theories to accrue wisdom.
You are here to learn to develop your verbal and written communication skills towards	You are here to learn to filter your research through your intuition and use your research of other people's

charismatic sharing of ideas and stories related to your specialism. You have the potential to be a great communicator	theories for your own needs. You can be too analytical and ignore your intuition. Or totally spiritual and ignore other theories. You must balance the two.
You are here to learn to be committed, dependable, to do what you say you are going to do. You often forget what you promise because you are so chaotic, scattered, and changeable, looking for the next new experience	You are here to be a free thinker, to be less interested in popular culture and following norms of fashion and appearance. This can make you feel different and out of place and lonely
You are here to develop your social skills and charisma, to have the potential to be fun loving, positive, and optimistic. You can be uptight and argumentative	You are here to develop the ability to focus on something long enough to develop it into something useful. You can be a little scattered and struggle to focus
You are here to develop consistent independence. You can swing from independence to dependence and back again. Risky behaviour and 'get rich quick' schemes can bring on dependence	You are here to develop interdependence, self-sufficiency but also a healthy dependence on other people. You like to do things for yourself but take care not to push others away
You are here to learn to develop fearlessness and help others to live fearlessly too. You can be fearful of many things, restriction, and boredom, to name but a few. You need to challenge yourself and others past your own comfort zone.	You are here to learn to deal with and reconcile your sensitive emotions. Others often think you are aloof, but you are a well of deep emotions. You need to connect emotionally, both to yourself and to other people
You are here to learn to make good use of your energy and drive, if you feel restricted and under confident, you will be restless, and you may turn into a drama queen. Use your energy for experience and adventure, be courageous	You are here to learn to balance your need to be alone and work alone with social contact. You love to be alone, but you must ensure that you do not isolate yourself beyond what is healthy

Life Path 5 with Birthday Number 8

Life Path Number 5 (90% Focus)	Birthday Number 8 (10% Focus)
You are easily bored and want to look at or study lots of topics. Initial varied experience is needed in order to choose a specialism, you are here to learn to be disciplined, to continue with a topic or activity beyond the boredom of the detail, towards mastery and specialism	You are both spiritual and worldly. But you are here to learn the secrets of worldly financial success. You seek the freedom that comes from financial success. But freedom brings responsibility, your ethics will be tested multiple times
You are here to develop the ability to balance variety, change and adventure with the stability of family and skill mastery. You can be totally spontaneous and take risks, jumping from one experience to another, but never settling or progressing	You are here to learn to use your financial success as a tool to help others achieve the same financial success. You often spend your abundance on materialistic status symbols rather than helping others
You need to learn to be extremely intuitive and access your intuitive wisdom when making decisions, assessing people and situations.	You are here to develop a healthy attitude towards money. You may resent or hate wealthy people, or you may feel guilty about your own wealth. You must understand that financial wealth does not equate to poor ethics
You are here to develop your ability to attain inner and outer freedom by doing things you might not want to do. Doing what you want is not necessarily freedom, you can become a slave to your desires. Freedom and discipline are inherently linked	You are here to develop balanced determination for achievement but with integrity and for the good of others. You can be either obsessed with achievement or fearful of achievement from low self-esteem. It is important that you develop a positive mindset because you attract what you think about.
You are here to learn to develop your verbal and written communication skills towards charismatic sharing of ideas and stories related to your specialism. You have the potential to be a great	You are here to develop inner confidence and balanced personal power. You can swing from over dominance or misuse of power to hiding away or submission to

communicator	others
You are here to learn to be committed, dependable, to do what you say you are going to do. You often forget what you promise because you are so chaotic, scattered, and changeable, looking for the next new experience	You are here to develop skilled leadership, which consists of subject competence coupled with excellent social skills and charisma
You are here to develop your social skills and charisma, to have the potential to be fun loving, positive, and optimistic. You can be uptight and argumentative	You are here to work hard as an excellent practical businessperson, but you must ensure that you do not work too hard, you need time out and time for your family
You are here to develop consistent independence. You can swing from independence to dependence and back again. Risky behaviour and 'get rich quick' schemes can bring on dependence	You are here to be worldly, strong, resilient, disciplined, and realistic. To be successful you need to be strong, tough, and able to cope with The ups and downs of the world
You are here to learn to develop fearlessness and help others to live fearlessly too. You can be fearful of many things, restriction, and boredom, to name but a few. You need to challenge yourself and others past your own comfort zone.	You are here to develop bravery and the courage to take risks to progress. Success comes from having the bravery to take risks
You are here to learn to make good use of your energy and drive, if you feel restricted and under confident, you will be restless, and you may turn into a drama queen. Use your energy for experience and adventure, be courageous	You are here to develop organisation and management skills, resolve to making things happen and to define and meet your goals.

Life Path 5 with Birthday Number 9

Life Path Number 5 (90% Focus)	Birthday Number 9 (10% Focus)

You are easily bored and want to look at or study lots of topics. Initial varied experience is needed in order to choose a specialism, you are here to learn to be disciplined, to continue with a topic or activity beyond the boredom of the detail, towards mastery and specialism

You are here to learn to follow your intuitive wisdom and live to spiritual laws, rather than worldly laws, conventions, and ideals. You tend to follow worldly laws and prejudices as an excuse for your actions. But if you had followed your intuitive spiritual wisdom, you would not have acted that way. Focus on faith over logic

You are here to develop the ability to balance variety, change and adventure with the stability of family and skill mastery. You can be totally spontaneous and take risks, jumping from one experience to another, but never settling or progressing

You are here to learn to act with integrity for the benefit of others. You are powerful and you must use your power for the benefit of others. You can act for selfish or nefarious reasons

You need to learn to be extremely intuitive and access your intuitive wisdom when making decisions, assessing people and situations.

You are here to learn to lead by example, do you practise what you preach? You can be quite domineering, an adviser with all the answers. But you must let others make their own mistakes

You are here to develop your ability to attain inner and outer freedom by doing things you might not want to do. Doing what you want is not necessarily freedom, you can become a slave to your desires. Freedom and discipline are inherently linked

You are here to make your life your teaching, you need to counsel with wisdom. You are a developed soul, the totality of all the numbers, full of cellular experience and higher knowledge

You are here to learn to develop your verbal and written communication skills towards charismatic sharing of ideas and stories related to your specialism. You have the potential to be a great communicator

You are here to develop broad mindedness, meet and accept diverse people. You must learn to be a humanitarian and make the world a better place. You need a global consciousness, as you can be narrow minded, judgemental, and even bigoted.

You are here to learn to be committed, dependable, to do what you say you are going to do. You often forget what you promise because you are so chaotic, scattered, and changeable, looking for the next new experience	You are here to learn to take responsibility for your powerful choices. You sometimes run away from the consequences of your actions
You are here to develop your social skills and charisma, to have the potential to be fun loving, positive, and optimistic. You can be uptight and argumentative	You need to develop towards being a successful entrepreneur or businessperson if it is with something you feel passionate about. You must choose work that has meaning for you. You are a powerful force for change
You are here to develop consistent independence. You can swing from independence to dependence and back again. Risky behaviour and 'get rich quick' schemes can bring on dependence	You are here to develop excellent social skills and charisma. You could develop the skills of a powerful speaker and influencer of others. People will hang on your every word
You are here to learn to develop fearlessness and help others to live fearlessly too. You can be fearful of many things, restriction, and boredom, to name but a few. You need to challenge yourself and others past your own comfort zone.	You are here to look after the wellbeing of others. But when you are in trouble or need support, people do not notice. You must ask for what you need, you must ask for help
You are here to learn to make good use of your energy and drive, if you feel restricted and under confident, you will be restless, and you may turn into a drama queen. Use your energy for experience and adventure, be courageous	You are here to wrap things up, let go and surrender. You can have a victim mentality, holding onto feelings that no longer serve you, unable to move on from perceived injustice, normally rooted in family issues.

Life Path 5 with Birthday Master 11

Life Path Number 5 (90% Focus)	Birthday Master 11 (10% Focus)

You are easily bored and want to look at or study lots of topics. Initial varied experience is needed in order to choose a specialism, you are here to learn to be disciplined, to continue with a topic or activity beyond the boredom of the detail, towards mastery and specialism

You are an old soul, with higher potential and higher responsibility to improve the world. You are here to learn to connect to source energy to channel unique new ideas and messages to change the world. You are here to learn to be happy in the limelight expressing new ideas for an audience. You need to develop and trust your massive intuitive potential. You often hide your ideas due to low confidence

You are here to develop the ability to balance variety, change and adventure with the stability of family and skill mastery. You can be totally spontaneous and take risks, jumping from one experience to another, but never settling or progressing

You are here to learn to be the ideas person, but you struggle to bring your unique ideas to reality because you lose interest quickly after the initial idea of sabotage yourself due to crippling low confidence. You are an idealistic dreamer whose ideas are often not grounded in reality

You need to learn to be extremely intuitive and access your intuitive wisdom when making decisions, assessing people and situations.

You are here to learn to be confident in your uniqueness because unique people have unique ground-breaking ideas. It is important that you are not craving validation from others. Your validation should come from your intuition.

You are here to develop your ability to attain inner and outer freedom by doing things you might not want to do. Doing what you want is not necessarily freedom, you can become a slave to your desires. Freedom and discipline are inherently linked

You need to bring unique, new ideas that break barriers, or challenge others comfort zone. You must learn to be brave, confident and be willing to take risks

You are here to learn to develop your verbal and written communication skills towards

You need to be a practical initiator, a doer, action orientated that learns by experience. Ideas will stay

charismatic sharing of ideas and stories related to your specialism. You have the potential to be a great communicator	unmanifested until you act! Only action brings change
You are here to learn to be committed, dependable, to do what you say you are going to do. You often forget what you promise because you are so chaotic, scattered, and changeable, looking for the next new experience	You need to set intentions then use spiritual practice and visualisation to channel your advanced, intense master energy into initiation and action. Unchanneled or mismanaged energy can cause intense nervous energy and anxiety. You may medicate these with unhealthy substances.
You are here to develop your social skills and charisma, to have the potential to be fun loving, positive, and optimistic. You can be uptight and argumentative	You are here to learn to be interdependent, not so independent that you push others away and refuse to delegate. You cannot do everything alone. Independence is an illusion; we are all interconnected
You are here to develop consistent independence. You can swing from independence to dependence and back again. Risky behaviour and 'get rich quick' schemes can bring on dependence	You need to be determined to succeed. Constant self-discovery and intuitive spiritual development is key for you to develop complete trust in the skills you have learned and mastered to serve as a kind of "security blanket" for you when you are feeling insecure
You are here to learn to develop fearlessness and help others to live fearlessly too. You can be fearful of many things, restriction, and boredom, to name but a few. You need to challenge yourself and others past your own comfort zone.	You need to learn to be a supportive, nurturing leader, be firm and assertive but also empathic and supportive. You must lead others to the fruition of your ideas, but with balanced personal power
You are here to learn to make good use of your energy and drive, if you feel restricted and under confident, you will be restless, and you may	Your power causes ripples, both positive and negative, you must remember that great power brings great responsibility. You must

turn into a drama queen. Use your energy for experience and adventure, be courageous	ensure that your intentions are good
	You are here to learn to be responsible to others, your family, team, or group but in a balanced way. You can be too responsible and do too much. You are irresponsible if you feel undervalued, resentful, and exhausted.
	You must develop and improve your social skills, focus on widening and deepening your relationships and make decisions subjectively. It is important that you deepen your relationships and connect 121 You may struggle to maintain long term close and romantic relationships.
	You must learn not to smother your loved ones or have expectations that can never be met. OR back away from wanting love because it hurts too badly. You need to balance your intense need for love for healthy relationships.
	You are here to learn to be intuitive and sensitive to the needs of others. You are here to be of service to others, the development of intuition will aid you in this journey
	You are here to learn to be a cooperative team player to get the job done as part of a cohesive team. You can be a disruptive, uncooperative drama queen.

	You must develop the assertiveness to demand boundaries to being overworked, walked all over, taken advantage of, and/or taken for granted. You must not be a "shape shifter" who changes who you are in order to please others or keep the peace. Be you and consider yourself too.
	You are here to serve the world, help the team, the task and be dependable. You can always be relied upon to keep the cogs turning behind the scenes
	You are here to be the tactful mediator of the team/group/family, helping to resolve conflicts fairly and for the good of everyone involved. You hate conflict and often run and hide until it is over
	You are here to learn to plan the next steps after channelling your message or idea & build a team to achieve it. The energy of the 11/2 needs to be the nurturer of ideas and a builder of teams
	You must learn to give yourself your own kudos. Oftentimes you judge yourself on what everyone else says or thinks about you. You need to develop your internal compass and turn inward for validation, do what YOU think you should do

Life Path 5 with Birthday Master 22/4

Life Path Number 5 (90% Focus)	Birthday Master 22/4 (10%

	Focus)
You are easily bored and want to look at or study lots of topics. Initial varied experience is needed in order to choose a specialism, you are here to learn to be disciplined, to continue with a topic or activity beyond the boredom of the detail, towards mastery and specialism	You are an old soul, as spiritual as you are practical, here to channel and then manifest ideas in reality to build world safety, stability, and security. You must learn to handle the master builder energy and focus it to manifestation. You have a big responsibility to the team and the world to build structures (buildings, concepts, body, mind, spirit, businesses, organisations, even an empire for the purpose of world stability and security
You are here to develop the ability to balance variety, change and adventure with the stability of family and skill mastery. You can be totally spontaneous and take risks, jumping from one experience to another, but never settling or progressing	You must develop and improve your social skills, focus on widening and deepening your relationships to assist you to manifest your big ideas. It is important that you learn to deepen your relationships and connect 121, you cannot do this alone!
You need to learn to be extremely intuitive and access your intuitive wisdom when making decisions, assessing people and situations.	You must learn to have balanced, healthy relationships with others that are part of your sense of security. You must learn not to smother your loved ones and your team or have expectations that can never be met. OR Your big task in this lifetime may disrupt your love relationships. You may back away from wanting love because it hurts too badly or attacks your sense of security
You are here to develop your ability	You are here to learn to listen to and

to attain inner and outer freedom by doing things you might not want to do. Doing what you want is not necessarily freedom, you can become a slave to your desires. Freedom and discipline are inherently linked	follow your intuition. Intuition is needed for you to be sensitive to the needs of others. You are here to be of service to change the world, the development of intuition will aid you in this journey
You are here to learn to develop your verbal and written communication skills towards charismatic sharing of ideas and stories related to your specialism. You have the potential to be a great communicator	You are here to learn to be a cooperative team player to get the job done as part of a cohesive team. You may fail to communicate effectively with others. You can be a hard-headed and high handed at times.
You are here to learn to be committed, dependable, to do what you say you are going to do. You often forget what you promise because you are so chaotic, scattered, and changeable, looking for the next new experience	You must develop the assertiveness to demand boundaries to being overworked, walked all over, taken advantage of, and/or taken for granted. You must also develop your ability to respect other people's boundaries and not be high handed.
You are here to develop your social skills and charisma, to have the potential to be fun loving, positive, and optimistic. You can be uptight and argumentative	You are here to be of service to the world, the leader, the team, the task and be dependable. You can always be counted upon to keep the cogs turning behind the scenes
You are here to develop consistent independence. You can swing from independence to dependence and back again. Risky behaviour and 'get rich quick' schemes can bring on dependence	You are extremely sensitive, and you hate and run away from conflict. But you are here to learn to be a tactful mediator, helping to resolve conflicts fairly and for the good of the team/family/group
You are here to learn to develop fearlessness and help others to live fearlessly too. You can be fearful of	You are here to learn to stay focused and plan the next steps after you have channelled a new idea & build

many things, restriction, and boredom, to name but a few. You need to challenge yourself and others past your own comfort zone.

a team to achieve it. The energy of the 22 needs to be the nurturer, the builder of ideas and teams.

You are here to learn to make good use of your energy and drive, if you feel restricted and under confident, you will be restless, and you may turn into a drama queen. Use your energy for experience and adventure, be courageous

You must learn to give yourself your own kudos. Oftentimes you judge yourself on what everyone else says or thinks about you. You need to develop your internal compass and turn inward for validation, do what you think you should do

You are here to learn to commit to a person and/or place, so that you can put down roots and dig the foundations for security. You can be uncommitted and therefore unable to build stability and security

You are here to learn to set and achieve goals to take you on your journey towards inner and outer stability and security.

Foundations, structures, families, and business empires are built 1 goal at a time.

You are here to learn to plan, create a process and/or procedure to ensure the achievement of your goals and bring strength and stability to dynamic ideas. You can be directionless, lazy and block your own progression.

You are here to develop deep meticulous focus on achieving stability, like a stable home, business or income and building your inner security. You can be scattered and miss steps in your impatience.

	You are here to learn to be detail orientated, analytical, organised, and accurate to ensure your plans and processes are watertight. You can be disorganised, flaky and miss steps in your plan
	Your master 22/4 Birthday means that you are an old soul and you have agreed to bring safety, stability, and security to the world. You innovate and build empires, organisations, and businesses. This involves hard work, detail focus, routine work, and tasks. You are here to develop a work ethic, to work hard and develop enjoyment of routine work and tasks
	You are here to develop patient perseverance, so that every step in the process towards your goals for your stable foundation are taken. You are prone to impatience and corner cutting.
	You are here to develop determination and the perseverance to keep going past obstacles to achieve your goals. You are prone to giving up at the first hurdle.
	You are here to learn to come to terms with limitation — both the limitations that are externally imposed on you and the limitations that you impose upon yourself.
	You are here to look at your wounded or problematic relationships and work through the feelings of lack and pain they have

	brought to you. All experiences have lessons embedded within them
	Avoid social isolation by socialising regularly in familiar groups and with likeminded friends.

Your Life Path and Birthday Number Six (6)

You have chosen to incarnate to learn the lessons of the 6 life path energy because when speaking to your spirit guide before this life, you highlighted that you needed to learn the lessons of the 6 energy. You are here to overcome issues in the area of idealism and perfectionism and gain a healthy balance between giving and receiving. You must reconcile your high ideals with practical reality, to accept yourself and the world as it is now for your own happiness and inner peace.

When you are developing well on your path, you are non-judgemental, accepting, friendly, and outgoing. Your ideals make you reliable, trustworthy, caring and an excellent team player. You love home, family, and community, and you must keep in close contact with them. You have great potential in art and aesthetics with your eye for colour and beauty. You may like home decoration, fashion, jewellery and impressing others with your beautiful things. You are a practical visionary, pointing the way to an ideal world. You do this very effectively because you have accepted yourself, others, and the world as they are now, while applying more realism. You have realised that it is who you are that matters, not how well you do or what you know. You will have released judgements that follow ideals and help all of us see our own perfection, while realising and pointing out, how problems are actually opportunities for development.

Your challenges are that you can be materialistic and want lots of stuff, mistakenly thinking that stuff and fast cars will finally make you happy. You can also be vain, compare yourself to others and manifest jealousy, you are best to stay away from social media. You tend to see the world and other people as perfect or flawed and you use your ideals as a benchmark for your happiness and inner peace. When you meet someone, you can see an idealised version of the person and not see the signs to the contrary, leading to disappointment. Or sometimes no one is perfect enough, you look for flaws in everything and you get lost in petty detail, dwelling on one tiny flaw. Your perfectionism brings you internal self-imposed pressure stemming from your own high sometimes unreachable standards. This leads to stress, low mood, low self-esteem, and judgement that you project onto others. You may tend towards asthma and complaints in the chest area.

You must learn to be a practical visionary of an ideal world, to visualise a world where no one is vulnerable, starving or at risk of harm. You thrive on your ideals and strive to manifest them as an avid nurturer, and a perfectionist. But this may cause you to be disappointed, unhappy, and judgemental when reality does not live up to your utopian dream. You reserve your biggest judgement for yourself because you set the bar too high, set yourself up for disappointment and failure. You need to reconcile your high ideals with reality and accept reality as it is now, as perfect imperfection. It is who you are that matters, not what you do or who you know.

You must develop your sense of responsibility, ethics, and ideals to make you reliable, trustworthy, and generally happy. You must learn to be a nurturer, extremely solid, reliable, and balanced, have the characteristics of the 3 but on a deeper level, bringing deep insight and wisdom. You must overcome shyness to develop excellent social skills, be non-judgemental, warm, compassionate, caring, fun loving, talkative and learn to nurture and support others. Shyness, low confidence, anxiety, or depression could stop you from developing your social skills further, if you let it.

You need to develop towards being an amazing adviser, counsellor, and responsible leader. Build close sincere relationships, be social, friendly, compassionate, kind, nurturing, peaceful, helpful, and supportive. You are here to create peaceful nurturing environments so you may need to be a tactful, mediator and resolver of conflict. You dislike disharmony which makes you either jump in to sort it out and sometimes offer unsolicited advice or run away and hide until it is over. You need to learn to be the trustworthy, 'sensible one' that steps back from petty drama and conflict to become a confidant, trusted listener, and adviser. You must be sincere, loving, warm, harmonious, responsible, and put others first, you are a loyal friend.

You are developing towards having deep concern for those less fortunate but also keeping a healthy focus on your self-care too. You need to find a healthy balance between giving and receiving by having boundaries for how much you will do for others to protect your own wellbeing. Your development of a strong sense of responsibility may cause you give too much and forget your own needs, this may cause burn out and illness. You must develop boundaries and look after yourself with as much vigour as you take care and responsibility for others.

You need to be nurturing, parental and compassionate, and strive to help and nurture those that are vulnerable, human, or animal. You also have, via your ideals, the potential to be an avid cause fighter and justice seeker, but you must focus attention first, on your loved ones, close friends, and caring in the community.

You are here to create a stable, nurturing home and learn to be a very family orientated home bird, who loves familiarity, helps close friends and the wider community. You need to be needed, your path is to learn to nurture, be a loyal friend and treat relationships with the utmost importance.

You have a liking for all aesthetic matters. Your love of your home blends with this towards a love of home decoration and furnishings, you also love beauty, fashion and making yourself look nice. You need to explore your creative artistry, you could be a singer, musician, actor, artist and/or writer. You have excellent musical potential and music may be a big part of your life. You may take to playing musical instruments easily and/or you may have an excellent singing voice. However, you may not take advantage of this potential until later in your life because of shyness and your preoccupation with organising your environment and the people in your life.

You can become too self-satisfied and complacent, bordering on the obsessional or even fanatical, with fixations and neurosis. You are very demanding, high maintenance and perfectionistic. You can miss big picture success by obsessing over petty details and imperfections. It is very important that you ground yourself in reality and realise that all is perfection exactly how it is. You compare yourself to others and you can be very pessimistic, judging yourself and others by extremely high, sometimes unreachable standards. Setting the bar too high for yourself and setting yourself up to fail will compound your self-judgment and low confidence. Focusing more on the positives and the big picture rather than small petty detail that does not matter will help you overcome your perfectionism. You judge yourself most harshly and this can cause the development of asthma, chest complaints and anxiety from never feeling good enough. You sometimes judge others as 'perfection,' dismiss the warning signs and as a result, become too trusting, leading to disappointment. Additionally, Your nurturing and caring nature can put you at risk of being taken for granted, as you worry so much about others welfare, you can end up being run ragged. You must stay in touch with how you really feel, rather than what you think you 'should' feel, take care of yourself as well as you care for others.

Careers that would help you achieve your Life Path are:

Fashion, Theatre, Charity work, Beauty, Music and the caring or health professions.

Key Attributes – Romantic, Idealistic and Sensual

Socially – Friendly, Outgoing, and harmonious.

Colour – Violet and Gold

Subtle body – Throat and Brow Chakra

Day – Friday

Astrologically – Venus, zodiac sign Taurus

Life Path 6 with Birthday Number 1

Life Path Number 6 (90% Focus)	Birthday Number 1 (10% Focus)
You are here to be a visionary of the ideal, the dreamer of a utopian world. You must act practically to create a better world with your ideals.	You are here to learn to connect to source energy to download / channel unique new ideas. You often hide your ideas due to low confidence. You are here to learn to be happy in the limelight expressing new ideas for an audience.
You are here to learn to not use your ideals as a benchmark for your happiness. You must not base your emotional wellbeing on the achievement of your ideals. You often judge yourself and others for not hitting perfection, causing you great unhappiness	You are here to learn to be the ideas person, but you struggle to bring your unique ideas to reality because you lose interest quickly after the initial idea.
Your perfectionism can make you an over achiever due to your constant self-judgement. You never meet your own standards. You must keep your big picture in mind and not get stuck in petty detail. You can often judge small imperfections and ruin or miss your successes.	You are here to learn to be confident in your uniqueness because unique people have unique ground-breaking ideas. It is important that you are not craving validation from others.
You are here to learn to be a nurturer, compassionate caring and giving, especially to those that are vulnerable or struggling within your close relationships, your community, and the wider world. Your judgemental nature can make you cruel and neglectful.	You need to be a practical initiator, a doer, action orientated that learns by experience. Only action makes the difference.
You are here to develop boundaries to ensure your mental and physical health. You do a lot for others, sometimes too much, which can	You need to learn to trust your intuitive voice within. You must achieve balanced confidence in yourself & your abilities, fed by

make you feel undervalued, unappreciated, and ill with exhaustion. You may force unsolicited advice and meddle in other people's affairs.

You are here to develop your social skills and be a team player. You must break through low self-esteem to be talkative, fun loving and relaxed around others. You can be shy and hide in the background.

You are here to create a stable, nurturing, tranquil home to maintain your security and well-being. Then nurture a family in an environment of stability and love. When low you can be a selfish, neglectful drama queen.

You are here to learn to be responsible and do good for those you care for. People naturally put you in positions of responsibility, but you often resent always being the 'responsible one.' Have boundaries on your responsibility so that you do not do too much.

You are here to learn to develop and use your artistic and aesthetic potential. Artistic, enhancing make up, great art and home designs. You have great musical potential that you may not develop.

strong connection & trust in your intuition. You bring your ideas without fear. You must not seek validation from others or base your confidence on what others say.

You need to bring unique, new ideas that break barriers, or challenge others comfort zones, you must learn to be brave, confident and be willing to take risks

You are here to learn to be interdependent, not so independent that you push others away and refuse to delegate. You cannot do everything alone. Independence is an illusion; we are all interconnected

You need to be determined to succeed. Constant self-discovery and development is key for you to develop complete trust in the skills you have learned and mastered to serve as a kind of "security blanket" for you when you are feeling insecure

You need to learn to be a powerful leader, be dominant and assertive. You must lead others to the fruition of your ideas, but with balanced personal power.

Your power causes ripples, both positive and negative, you must remember that great power brings great responsibility. You must ensure that your intentions are good

Life Path 6 with Birthday Number 2

Life Path Number 6 (90% Focus)	Birthday Number 2 (10% Focus)
You are here to be a visionary of the ideal, the dreamer of a utopian world. You must act to create a better world with your ideals.	You are here to learn to be responsible to others and the team. You can be too responsible and do too much. You are irresponsible if you feel undervalued and resentful
You are here to learn to not use your ideals as a benchmark for your happiness. You must not base your emotional wellbeing on the achievement of your ideals. You often judge yourself and others for not hitting perfection, causing you great unhappiness	You must learn to improve your social skills, focus on widening and deepening your relationships and make decisions subjectively. It is important that you deepen your relationships and connect 121
Your perfectionism can make you an over achiever due to your constant self-judgement. You never meet your own standards. You must keep your big picture in mind and not get stuck in petty detail. You can often judge small imperfections and ruin or miss your successes.	You must learn not to smother your loved ones or have expectations that can never be met. OR you may back away from wanting love because it hurts too badly. You need to balance your intense need for love
You are here to learn to be a nurturer, compassionate caring and giving, especially to those that are vulnerable or struggling within your close relationships, your community, and the wider world. Your judgemental nature can make you cruel and neglectful.	You are here to learn to be intuitive and sensitive to the needs of others. You are here to be of service to others, the development of intuition will aid you in this journey
You are here to develop boundaries to ensure your mental and physical health. You do a lot for others, sometimes too much, which can make you feel undervalued, unappreciated, and ill with exhaustion. You may force	You are here to learn to be a cooperative team player to get the job done as part of a cohesive team. You can be a disruptive, uncooperative drama queen.

unsolicited advice and meddle in other people's affairs.	
You are here to develop your social skills and be a team player. You must break through low self-esteem to be talkative, fun loving and relaxed around others. You can be shy and hide in the background.	You must develop the assertiveness to demand boundaries to being overworked, walked all over, taken advantage of, and/or taken for granted. You must not be a "shape shifter" who changes who you are in order to please others or keep the peace.
You are here to create a stable, nurturing, tranquil home to maintain your security and well-being. Then nurture a family in an environment of stability and love. When low you can be a selfish, neglectful drama queen.	You are here to serve the leader, the team, the task and be dependable. You can always be counted upon to keep the cogs turning behind the scenes
You are here to learn to be responsible and do good for those you care for. People naturally put you in positions of responsibility, but you often resent always being the 'responsible one.' Have boundaries on your responsibility so that you do not do too much.	You are here to be the tactful mediator of the team, helping to resolve conflicts fairly and for the good of the team. You hate conflict and often run and hide until it is over
You are here to learn to develop and use your artistic and aesthetic potential. Artistic, enhancing make up, great art and home designs. You have great musical potential that you may not develop.	You are here to learn to plan the next steps after the initial idea & build a team to achieve it. The energy of the two is the nurturer of ideas and a builder of teams
	You must learn to give yourself your own kudos. Oftentimes you judge yourself on what everyone else says or thinks about you. You need to develop your internal compass and turn inward for validation, do what you think you should do

Life Path 6 with Birthday Number 3

Life Path Number 6 (90% Focus)	Birthday Number 3 (10% Focus)
You are here to be a visionary of the ideal, the dreamer of a utopian world. You must act to create a better world with your ideals.	You are here to learn to express yourself verbally to inspire, inform and delight. You may struggle in some way verbally, chronic shyness, speech delay, stutter or struggling to find the words
You are here to learn to not use your ideals as a benchmark for your happiness. You must not base your emotional wellbeing on the achievement of your ideals. You often judge yourself and others for not hitting perfection, causing you great unhappiness	You are here to learn to express yourself creatively to inspire, inform and delight. But you may struggle to progress, execute, and finish creative projects, due to lack of self-belief
Your perfectionism can make you an over achiever due to your constant self-judgement. You never meet your own standards. You must keep your big picture in mind and not get stuck in petty detail. You can often judge small imperfections and ruin or miss your successes.	You must learn to be dynamic, take risks and be confident to enjoy the attention and limelight of an audience. You can be shy, under confident and feel unable to take risks.
You are here to learn to be a nurturer, compassionate caring and giving, especially to those that are vulnerable or struggling within your close relationships, your community, and the wider world. Your judgemental nature can make you cruel and neglectful.	You need to develop as an entrepreneur who is able to promote, network and make money creatively. But you may procrastinate and fail to stay focused and work inconsistently.
You are here to develop boundaries to ensure your mental and physical health. You do a lot for others, sometimes too much, which can make you feel undervalued,	You are here to learn to express your emotions positively. You can be extremely sensitive to criticism and other people's emotions, causing you to express emotions

unappreciated, and ill with exhaustion. You may force unsolicited advice and meddle in other people's affairs.	negatively
You are here to develop your social skills and be a team player. You must break through low self-esteem to be talkative, fun loving and relaxed around others. You can be shy and hide in the background.	You are here to develop the habit of acting, be a doer and executer of ideas. When low, you can struggle with apathy, laziness and lack of focus and direction
You are here to create a stable, nurturing, tranquil home to maintain your security and well-being. Then nurture a family in an environment of stability and love. When low you can be a selfish, neglectful drama queen.	You are here to learn to be social, talkative, the life of the party and bringer of fun & positivity. You need to be the networker, communicating an emotional message. You can be quiet and struggle to speak
You are here to learn to be responsible and do good for those you care for. People naturally put you in positions of responsibility, but you often resent always being the 'responsible one.' Have boundaries on your responsibility so that you do not do too much.	You must develop interdependence, life path 3's like to be looked after and can be prone to avoiding work or anything needing routine and commitment
You are here to learn to develop and use your artistic and aesthetic potential. Artistic, enhancing make up, great art and home designs. You have great musical potential that you may not develop.	You are here to be opportunistic, to network, make useful connections and snap up opportunities to spread the word and progress ideas and projects
	You must learn to take responsibility and listen to guidance; you can be irresponsible. You must think before you act, and take full responsibility for what you do

Life Path 6 with Birthday Number 4

Life Path Number 6 (90% Focus)	Birthday Number 4 (10% Focus)
You are here to be a visionary of the ideal, the dreamer of a utopian world. You must act to create a better world with your ideals.	You are here to learn to commit to a person and/or place, so that you can put down roots and dig the foundations for security. You can be uncommitted and therefore unable to build stability and security
You are here to learn to not use your ideals as a benchmark for your happiness. You must not base your emotional wellbeing on the achievement of your ideals. You often judge yourself and others for not hitting perfection, causing you great unhappiness	You are here to learn to set and achieve goals to take you on your journey towards inner and outer stability and security. Foundations, structures, families, and business empires are built 1 goal at a time.
Your perfectionism can make you an over achiever due to your constant self-judgement. You never meet your own standards. You must keep your big picture in mind and not get stuck in petty detail. You can often judge small imperfections and ruin or miss your successes.	You are here to learn to plan, create a process and/or procedure to ensure the achievement of your goals. You can be directionless, lazy and block your own progression
You are here to learn to be a nurturer, compassionate caring and giving, especially to those that are vulnerable or struggling within your close relationships, your community, and the wider world. Your judgemental nature can make you cruel and neglectful.	You are here to develop deep meticulous focus on achieving stability, like a stable home, business or income and building your inner security. You can be scattered
You are here to develop boundaries to ensure your mental and physical health. You do a lot for others, sometimes too much, which can make you feel undervalued,	You are here to learn to be detail orientated, analytical, organised, and accurate to ensure your plans and processes are watertight. You can be disorganised and miss steps in the

unappreciated, and ill with exhaustion. You may force unsolicited advice and meddle in other people's affairs.	plan
You are here to develop your social skills and be a team player. You must break through low self-esteem to be talkative, fun loving and relaxed around others. You can be shy and hide in the background.	You are here to develop a work ethic, to work hard and develop enjoyment of routine work and tasks. When low you can be lazy and stuck in 1 place, without progression
You are here to create a stable, nurturing, tranquil home to maintain your security and well-being. Then nurture a family in an environment of stability and love. When low you can be a selfish, neglectful drama queen.	You are here to develop patient perseverance, so that every step in the process towards your goals for your stable foundation are taken. You are prone to impatience and missing steps
You are here to learn to be responsible and do good for those you care for. People naturally put you in positions of responsibility, but you often resent always being the 'responsible one.' Have boundaries on your responsibility so that you do not do too much.	You are here to learn to come to terms with limitation — both the limitations that are externally imposed on you and the limitations that you impose upon yourself.
You are here to learn to develop and use your artistic and aesthetic potential. Artistic, enhancing make up, great art and home designs. You have great musical potential that you may not develop.	You are here to look at your wounded or problematic relationships and work through the feelings of lack and pain they have brought to you.
	You are prone to choosing social isolation, avoiding social situations due to social anxiety. It is important that you socialise regularly in familiar groups and with likeminded friends.

Life Path 6 with Birthday Number 5

Life Path Number 6 (90% Focus)	Birthday Number 5 (10% Focus)
You are here to be a visionary of the ideal, the dreamer of a utopian world. You must act to create a better world with your ideals.	You are easily bored and want to look at or study lots of topics. Initial varied experience is needed in order to choose a specialism, you are here to learn to be disciplined, to continue with a topic or activity beyond the boredom of the detail, towards mastery and specialism.
You are here to learn to not use your ideals as a benchmark for your happiness. You must not base your emotional wellbeing on the achievement of your ideals. You often judge yourself and others for not hitting perfection, causing you great unhappiness	You are here to develop the ability to balance variety, change and adventure with the stability of family and skill mastery. You can be totally spontaneous and take risks, jumping from one experience to another, but never settling or progressing
Your perfectionism can make you an over achiever due to your constant self-judgement. You never meet your own standards. You must keep your big picture in mind and not get stuck in petty detail. You can often judge small imperfections and ruin or miss your successes.	You need to learn to be extremely intuitive and access your intuitive wisdom when making decisions, assessing people and situations.
You are here to learn to be a nurturer, compassionate caring and giving, especially to those that are vulnerable or struggling within your close relationships, your community, and the wider world. Your judgemental nature can make you cruel and neglectful.	You are here to develop your ability to attain inner freedom and outer freedom by doing things you might not want to do. Doing what you want is not necessarily freedom, you can become a slave to your desires. Freedom and discipline are inherently linked.
You are here to develop boundaries to ensure your mental and physical	You are here to learn to develop your verbal and written

health. You do a lot for others, sometimes too much, which can make you feel undervalued, unappreciated, and ill with exhaustion. You may force unsolicited advice and meddle in other people's affairs.

communication skills towards charismatic sharing of ideas and stories related to your specialism. You have the potential to be a great communicator

You are here to develop your social skills and be a team player. You must break through low self-esteem to be talkative, fun loving and relaxed around others. You can be shy and hide in the background.

You are here to learn to be committed, dependable, to do what you say you are going to do. You often forget what you promise because you are so chaotic, scattered, and changeable, looking for the next new experience

You are here to create a stable, nurturing, tranquil home to maintain your security and well-being. Then nurture a family in an environment of stability and love. When low you can be a selfish, neglectful drama queen.

You are here to develop your social skills and charisma, to have the potential to be fun loving, positive, and optimistic. You can be uptight and argumentative

You are here to learn to be responsible and do good for those you care for. People naturally put you in positions of responsibility, but you often resent always being the 'responsible one.' Have boundaries on your responsibility so that you do not do too much.

You are here to develop consistent independence. You can swing from independence to dependence and back again. Risky behaviour and 'get rich quick' schemes can bring on dependence

You are here to learn to develop and use your artistic and aesthetic potential. Artistic, enhancing make up, great art and home designs. You have great musical potential that you may not develop.

You are here to learn to develop fearlessness and help others to live fearlessly. You can be fearful of many things, restriction, and boredom, to name but a few. You need to challenge yourself and others past your own comfort zone

You are here to learn to make good use of your energy and drive, if you

	feel restricted and under confident, you will be restless, and you may turn into a drama queen. Use your energy for experience and adventure, be courageous

Life Path 6 with Birthday Number 7

Life Path Number 6 (90% Focus)	Birthday Number 7 (10% Focus)
You are here to be a visionary of the ideal, the dreamer of a utopian world. You must act to create a better world with your ideals.	You are here to learn to have faith that you are an immortal soul that has experience from previous lives. You must trust the soul within you by listening to and following your intuition without over thinking and applying logic. Listen to and follow your inner voice and feel safe enough to communicate your soul wisdom to the world without fear of ridicule
You are here to learn to not use your ideals as a benchmark for your happiness. You must not base your emotional wellbeing on the achievement of your ideals. You often judge yourself and others for not hitting perfection, causing you great unhappiness	You are here to trust that the world is not against you. The universe is everything existing in perfect balance, it is like a cosmic library of all knowledge and experience. We must experience it all to learn and evolve
Your perfectionism can make you an over achiever due to your constant self-judgement. You never meet your own standards. You must keep your big picture in mind and not get stuck in petty detail. You can often judge small imperfections and ruin or miss your successes.	Your focus for this lifetime must be Inner development rather than outer development and success. You must develop yourself constantly with self-discovery and spiritual wisdom. Meditation and time in nature is imperative for you
You are here to learn to be a nurturer, compassionate caring and giving, especially to those that are vulnerable or struggling within your close relationships, your community, and the wider world. Your judgemental nature can make you cruel and neglectful.	You are here to learn to be a problem solver, thinker, a studier of the metaphysical and the big questions. You need to research, learn, and analyse theories to accrue wisdom.

You are here to develop boundaries to ensure your mental and physical health. You do a lot for others, sometimes too much, which can make you feel undervalued, unappreciated, and ill with exhaustion. You may force unsolicited advice and meddle in other people's affairs.

You are here to learn to filter your research through your intuition and use your research of other people's theories for your own needs. You can be too analytical and ignore your intuition. Or totally spiritual and ignore other theories. You must balance the two.

You are here to develop your social skills and be a team player. You must break through low self-esteem to be talkative, fun loving and relaxed around others. You can be shy and hide in the background.

You are here to be a free thinker, to be less interested in popular culture and following norms of fashion and appearance. This can make you feel different and out of place and lonely

You are here to create a stable, nurturing, tranquil home to maintain your security and well-being. Then nurture a family in an environment of stability and love. When low you can be a selfish, neglectful drama queen.

You are here to develop the ability to focus on something long enough to develop it into something useful. You can be a little scattered and struggle to focus

You are here to learn to be responsible and do good for those you care for. People naturally put you in positions of responsibility, but you often resent always being the 'responsible one.' Have boundaries on your responsibility so that you do not do too much.

You are here to develop interdependence, self-sufficiency but also a healthy dependence on other people. You like to do things for yourself but take care not to push others away

You are here to learn to develop and use your artistic and aesthetic potential. Artistic, enhancing make up, great art and home designs. You have great musical potential that you may not develop.

You are here to learn to deal with and reconcile your sensitive emotions. Others often think you are aloof, but you are a well of deep emotions. You need to connect emotionally, both to yourself and to other people

180

You are here to learn to balance your need to be alone and work alone with social contact. You love to be alone, but you must ensure that you do not isolate yourself beyond what is healthy

Life Path 6 with Birthday Number 8

Life Path Number 6 (90% Focus)	Birthday Number 8 (10% Focus)
You are here to be a visionary of the ideal, the dreamer of a utopian world. You must act to create a better world with your ideals.	You are both spiritual and worldly. But you are here to learn the secrets of worldly financial success. You seek the freedom that comes from financial success. But freedom brings responsibility, your ethics will be tested multiple times
You are here to learn to not use your ideals as a benchmark for your happiness. You must not base your emotional wellbeing on the achievement of your ideals. You often judge yourself and others for not hitting perfection, causing you great unhappiness	You are here to learn to use your financial success as a tool to help others achieve the same financial success. You often spend your abundance on materialistic status symbols rather than helping others
Your perfectionism can make you an over achiever due to your constant self-judgement. You never meet your own standards. You must keep your big picture in mind and not get stuck in petty detail. You can often judge small imperfections and ruin or miss your successes.	You are here to develop a healthy attitude towards money. You may resent or hate wealthy people, or you may feel guilty about your own wealth. You must understand that financial wealth does not equate to poor ethics
You are here to learn to be a nurturer, compassionate caring and giving, especially to those that are vulnerable or struggling within your close relationships, your community, and the wider world. Your judgemental nature can make you cruel and neglectful.	You are here to develop balanced determination for achievement but with integrity and for the good of others. You can be either obsessed with achievement or fearful of achievement from low self-esteem. It is important that you develop a positive mindset because you attract what you think about.
You are here to develop boundaries to ensure your mental and physical health. You do a lot for others,	You are here to develop inner confidence and balanced personal power. You can swing from over

182

sometimes too much, which can make you feel undervalued, unappreciated, and ill with exhaustion. You may force unsolicited advice and meddle in other people's affairs.	dominance or misuse of power to hiding away or submission to others
You are here to develop your social skills and be a team player. You must break through low self-esteem to be talkative, fun loving and relaxed around others. You can be shy and hide in the background.	You are here to develop skilled leadership, which consists of subject competence coupled with excellent social skills and charisma
You are here to create a stable, nurturing, tranquil home to maintain your security and well-being. Then nurture a family in an environment of stability and love. When low you can be a selfish, neglectful drama queen.	You are here to work hard as an excellent practical businessperson, but you must ensure that you do not work too hard, you need time out and time for your family
You are here to learn to be responsible and do good for those you care for. People naturally put you in positions of responsibility, but you often resent always being the 'responsible one.' Have boundaries on your responsibility so that you do not do too much.	You are here to be worldly, strong, resilient, disciplined, and realistic. To be successful you need to be strong, tough, and able to cope with

The ups and downs of the world |
| You are here to learn to develop and use your artistic and aesthetic potential. Artistic, enhancing make up, great art and home designs. You have great musical potential that you may not develop. | You are here to develop bravery and the courage to take risks to progress. Success comes from having the bravery to take risks |
| | You are here to develop organisation and management skills, resolve to making things happen and to define and meet your goals. |

Life Path 6 with Birthday Number 9

Life Path Number 6 (90% Focus)	Birthday Number 9 (10% Focus)
You are here to be a visionary of the ideal, the dreamer of a utopian world. You must act to create a better world with your ideals.	You are here to learn to follow your intuitive wisdom and live to spiritual laws, rather than worldly laws, conventions, and ideals. You tend to follow worldly laws and prejudices as an excuse for your actions. But if you had followed your intuitive spiritual wisdom, you would not have acted that way. Focus on faith over logic
You are here to learn to not use your ideals as a benchmark for your happiness. You must not base your emotional wellbeing on the achievement of your ideals. You often judge yourself and others for not hitting perfection, causing you great unhappiness	You are here to learn to act with integrity for the benefit of others. You are powerful and you must use your power for the benefit of others. You can act for selfish or nefarious reasons
Your perfectionism can make you an over achiever due to your constant self-judgement. You never meet your own standards. You must keep your big picture in mind and not get stuck in petty detail. You can often judge small imperfections and ruin or miss your successes.	You are here to learn to lead by example, do you practise what you preach? You can be quite domineering, an adviser with all the answers. But you must let others make their own mistakes
You are here to learn to be a nurturer, compassionate caring and giving, especially to those that are vulnerable or struggling within your close relationships, your community, and the wider world. Your judgemental nature can make you cruel and neglectful.	You are here to make your life your teaching, you need to counsel with wisdom. You are a developed soul, the totality of all the numbers, full of cellular experience and higher knowledge
You are here to develop boundaries	You are here to develop broad

to ensure your mental and physical health. You do a lot for others, sometimes too much, which can make you feel undervalued, unappreciated, and ill with exhaustion. You may force unsolicited advice and meddle in other people's affairs.

You are here to develop your social skills and be a team player. You must break through low self-esteem to be talkative, fun loving and relaxed around others. You can be shy and hide in the background.

You are here to create a stable, nurturing, tranquil home to maintain your security and well-being. Then nurture a family in an environment of stability and love. When low you can be a selfish, neglectful drama queen.

You are here to learn to be responsible and do good for those you care for. People naturally put you in positions of responsibility, but you often resent always being the 'responsible one.' Have boundaries on your responsibility so that you do not do too much.

You are here to learn to develop and use your artistic and aesthetic potential. Artistic, enhancing make up, great art and home designs. You have great musical potential that you may not develop.

mindedness, meet and accept diverse people. You must learn to be a humanitarian and make the world a better place. You need a global consciousness, as you can be narrow minded, judgemental, and even bigoted.

You are here to learn to take responsibility for your powerful choices. You sometimes run away from the consequences of your actions

You need to develop towards being a successful entrepreneur or businessperson if it is with something you feel passionate about. You must choose work that has meaning for you. You are a powerful force for change

You are here to develop excellent social skills and charisma. You could develop the skills of a powerful speaker and influencer of others. People will hang on your every word

You are here to look after the wellbeing of others. But when you are in trouble or need support, people do not notice. You must ask for what you need, you must ask for help

You are here to wrap things up, let go and surrender. You can have a victim mentality, holding onto

	feelings that no longer serve you, unable to move on from perceived injustice, normally rooted in family issues.

Life Path 6 with Birthday Master 11

Life Path Number 6 (90% Focus)	Birthday Master 11 (10% Focus)
You are here to be a visionary of the ideal, the dreamer of a utopian world. You must act to create a better world with your ideals.	You are an old soul, with higher potential and higher responsibility to improve the world. You are here to learn to connect to source energy to channel unique new ideas and messages to change the world. You are here to learn to be happy in the limelight expressing new ideas for an audience. You need to develop and trust your massive intuitive potential. You often hide your ideas due to low confidence
You are here to learn to not use your ideals as a benchmark for your happiness. You must not base your emotional wellbeing on the achievement of your ideals. You often judge yourself and others for not hitting perfection, causing you great unhappiness	You are here to learn to be the ideas person, but you struggle to bring your unique ideas to reality because you lose interest quickly after the initial idea of sabotage yourself due to crippling low confidence. You are an idealistic dreamer whose ideas are often not grounded in reality
Your perfectionism can make you an over achiever due to your constant self-judgement. You never meet your own standards. You must keep your big picture in mind and not get stuck in petty detail. You can often judge small imperfections and ruin or miss your successes.	You are here to learn to be confident in your uniqueness because unique people have unique ground-breaking ideas. It is important that you are not craving validation from others. Your validation should come from your intuition.
You are here to learn to be a nurturer, compassionate caring and giving, especially to those that are vulnerable or struggling within your close relationships, your community, and the wider world. Your judgemental nature can make	You need to bring unique, new ideas that break barriers, or challenge others comfort zone. You must learn to be brave, confident and be willing to take risks

you cruel and neglectful.	
You are here to develop boundaries to ensure your mental and physical health. You do a lot for others, sometimes too much, which can make you feel undervalued, unappreciated, and ill with exhaustion. You may force unsolicited advice and meddle in other people's affairs.	You need to be a practical initiator, a doer, action orientated that learns by experience. Ideas will stay unmanifested until you act! Only action brings change
You are here to develop your social skills and be a team player. You must break through low self-esteem to be talkative, fun loving and relaxed around others. You can be shy and hide in the background.	You need to set intentions then use spiritual practice and visualisation to channel your advanced, intense master energy into initiation and action. Unchanneled or mismanaged energy can cause intense nervous energy and anxiety. You may medicate these with unhealthy substances.
You are here to create a stable, nurturing, tranquil home to maintain your security and well-being. Then nurture a family in an environment of stability and love. When low you can be a selfish, neglectful drama queen.	You are here to learn to be interdependent, not so independent that you push others away and refuse to delegate. You cannot do everything alone. Independence is an illusion; we are all interconnected
You are here to learn to be responsible and do good for those you care for. People naturally put you in positions of responsibility, but you often resent always being the 'responsible one.' Have boundaries on your responsibility so that you do not do too much.	You need to be determined to succeed. Constant self-discovery and intuitive spiritual development is key for you to develop complete trust in the skills you have learned and mastered to serve as a kind of "security blanket" for you when you are feeling insecure
You are here to learn to develop and use your artistic and aesthetic potential. Artistic, enhancing make up, great art and home designs. You have great musical potential	You need to learn to be a supportive, nurturing leader, be firm and assertive but also empathic and supportive. You must lead others to the fruition of your ideas, but with balanced personal

that you may not develop.	power
	Your power causes ripples, both positive and negative, you must remember that great power brings great responsibility. You must ensure that your intentions are good
	You are here to learn to be responsible to others, your family, team, or group but in a balanced way. You can be too responsible and do too much. You are irresponsible if you feel undervalued, resentful, and exhausted.
	You must develop and improve your social skills, focus on widening and deepening your relationships and make decisions subjectively. It is important that you deepen your relationships and connect 121
	You may struggle to maintain long term close and romantic relationships.
	You must learn not to smother your loved ones or have expectations that can never be met. OR back away from wanting love because it hurts too badly. You need to balance your intense need for love for healthy relationships.
	You are here to learn to be intuitive and sensitive to the needs of others. You are here to be of service to others, the development of intuition will aid you in this journey
	You are here to learn to be a cooperative team player to get the job done as part of a cohesive team. You can be a disruptive, uncooperative

	drama queen.
	You must develop the assertiveness to demand boundaries to being overworked, walked all over, taken advantage of, and/or taken for granted. You must not be a "shape shifter" who changes who you are in order to please others or keep the peace. Be you and consider yourself too.
	You are here to serve the world, help the team, the task and be dependable. You can always be relied upon to keep the cogs turning behind the scenes
	You are here to be the tactful mediator of the team/group/family, helping to resolve conflicts fairly and for the good of everyone involved. You hate conflict and often run and hide until it is over
	You are here to learn to plan the next steps after channelling your message or idea & build a team to achieve it. The energy of the 11/2 needs to be the nurturer of ideas and a builder of teams
	You must learn to give yourself your own kudos. Oftentimes you judge yourself on what everyone else says or thinks about you. You need to develop your internal compass and turn inward for validation, do what YOU think you should do

Life Path 6 with Birthday Master 22/4

Life Path Number 6 (90% Focus)	Birthday Master 22/4 (10% Focus)
You are here to be a visionary of the ideal, the dreamer of a utopian world. You must act to create a better world with your ideals.	You are an old soul, as spiritual as you are practical, here to channel and then manifest ideas in reality to build world safety, stability, and security.
	You must learn to handle the master builder energy and focus it to manifestation.
	You have a big responsibility to the team and the world to build structures (buildings, concepts, body, mind, spirit, businesses, organisations, even an empire for the purpose of world stability and security
You are here to learn to not use your ideals as a benchmark for your happiness. You must not base your emotional wellbeing on the achievement of your ideals. You often judge yourself and others for not hitting perfection, causing you great unhappiness	You must develop and improve your social skills, focus on widening and deepening your relationships to assist you to manifest your big ideas. It is important that you learn to deepen your relationships and connect 121, you cannot do this alone!
Your perfectionism can make you an over achiever due to your constant self-judgement. You never meet your own standards. You must keep your big picture in mind and not get stuck in petty detail. You can often judge small imperfections and ruin or miss your successes.	You must learn to have balanced, healthy relationships with others that are part of your sense of security. You must learn not to smother your loved ones and your team or have expectations that can never be met.
	OR Your big task in this lifetime may disrupt your love relationships. You may back away from wanting love because it hurts too badly or attacks your sense of security

You are here to learn to be a nurturer, compassionate caring and giving, especially to those that are vulnerable or struggling within your close relationships, your community, and the wider world. Your judgemental nature can make you cruel and neglectful.	You are here to learn to listen to and follow your intuition. Intuition is needed for you to be sensitive to the needs of others. You are here to be of service to change the world, the development of intuition will aid you in this journey
You are here to develop boundaries to ensure your mental and physical health. You do a lot for others, sometimes too much, which can make you feel undervalued, unappreciated, and ill with exhaustion. You may force unsolicited advice and meddle in other people's affairs.	You are here to learn to be a cooperative team player to get the job done as part of a cohesive team. You may fail to communicate effectively with others. You can be a hard-headed and high handed at times.
You are here to develop your social skills and be a team player. You must break through low self-esteem to be talkative, fun loving and relaxed around others. You can be shy and hide in the background.	You must develop the assertiveness to demand boundaries to being overworked, walked all over, taken advantage of, and/or taken for granted. You must also develop your ability to respect other people's boundaries and not be high handed.
You are here to create a stable, nurturing, tranquil home to maintain your security and well-being. Then nurture a family in an environment of stability and love. When low you can be a selfish, neglectful drama queen.	You are here to be of service to the world, the leader, the team, the task and be dependable. You can always be counted upon to keep the cogs turning behind the scenes
You are here to learn to be responsible and do good for those you care for. People naturally put you in positions of responsibility, but you often resent always being the 'responsible one.' Have boundaries on your responsibility so that you do	You are extremely sensitive, and you hate and run away from conflict. But you are here to learn to be a tactful mediator, helping to resolve conflicts fairly and for the good of the team/family/group

not do too much.	
You are here to learn to develop and use your artistic and aesthetic potential. Artistic, enhancing make up, great art and home designs. You have great musical potential that you may not develop.	You are here to learn to stay focused and plan the next steps after you have channelled a new idea & build a team to achieve it. The energy of the 22 needs to be the nurturer, the builder of ideas and teams.
	You must learn to give yourself your own kudos. Oftentimes you judge yourself on what everyone else says or thinks about you. You need to develop your internal compass and turn inward for validation, do what you think you should do
	You are here to learn to commit to a person and/or place, so that you can put down roots and dig the foundations for security. You can be uncommitted and therefore unable to build stability and security
	You are here to learn to set and achieve goals to take you on your journey towards inner and outer stability and security. Foundations, structures, families, and business empires are built 1 goal at a time.
	You are here to learn to plan, create a process and/or procedure to ensure the achievement of your goals and bring strength and stability to dynamic ideas. You can be directionless, lazy and block your own progression.
	You are here to develop deep meticulous focus on achieving stability, like a stable home, business

	or income and building your inner security. You can be scattered and miss steps in your impatience.
	You are here to learn to be detail orientated, analytical, organised, and accurate to ensure your plans and processes are watertight. You can be disorganised, flaky and miss steps in your plan
	Your master 22/4 Birthday means that you are an old soul and you have agreed to bring safety, stability, and security to the world. You innovate and build empires, organisations, and businesses. This involves hard work, detail focus, routine work, and tasks. You are here to develop a work ethic, to work hard and develop enjoyment of routine work and tasks
	You are here to develop patient perseverance, so that every step in the process towards your goals for your stable foundation are taken. You are prone to impatience and corner cutting.
	You are here to develop determination and the perseverance to keep going past obstacles to achieve your goals. You are prone to giving up at the first hurdle.
	You are here to learn to come to terms with limitation — both the limitations that are externally imposed on you and the limitations that you impose upon yourself.
	You are here to look at your wounded or problematic

	relationships and work through the feelings of lack and pain they have brought to you. All experiences have lessons embedded within them
	Avoid social isolation by socialising regularly in familiar groups and with likeminded friends.

Your Life Path and Birthday Number Seven (7)

You have chosen to incarnate and learn the lessons of the 7 life path energy because when speaking to your spirit guide before this life, you highlighted that you needed to learn the lessons of the 7 energy. You are here to learn to walk a spiritual path, trust the soul within you, the soul within others and in the process of your life, so that you feel safe enough to open up and share your inner beauty with the world. Trust meaning, the feeling of confidence or protection from shame and ridicule.

At your highest vibration, you are a spiritual truth seeker, you focus on your own evolution and the journey within for knowledge of yourself and increased awareness at a deeper level. You use research and investigation to challenge the accepted truth, but you filter your research through your own inner guidance and intuition for its authenticity. You have stopped looking for evidence of betrayal, you see the deeper wisdom and order emanating from everyone and every circumstance. You have gratitude through difficulties, safe in the knowledge that all experience, good and bad brings wisdom.

When you realise that the universe has your back, you will feel more able to open up and say what you really feel, communicate emotionally, and learn. You must trust the universe enough to share what is really in your heart and trust your own instinct, abilities, and intuition, you are the expert in your life.

Your challenges begin with a lack of self-trust, you may think you trust yourself, but you are trusting the thinking mind and the theories of others over your own inner knowing or intuitive wisdom. You gain knowledge through the mind, through books and experts, fitting yourself into others approaches rather than tailoring it to fit your own needs. You must measure what you read with your own intuition and rely on your own instincts and wisdom rather than other people's ideas.

When you are lacking trust in yourself and the world, you can isolate yourself beyond what is healthy to protect yourself from perceived threats. Your lack of trust can cause you to make others feel uncomfortable in your presence because you seem aloof and disinterested.

At your lowest, you can be either totally detached from spirituality and the journey within causing pessimism and distress or totally obsessed with spirituality and detached from the world. You must find balance, be an intuitive researcher, looking at other people's theories but only keeping research that resonates with the soul within you.

Your 7 energy needs you to develop your spirituality, to understand and trust your soul, to have faith that your soul, intuition and inner voice has your back. You must realise that you are an immortal spiritual being residing in a temporary body, so that you can experience the world, learn, and evolve your soul.

When you start to trust the soul within you, you will trust your soul's intuition above all else. Currently, you may second guess your intuition, over analyse, and talk yourself out of following your inner messages and intuitive wisdom.

You are here to be a bit of a scholar, you need to spend time analysing other people's theories, but you may use all their ideas to live your life. Living by others theories entirely just shows that you are staying firmly in the mind without any awareness as to whether the information resonates with your soul. Your lesson here, is to listen to, and trust, your inner voice as your yardstick for your beliefs, rather than just your mind and other people's theories. Balance your ability to analyse with your intuition by filtering what you learn through your intuition, pick out what resonates and use it for your own purposes.

Your 7 life path suggests that you struggle to trust the world, other people and above all, yourself. You often feel that the world is against you. You read alternative media and you may immerse yourself in conspiracy theories that further entrenches your mistrust for the world and everyone around you. The universe is not against you, it is in balance, it is everything, selfishness and selflessness, love, and hate, we must experience it all, to learn. You cannot deeply appreciate love if you have not experienced hate or heartbreak. The media focuses on the negative and discards the immense love, altruism and compassion that exists in this world. If your mindset says that the world is against you, then you will filter your perceptions through this belief or only connect with information that supports this. Try looking for evidence of compassion and altruism in the world.

Your development of your 7 energy needs you to be a thinker, focused on your inner development, self-discovery, spiritual development, and the development of your intuitive wisdom. Study metaphysical subjects that resonate with your soul, look at the underlying meaning and analyse the big questions. You could research the paranormal, spirituality, the occult and the unexplained, read metaphysics, mystical or ghost and fantasy stories. Look into spirituality, psychology, and philosophy, you need time alone to think, contemplate and decide what resonates with you.

You are an old soul who has lived many previous lives, so you have lots of cellular memory and inner knowing. When you trust this inner knowing, instinct and intuition, you understand that the world is a school, a learning environment and that every difficulty is an opportunity to learn, develop then soar higher.

Your love of knowledge is linked to your need for wisdom, meaning and truth. All this is part of your path to finally 'knowing' that the information you search for is already within you, stored within your soul's previous experience and wisdom.

Your destiny is centred on developing your inner processes rather than external success, so, meditation is important. Self-trust can be built through meditation, spiritual development and physical practise like dance, martial arts, music, or dancing.

When you are unbalanced, you may have an inner urge to run away into the forest, live in an ashram, resonate with nature, and live with the native American Indians, you could become a back packer or spiritual tramp. But you must remember to keep a connection to the world and what other people do or say. You do not have to follow it, but it is important that you still stay connected to it to prevent total isolation. You are not one to follow fashions or stand in front of the mirror for long periods, because you are unconcerned with following the crowd or fitting in, so you can be perceived as eccentric. You are here to be a free thinker, to do things differently, think differently, you see no value in doing what everyone else is doing. But it is vital that you look to the world too, connect with it and listen to it, then consult your intuition for its validity and usefulness for you.

Your 7 life path means that you are a potentially intelligent, deep thinker and spiritual truth seeker, possessing an affinity with nature and the ocean. Energise yourself by walking or relaxing by the sea, surrounded by rolling fields and mountains, pondering the big questions alone.

You prefer to work alone; you are a potential strategist with the capacity to see the big picture. You could be an excellent problem solver, helped by high intelligence and a vivid imagination. You are scattered by nature, so you may find it hard to focus on one thing when researching. Take care not to study too many subjects at once, focus on one subject at a time to really gain a deep understanding, meditation and time in nature will help this.

You are fiercely independent, a quiet, shy loner who thinks with your head and avoids emotions, which can make you come across as aloof and serious. People may think you are devoid of emotion but that could not be further from the truth, you are a well of deep sensitive emotions that you hide from those that you do not trust. You need privacy and introspection leaving precious little time for a relationship, commitment or staying in one place. You struggle to settle and commit to any person, group, or idea because you are a free thinker and a rebel with truly little interest in popular culture, mirror fuss or money worship.

Relationships can be difficult as you can be closed, aloof, cold hearted, pessimistic, cynical, and suspicious. You want a relationship, but you don't at the same time because you like to be alone, and you may not trust another enough not to be fearful of sharing your inner processes for fear of ridicule. You fear that other people may betray you, so you put up a protective shield and look for evidence of betrayal or conspiracy theories to confirm your beliefs. On the flip side, some 7's are naïve, believe blind faith, setting themselves up for betrayal, which further enforces their negative belief that others can't be trusted. Your energy of mistrust in others and your mysterious, disconnected, aloof demeanour causes other people to mistrust you in return, exacerbating your tendency for self-isolation.

You are here to be an eternal seeker until the day you realise that all you need is within you already! It is okay to look at other's ideas, but you must filter those ideas through your own intuition before buying into them. You are the expert in your own life, and you are here to be a spiritual teacher and teach others to be the expert in their own life. Take care not to become too involved in worldly matters and disconnecting from the spiritual or too spiritual and disconnected with the world. Your biggest problem however is trusting yourself!

Careers that will support your life path:

Spiritual teacher, Guru, Priest, Clairvoyant, Clairsentient, Clairaudient, Astrologer, Numerologist, yoga teacher, Healer, Counsellor, Therapist, Instructor, health and wellbeing practitioner, Scientist, Psychologist, Researcher, Astrophysicist, Teacher, Accountant or Engineer.

Key Attributes – Intuitive, Intellectual, Psychic and Unique

Socially – Aloof, Reserved, Spiritual.

Colour – Violet

Subtle body – Brow Chakra with the Third Eye Chakra, intuitive with the ability to 'see'

Day – Monday

Astrologically – Uranus, zodiac sign Aquarius

Life Path 7 with Birthday Number 1

Life Path Number 7 (90% Focus)	Birthday Number 1 (10% Focus)
You are here to learn to have faith that you are an immortal soul that has experience from your other multiple lives. You must trust the soul within you by listening to and following your intuition without over thinking and applying too much worldly logic. Listen to and follow your inner voice and feel safe enough to communicate your soul wisdom to the world without fear of ridicule	You are here to learn to connect to source energy to download / channel unique new ideas. You often hide your ideas due to low confidence. You are here to learn to be happy in the limelight expressing new ideas for an audience.
You are here to trust that the world is not against you. The universe is everything existing in perfect balance, it is like a cosmic library of all knowledge and experience. We must experience it all to learn and evolve	You are here to learn to be the ideas person, but you struggle to bring your unique ideas to reality because you lose interest quickly after the initial idea.
Your focus for this lifetime must be Inner development rather than outer development and success. You must develop yourself constantly with self-discovery and spiritual wisdom. Meditation and time in nature is imperative for you	You are here to learn to be confident in your uniqueness because unique people have unique ground-breaking ideas. It is important that you are not craving validation from others.
You are here to learn to be a problem solver, thinker, a studier of the metaphysical and the big questions. You need to research, learn, and analyse theories to accrue wisdom.	You need to be a practical initiator, a doer, action orientated that learns by experience. Only action makes the difference.
You are here to learn to filter your researched wisdom through your intuition and use your research of	You need to learn to trust your intuitive voice within. You must achieve balanced confidence in

other people's theories for your own needs. You can be too analytical and ignore your intuition. Or totally spiritual and ignore other theories. You must balance the two.	yourself & your abilities, fed by strong connection & trust in your intuition. You bring your ideas without fear. You must not seek validation from others or base your confidence on what others say.
You are here to be a free thinker, to be less interested in popular culture and following norms of fashion and appearance. This can make you feel different and out of place and lonely	You need to bring unique, new ideas that break barriers, or challenge others comfort zones, you must learn to be brave, confident and be willing to take risks
You are here to develop the ability to focus on something long enough to develop it into something useful. You can be a little scattered and struggle to focus on one spiritual or self-discovery topic at a time.	You are here to learn to be interdependent, not so independent that you push others away and refuse to delegate. You cannot do everything alone. Independence is an illusion; we are all interconnected
You are here to develop interdependence, self-sufficiency but also a healthy dependence on other people. You like to do things for yourself but take care not to push others away	You need to be determined to succeed. Constant self-discovery and development is key for you to develop complete trust in the skills you have learned and mastered to serve as a kind of "security blanket" for you when you are feeling insecure
You are here to learn to deal with and reconcile your sensitive emotions. Others often think you are aloof, but you are a well of deep emotions. You need to connect emotionally, both to yourself and to other people	You need to learn to be a powerful leader, be dominant and assertive. You must lead others to the fruition of your ideas, but with balanced personal power
You are here to learn to balance your need to be alone and work alone with social contact. You love to be alone, but you must ensure that you do not isolate yourself beyond what is healthy	Your power causes ripples, both positive and negative, you must remember that great power brings great responsibility. You must ensure that your intentions are good

Life Path 7 with Birthday Number 2

Life Path Number 7 (90% Focus)	Birthday Number 2 (10% Focus)
You are here to learn to have faith that you are an immortal soul that has experience from your other multiple lives. You must trust the soul within you by listening to and following your intuition without over thinking and applying worldly logic. Listen to and follow your inner voice and feel safe enough to communicate your soul wisdom to the world without fear of ridicule	You are here to learn to be responsible to others and the team. You can be too responsible and do too much. You are irresponsible if you feel undervalued and resentful
You are here to trust that the world is not against you. The universe is everything existing in perfect balance, it is like a cosmic library of all knowledge and experience. We must experience it all to learn and evolve	You must learn to improve your social skills, focus on widening and deepening your relationships and make decisions subjectively. It is important that you deepen your relationships and connect 121
Your focus for this lifetime must be Inner development rather than outer development and success. You must develop yourself constantly with self-discovery and spiritual wisdom. Meditation and time in nature is imperative for you	You must learn not to smother your loved ones or have expectations that can never be met. OR you may back away from wanting love because it hurts too badly. You need to balance your intense need for love
You are here to learn to be a problem solver, thinker, a studier of the metaphysical and the big questions. You need to research, learn, and analyse theories to accrue wisdom.	You are here to learn to be intuitive and sensitive to the needs of others. You are here to be of service to others, the development of intuition will aid you in this journey
You are here to learn to filter your researched wisdom through your intuition and use your research of other people's theories for your own needs. You can be too analytical and ignore your intuition. Or totally	You are here to learn to be a cooperative team player to get the job done as part of a cohesive team. You can be a disruptive, uncooperative drama queen.

spiritual and ignore other theories. You must balance the two.	
You are here to be a free thinker, to be less interested in popular culture and following norms of fashion and appearance. This can make you feel different and out of place and lonely	You must develop the assertiveness to demand boundaries to being overworked, walked all over, taken advantage of, and/or taken for granted. You must not be a "shape shifter" who changes who you are in order to please others or keep the peace.
You are here to develop the ability to focus on something long enough to develop it into something useful. You can be a little scattered and struggle to focus on one spiritual or self-discovery topic at a time.	You are here to serve the leader, the team, the task and be dependable. You can always be counted upon to keep the cogs turning behind the scenes
You are here to develop interdependence, self-sufficiency but also a healthy dependence on other people. You like to do things for yourself but take care not to push others away	You are here to be the tactful mediator of the team, helping to resolve conflicts fairly and for the good of the team. You hate conflict and often run and hide until it is over
You are here to learn to deal with and reconcile your sensitive emotions. Others often think you are aloof, but you are a well of deep emotions. You need to connect emotionally, both to yourself and to other people	You are here to learn to plan the next steps after the initial idea & build a team to achieve it. The energy of the two is the nurturer of ideas and a builder of teams
You are here to learn to balance your need to be alone and work alone with social contact. You love to be alone, but you must ensure that you do not isolate yourself beyond what is healthy	You must learn to give yourself your own kudos. Oftentimes you judge yourself on what everyone else says or thinks about you. You need to develop your internal compass and turn inward for validation, do what you think you should do

Life Path 7 with Birthday Number 3

Life Path Number 7 (90% Focus)	Birthday Number 3 (10% Focus)
You are here to learn to have faith that you are an immortal soul that has experience from your other multiple lives. You must trust the soul within you by listening to and following your intuition without over thinking and applying worldly logic. Listen to and follow your inner voice and feel safe enough to communicate your soul wisdom to the world without fear of ridicule	You are here to learn to express yourself verbally to inspire, inform and delight. You may struggle in some way verbally, chronic shyness, speech delay, stutter or struggling to find the words.
You are here to trust that the world is not against you. The universe is everything existing in perfect balance, it is like a cosmic library of all knowledge and experience. We must experience it all to learn and evolve	You are here to learn to express yourself creatively to inspire, inform and delight. But you may struggle to progress, execute, and finish creative projects, due to lack of self-belief
Your focus for this lifetime must be Inner development rather than outer development and success. You must develop yourself constantly with self-discovery and spiritual wisdom. Meditation and time in nature is imperative for you	You must learn to be dynamic, take risks and be confident to enjoy the attention and limelight of an audience. You can be shy, under confident and feel unable to take risks.
You are here to learn to be a problem solver, thinker, a studier of the metaphysical and the big questions. You need to research, learn, and analyse theories to accrue wisdom.	You need to develop as an entrepreneur who is able to promote, network and make money creatively. But you may procrastinate and fail to stay focused and work inconsistently.
You are here to learn to filter your researched wisdom through your intuition and use your research of other people's theories for your own	You are here to learn to express your emotions positively. You can be extremely sensitive to criticism and other people's emotions, causing

needs. You can be too analytical and ignore your intuition. Or totally spiritual and ignore other theories. You must balance the two.	you to express emotions negatively
You are here to be a free thinker, to be less interested in popular culture and following norms of fashion and appearance. This can make you feel different and out of place and lonely	You are here to develop the habit of acting, be a doer and executer of ideas. When low, you can struggle with apathy, laziness and lack of focus and direction
You are here to develop the ability to focus on something long enough to develop it into something useful. You can be a little scattered and struggle to focus on one spiritual or self-discovery topic at a time.	You are here to learn to be social, talkative, the life of the party and bringer of fun & positivity. You need to be the networker, communicating an emotional message. You can be quiet and struggle to speak
You are here to develop interdependence, self-sufficiency but also a healthy dependence on other people. You like to do things for yourself but take care not to push others away	You must develop interdependence, life path 3's like to be looked after and can be prone to avoiding work or anything needing routine and commitment
You are here to learn to deal with and reconcile your sensitive emotions. Others often think you are aloof, but you are a well of deep emotions. You need to connect emotionally, both to yourself and to other people	You are here to be opportunistic, to network, make useful connections and snap up opportunities to spread the word and progress ideas and projects
You are here to learn to balance your need to be alone and work alone with social contact. You love to be alone, but you must ensure that you do not isolate yourself beyond what is healthy	You must learn to take responsibility and listen to guidance; you can be irresponsible. You must think before you act, and take full responsibility for what you do

Life Path 7 with Birthday Number 4

Life Path Number 7 (90% Focus)	Birthday Number 4 (10% Focus)
You are here to learn to have faith that you are an immortal soul that has experience from your other multiple lives. You must trust the soul within you by listening to and following your intuition without over thinking and applying worldly logic. Listen to and follow your inner voice and feel safe enough to communicate your soul wisdom to the world without fear of ridicule	You are here to learn to commit to a person and/or place, so that you can put down roots and dig the foundations for security. You can be uncommitted and therefore unable to build stability and security
You are here to trust that the world is not against you. The universe is everything existing in perfect balance, it is like a cosmic library of all knowledge and experience. We must experience it all to learn and evolve	You are here to learn to set and achieve goals to take you on your journey towards inner and outer stability and security. Foundations, structures, families, and business empires are built 1 goal at a time.
Your focus for this lifetime must be Inner development rather than outer development and success. You must develop yourself constantly with self-discovery and spiritual wisdom. Meditation and time in nature is imperative for you	You are here to learn to plan, create a process and/or procedure to ensure the achievement of your goals. You can be directionless, lazy and block your own progression
You are here to learn to be a problem solver, thinker, a studier of the metaphysical and the big questions. You need to research, learn, and analyse theories to accrue wisdom.	You are here to develop deep meticulous focus on achieving stability, like a stable home, business or income and building your inner security. You can be scattered
You are here to learn to filter your researched wisdom through your intuition and use your research of	You are here to learn to be detail orientated, analytical, organised, and accurate to ensure your plans

other people's theories for your own needs. You can be too analytical and ignore your intuition. Or totally spiritual and ignore other theories. You must balance the two.	and processes are watertight. You can be disorganised and miss steps in the plan
You are here to be a free thinker, to be less interested in popular culture and following norms of fashion and appearance. This can make you feel different and out of place and lonely	You are here to develop a work ethic, to work hard and develop enjoyment of routine work and tasks. When low you can be lazy and stuck in 1 place, without progression
You are here to develop the ability to focus on something long enough to develop it into something useful. You can be a little scattered and struggle to focus on one spiritual or self-discovery topic at a time.	You are here to develop patient perseverance, so that every step in the process towards your goals for your stable foundation are taken. You are prone to impatience and missing steps
You are here to develop interdependence, self-sufficiency but also a healthy dependence on other people. You like to do things for yourself but take care not to push others away	You are here to learn to come to terms with limitation — both the limitations that are externally imposed on you and the limitations that you impose upon yourself.
You are here to learn to deal with and reconcile your sensitive emotions. Others often think you are aloof, but you are a well of deep emotions. You need to connect emotionally, both to yourself and to other people	You are here to look at your wounded or problematic relationships and work through the feelings of lack and pain they have brought to you.
You are here to learn to balance your need to be alone and work alone with social contact. You love to be alone, but you must ensure that you do not isolate yourself beyond what is healthy	You are prone to choosing social isolation, avoiding social situations due to social anxiety. It is important that you socialise regularly in familiar groups and with likeminded friends.

Life Path 7 with Birthday Number 5

Life Path Number 7 (90% Focus)	Birthday Number 5 (10% Focus)
You are here to learn to have faith that you are an immortal soul that has experience from your other multiple lives. You must trust the soul within you by listening to and following your intuition without over thinking and applying worldly logic. Listen to and follow your inner voice and feel safe enough to communicate your soul wisdom to the world without fear of ridicule	You are easily bored and want to look at or study lots of topics. Initial varied experience is needed in order to choose a specialism, you are here to learn to be disciplined, to continue with a topic or activity beyond the boredom of the detail, towards mastery and specialism.
You are here to trust that the world is not against you. The universe is everything existing in perfect balance, it is like a cosmic library of all knowledge and experience. We must experience it all to learn and evolve	You are here to develop the ability to balance variety, change and adventure with the stability of family and skill mastery. You can be totally spontaneous and take risks, jumping from one experience to another, but never settling or progressing
Your focus for this lifetime must be Inner development rather than outer development and success. You must develop yourself constantly with self-discovery and spiritual wisdom. Meditation and time in nature is imperative for you	You need to learn to be extremely intuitive and access your intuitive wisdom when making decisions, assessing people and situations.
You are here to learn to be a problem solver, thinker, a studier of the metaphysical and the big questions. You need to research, learn, and analyse theories to accrue wisdom.	You are here to develop your ability to attain inner freedom and outer freedom by doing things you might not want to do. Doing what you want is not necessarily freedom, you can become a slave to your desires. Freedom and discipline are inherently linked.
You are here to learn to filter your	You are here to learn to develop

researched wisdom through your intuition and use your research of other people's theories for your own needs. You can be too analytical and ignore your intuition. Or totally spiritual and ignore other theories. You must balance the two.	your verbal and written communication skills towards charismatic sharing of ideas and stories related to your specialism. You have the potential to be a great communicator
You are here to be a free thinker, to be less interested in popular culture and following norms of fashion and appearance. This can make you feel different and out of place and lonely	You are here to learn to be committed, dependable, to do what you say you are going to do. You often forget what you promise because you are so chaotic, scattered, and changeable, looking for the next new experience
You are here to develop the ability to focus on something long enough to develop it into something useful. You can be a little scattered and struggle to focus on one spiritual or self-discovery topic at a time.	You are here to develop your social skills and charisma, to have the potential to be fun loving, positive, and optimistic. You can be uptight and argumentative
You are here to develop interdependence, self-sufficiency but also a healthy dependence on other people. You like to do things for yourself but take care not to push others away	You are here to develop consistent independence. You can swing from independence to dependence and back again. Risky behaviour and 'get rich quick' schemes can bring on dependence
You are here to learn to deal with and reconcile your sensitive emotions. Others often think you are aloof, but you are a well of deep emotions. You need to connect emotionally, both to yourself and to other people	You are here to learn to develop fearlessness and help others to live fearlessly. You can be fearful of many things, restriction, and boredom, to name but a few. You need to challenge yourself and others past your own comfort zone
You are here to learn to balance your need to be alone and work alone with social contact. You love to be alone, but you must ensure that you do not isolate yourself beyond what is	You are here to learn to make good use of your energy and drive, if you feel restricted and under confident, you will be restless, and you may turn into a drama queen. Use your

healthy	energy for experience and adventure, be courageous

Life Path 7 with Birthday Number 6

Life Path Number 7 (90% Focus)	Birthday Number 6 (10% Focus)
You are here to learn to have faith that you are an immortal soul that has experience from your other multiple lives. You must trust the soul within you by listening to and following your intuition without over thinking and applying worldly logic. Listen to and follow your inner voice and feel safe enough to communicate your soul wisdom to the world without fear of ridicule	You are here to be a visionary of the ideal, the dreamer of a utopian world. You must act to create a better world with your ideals.
You are here to trust that the world is not against you. The universe is everything existing in perfect balance, it is like a cosmic library of all knowledge and experience. We must experience it all to learn and evolve	You are here to learn to not use your ideals as a benchmark for your happiness. You must not base your emotional wellbeing on the achievement of your ideals. You often judge yourself and others for not hitting perfection, causing you great unhappiness
Your focus for this lifetime must be Inner development rather than outer development and success. You must develop yourself constantly with self-discovery and spiritual wisdom. Meditation and time in nature is imperative for you	Your perfectionism can make you an over achiever due to your constant self-judgement. You never meet your own standards. You must keep your big picture in mind and not get stuck in petty detail. You can often judge small imperfections and ruin or miss your successes.
You are here to learn to be a problem solver, thinker, a studier of the metaphysical and the big questions. You need to research, learn, and analyse theories to accrue wisdom.	You are here to learn to be a nurturer, compassionate caring and giving, especially to those that are vulnerable or struggling within your close relationships, your community, and the wider world. Your judgemental nature can make you cruel and neglectful.

You are here to learn to filter your researched wisdom through your intuition and use your research of other people's theories for your own needs. You can be too analytical and ignore your intuition. Or totally spiritual and ignore other theories. You must balance the two.

You are here to develop boundaries to ensure your mental and physical health. You do a lot for others, sometimes too much, which can make you feel undervalued, unappreciated, and ill with exhaustion. You may force unsolicited advice and meddle in other people's affairs.

You are here to be a free thinker, to be less interested in popular culture and following norms of fashion and appearance. This can make you feel different and out of place and lonely

You are here to develop your social skills and be a team player. You must break through low self-esteem to be talkative, fun loving and relaxed around others. You can be shy and hide in the background.

You are here to develop the ability to focus on something long enough to develop it into something useful. You can be a little scattered and struggle to focus on one spiritual or self-discovery topic at a time.

You are here to create a stable, nurturing, tranquil home to maintain your security and well-being. Then nurture a family in an environment of stability and love. When low you can be a selfish, neglectful drama queen.

You are here to develop interdependence, self-sufficiency but also a healthy dependence on other people. You like to do things for yourself but take care not to push others away

You are here to learn to be responsible and do good for those you care for. People naturally put you in positions of responsibility, but you often resent always being the 'responsible one.' Have boundaries on your responsibility so that you do not do too much.

You are here to learn to deal with and reconcile your sensitive emotions. Others often think you are aloof, but you are a well of deep emotions. You need to connect emotionally, both to yourself and to other people

You are here to learn to develop and use your artistic and aesthetic potential. Artistic, enhancing make up, great art and home designs. You have great musical potential that you may not develop.

You are here to learn to balance your need to be alone and work alone with social contact. You love to be alone, but you must ensure that you do not isolate yourself beyond what is healthy

Life Path 7 with Birthday Number 8

Life Path Number 7 (90% Focus)	Birthday Number 8 (10% Focus)
You are here to learn to have faith that you are an immortal soul that has experience from your other multiple lives. You must trust the soul within you by listening to and following your intuition without over thinking and applying worldly logic. Listen to and follow your inner voice and feel safe enough to communicate your soul wisdom to the world without fear of ridicule	You are both spiritual and worldly. But you are here to learn the secrets of worldly financial success. You seek the freedom that comes from financial success. But freedom brings responsibility, your ethics will be tested multiple times
You are here to trust that the world is not against you. The universe is everything existing in perfect balance, it is like a cosmic library of all knowledge and experience. We must experience it all to learn and evolve	You are here to learn to use your financial success as a tool to help others achieve the same financial success. You often spend your abundance on materialistic status symbols rather than helping others
Your focus for this lifetime must be Inner development rather than outer development and success. You must develop yourself constantly with self-discovery and spiritual wisdom. Meditation and time in nature is imperative for you	You are here to develop a healthy attitude towards money. You may resent or hate wealthy people, or you may feel guilty about your own wealth. You must understand that financial wealth does not equate to poor ethics
You are here to learn to be a problem solver, thinker, a studier of the metaphysical and the big questions. You need to research, learn, and analyse theories to accrue wisdom.	You are here to develop balanced determination for achievement but with integrity and for the good of others. You can be either obsessed with achievement or fearful of achievement from low self-esteem. It is important that you develop a positive mindset because you attract what you think about.
You are here to learn to filter your researched wisdom through your	You are here to develop inner confidence and balanced personal

intuition and use your research of other people's theories for your own needs. You can be too analytical and ignore your intuition. Or totally spiritual and ignore other theories. You must balance the two.	power. You can swing from over dominance or misuse of power to hiding away or submission to others
You are here to be a free thinker, to be less interested in popular culture and following norms of fashion and appearance. This can make you feel different and out of place and lonely	You are here to develop skilled leadership, which consists of subject competence coupled with excellent social skills and charisma
You are here to develop the ability to focus on something long enough to develop it into something useful. You can be a little scattered and struggle to focus on one spiritual or self-discovery topic at a time.	You are here to work hard as an excellent practical businessperson, but you must ensure that you do not work too hard, you need time out and time for your family
You are here to develop interdependence, self-sufficiency but also a healthy dependence on other people. You like to do things for yourself but take care not to push others away	You are here to be worldly, strong, resilient, disciplined, and realistic. To be successful you need to be strong, tough, and able to cope with The ups and downs of the world
You are here to learn to deal with and reconcile your sensitive emotions. Others often think you are aloof, but you are a well of deep emotions. You need to connect emotionally, both to yourself and to other people	You are here to develop bravery and the courage to take risks to progress. Success comes from having the bravery to take risks
You are here to learn to balance your need to be alone and work alone with social contact. You love to be alone, but you must ensure that you do not isolate yourself beyond what is healthy	You are here to develop organisation and management skills, resolve to making things happen and to define and meet your goals.

Life Path 7 with Birthday Number 9

Life Path Number 7 (90% Focus)	Birthday Number 9 (10% Focus)
You are here to learn to have faith that you are an immortal soul that has experience from your other multiple lives. You must trust the soul within you by listening to and following your intuition without over thinking and applying worldly logic. Listen to and follow your inner voice and feel safe enough to communicate your soul wisdom to the world without fear of ridicule	You are here to learn to follow your intuitive wisdom and live to spiritual laws, rather than worldly laws, conventions, and ideals. You tend to follow worldly laws and prejudices as an excuse for your actions. But if you had followed your intuitive spiritual wisdom, you would not have acted that way. Focus on faith over logic
You are here to trust that the world is not against you. The universe is everything existing in perfect balance, it is like a cosmic library of all knowledge and experience. We must experience it all to learn and evolve	You are here to learn to act with integrity for the benefit of others. You are powerful and you must use your power for the benefit of others. You can act for selfish or nefarious reasons
Your focus for this lifetime must be Inner development rather than outer development and success. You must develop yourself constantly with self-discovery and spiritual wisdom. Meditation and time in nature is imperative for you	You are here to learn to lead by example, do you practise what you preach? You can be quite domineering, an adviser with all the answers. But you must let others make their own mistakes
You are here to learn to be a problem solver, thinker, a studier of the metaphysical and the big questions. You need to research, learn, and analyse theories to accrue wisdom.	You are here to make your life your teaching, you need to counsel with wisdom. You are a developed soul, the totality of all the numbers, full of cellular experience and higher knowledge
You are here to learn to filter your researched wisdom through your intuition and use your research of other people's theories for your own	You are here to develop broad mindedness, meet and accept diverse people. You must learn to be a humanitarian and make the world

needs. You can be too analytical and ignore your intuition. Or totally spiritual and ignore other theories. You must balance the two.

a better place. You need a global consciousness, as you can be narrow minded, judgemental, and even bigoted.

You are here to be a free thinker, to be less interested in popular culture and following norms of fashion and appearance. This can make you feel different and out of place and lonely

You are here to learn to take responsibility for your powerful choices. You sometimes run away from the consequences of your actions

You are here to develop the ability to focus on something long enough to develop it into something useful. You can be a little scattered and struggle to focus on one spiritual or self-discovery topic at a time.

You need to develop towards being a successful entrepreneur or businessperson if it is with something you feel passionate about. You must choose work that has meaning for you. You are a powerful force for change

You are here to develop interdependence, self-sufficiency but also a healthy dependence on other people. You like to do things for yourself but take care not to push others away

You are here to develop excellent social skills and charisma. You could develop the skills of a powerful speaker and influencer of others. People will hang on your every word

You are here to learn to deal with and reconcile your sensitive emotions. Others often think you are aloof, but you are a well of deep emotions. You need to connect emotionally, both to yourself and to other people

You are here to look after the wellbeing of others. But when you are in trouble or need support, people do not notice. You must ask for what you need, you must ask for help

You are here to learn to balance your need to be alone and work alone with social contact. You love to be alone, but you must ensure that you do not isolate yourself beyond what is healthy

You are here to wrap things up, let go and surrender. You can have a victim mentality, holding onto feelings that no longer serve you, unable to move on from perceived injustice, normally rooted in family issues.

Life Path 7 with Birthday Master 11

Life Path Number 7 (90% Focus)	Birthday Master 11 (10% Focus)
You are here to learn to have faith that you are an immortal soul that has experience from your other multiple lives. You must trust the soul within you by listening to and following your intuition without over thinking and applying worldly logic. Listen to and follow your inner voice and feel safe enough to communicate your soul wisdom to the world without fear of ridicule	You are an old soul, with higher potential and higher responsibility to improve the world. You are here to learn to connect to source energy to channel unique new ideas and messages to change the world. You are here to learn to be happy in the limelight expressing new ideas for an audience. You need to develop and trust your massive intuitive potential. You often hide your ideas due to low confidence
You are here to trust that the world is not against you. The universe is everything existing in perfect balance, it is like a cosmic library of all knowledge and experience. We must experience it all to learn and evolve	You are here to learn to be the ideas person, but you struggle to bring your unique ideas to reality because you lose interest quickly after the initial idea of sabotage yourself due to crippling low confidence. You are an idealistic dreamer whose ideas are often not grounded in reality
Your focus for this lifetime must be Inner development rather than outer development and success. You must develop yourself constantly with self-discovery and spiritual wisdom. Meditation and time in nature is imperative for you	You are here to learn to be confident in your uniqueness because unique people have unique ground-breaking ideas. It is important that you are not craving validation from others. Your validation should come from your intuition.
You are here to learn to be a problem solver, thinker, a studier of the metaphysical and the big questions. You need to research, learn, and analyse theories to accrue wisdom.	You need to bring unique, new ideas that break barriers, or challenge others comfort zone. You must learn to be brave, confident and be willing to take risks
You are here to learn to filter your researched wisdom through your	You need to be a practical initiator, a doer, action orientated that learns by

intuition and use your research of other people's theories for your own needs. You can be too analytical and ignore your intuition. Or totally spiritual and ignore other theories. You must balance the two.	experience. Ideas will stay unmanifested until you act! Only action brings change
You are here to be a free thinker, to be less interested in popular culture and following norms of fashion and appearance. This can make you feel different and out of place and lonely	You need to set intentions then use spiritual practice and visualisation to channel your advanced, intense master energy into initiation and action. Unchanneled or mismanaged energy can cause intense nervous energy and anxiety. You may medicate these with unhealthy substances.
You are here to develop the ability to focus on something long enough to develop it into something useful. You can be a little scattered and struggle to focus on one spiritual or self-discovery topic at a time.	You are here to learn to be interdependent, not so independent that you push others away and refuse to delegate. You cannot do everything alone. Independence is an illusion; we are all interconnected
You are here to develop interdependence, self-sufficiency but also a healthy dependence on other people. You like to do things for yourself but take care not to push others away	You need to be determined to succeed. Constant self-discovery and intuitive spiritual development is key for you to develop complete trust in the skills you have learned and mastered to serve as a kind of "security blanket" for you when you are feeling insecure
You are here to learn to deal with and reconcile your sensitive emotions. Others often think you are aloof, but you are a well of deep emotions. You need to connect emotionally, both to yourself and to other people	You need to learn to be a supportive, nurturing leader, be firm and assertive but also empathic and supportive. You must lead others to the fruition of your ideas, but with balanced personal power
You are here to learn to balance your need to be alone and work	Your power causes ripples, both positive and negative, you must

alone with social contact. You love to be alone, but you must ensure that you do not isolate yourself beyond what is healthy

remember that great power brings great responsibility. You must ensure that your intentions are good

You are here to learn to be responsible to others, your family, team, or group but in a balanced way. You can be too responsible and do too much. You are irresponsible if you feel undervalued, resentful, and exhausted.

You must develop and improve your social skills, focus on widening and deepening your relationships and make decisions subjectively. It is important that you deepen your relationships and connect 121

You may struggle to maintain long term close and romantic relationships.

You must learn not to smother your loved ones or have expectations that can never be met. OR back away from wanting love because it hurts too badly. You need to balance your intense need for love for healthy relationships.

You are here to learn to be intuitive and sensitive to the needs of others. You are here to be of service to others, the development of intuition will aid you in this journey

You are here to learn to be a cooperative team player to get the job done as part of a cohesive team. You can be a disruptive, uncooperative drama queen.

	You must develop the assertiveness to demand boundaries to being overworked, walked all over, taken advantage of, and/or taken for granted. You must not be a "shape shifter" who changes who you are in order to please others or keep the peace. Be you and consider yourself too.
	You are here to serve the world, help the team, the task and be dependable. You can always be relied upon to keep the cogs turning behind the scenes
	You are here to be the tactful mediator of the team/group/family, helping to resolve conflicts fairly and for the good of everyone involved. You hate conflict and often run and hide until it is over
	You are here to learn to plan the next steps after channelling your message or idea & build a team to achieve it. The energy of the 11/2 needs to be the nurturer of ideas and a builder of teams
	You must learn to give yourself your own kudos. Oftentimes you judge yourself on what everyone else says or thinks about you. You need to develop your internal compass and turn inward for validation, do what YOU think you should do

Life Path 7 with Birthday Master 22/4

Life Path Number 7 (90 % Focus)	Birthday Master 22/4 (10% Focus)
You are here to learn to have faith that you are an immortal soul that has experience from your other multiple lives. You must trust the soul within you by listening to and following your intuition without over thinking and applying worldly logic. Listen to and follow your inner voice and feel safe enough to communicate your soul wisdom to the world without fear of ridicule	You are an old soul, as spiritual as you are practical, here to channel and then manifest ideas in reality to build world safety, stability, and security. You must learn to handle the master builder energy and focus it to manifestation. You have a big responsibility to the team and the world to build structures (buildings, concepts, body, mind, spirit, businesses, organisations, even an empire for the purpose of world stability and security
You are here to trust that the world is not against you. The universe is everything existing in perfect balance, it is like a cosmic library of all knowledge and experience. We must experience it all to learn and evolve	You must develop and improve your social skills, focus on widening and deepening your relationships to assist you to manifest your big ideas. It is important that you learn to deepen your relationships and connect 121, you cannot do this alone!
Your focus for this lifetime must be Inner development rather than outer development and success. You must develop yourself constantly with self-discovery and spiritual wisdom. Meditation and time in nature is imperative for you	You must learn to have balanced, healthy relationships with others that are part of your sense of security. You must learn not to smother your loved ones and your team or have expectations that can never be met. OR Your big task in this lifetime may disrupt your love relationships. You may back away from wanting love because it hurts too badly or attacks

	your sense of security
You are here to learn to be a problem solver, thinker, a studier of the metaphysical and the big questions. You need to research, learn, and analyse theories to accrue wisdom.	You are here to learn to listen to and follow your intuition. Intuition is needed for you to be sensitive to the needs of others. You are here to be of service to change the world, the development of intuition will aid you in this journey
You are here to learn to filter your researched wisdom through your intuition and use your research of other people's theories for your own needs. You can be too analytical and ignore your intuition. Or totally spiritual and ignore other theories. You must balance the two.	You are here to learn to be a cooperative team player to get the job done as part of a cohesive team. You may fail to communicate effectively with others. You can be a hard-headed and high handed at times.
You are here to be a free thinker, to be less interested in popular culture and following norms of fashion and appearance. This can make you feel different and out of place and lonely	You must develop the assertiveness to demand boundaries to being overworked, walked all over, taken advantage of, and/or taken for granted. You must also develop your ability to respect other people's boundaries and not be high handed.
You are here to develop the ability to focus on something long enough to develop it into something useful. You can be a little scattered and struggle to focus on one spiritual or self-discovery topic at a time.	You are here to be of service to the world, the leader, the team, the task and be dependable. You can always be counted upon to keep the cogs turning behind the scenes
You are here to develop interdependence, self-sufficiency but also a healthy dependence on other people. You like to do things for yourself but take care not to push	You are extremely sensitive, and you hate and run away from conflict. But you are here to learn to be a tactful mediator, helping to resolve conflicts fairly and for the good of

others away	the team/family/group
You are here to learn to deal with and reconcile your sensitive emotions. Others often think you are aloof, but you are a well of deep emotions. You need to connect emotionally, both to yourself and to other people	You are here to learn to stay focused and plan the next steps after you have channelled a new idea & build a team to achieve it. The energy of the 22 needs to be the nurturer, the builder of ideas and teams.
You are here to learn to balance your need to be alone and work alone with social contact. You love to be alone, but you must ensure that you do not isolate yourself beyond what is healthy	You must learn to give yourself your own kudos. Oftentimes you judge yourself on what everyone else says or thinks about you. You need to develop your internal compass and turn inward for validation, do what you think you should do
	You are here to learn to commit to a person and/or place, so that you can put down roots and dig the foundations for security. You can be uncommitted and therefore unable to build stability and security
	You are here to learn to set and achieve goals to take you on your journey towards inner and outer stability and security. Foundations, structures, families, and business empires are built 1 goal at a time.
	You are here to learn to plan, create a process and/or procedure to ensure the achievement of your goals and bring strength and stability to dynamic ideas. You can be directionless, lazy and block your own progression. You are here to develop deep meticulous focus on achieving

	stability, like a stable home, business or income and building your inner security. You can be scattered and miss steps in your impatience.
	You are here to learn to be detail orientated, analytical, organised, and accurate to ensure your plans and processes are watertight. You can be disorganised, flaky and miss steps in your plan
	Your master 22/4 Birthday means that you are an old soul and you have agreed to bring safety, stability, and security to the world. You innovate and build empires, organisations, and businesses. This involves hard work, detail focus, routine work, and tasks. You are here to develop a work ethic, to work hard and develop enjoyment of routine work and tasks
	You are here to develop patient perseverance, so that every step in the process towards your goals for your stable foundation are taken. You are prone to impatience and corner cutting.
	You are here to develop determination and the perseverance to keep going past obstacles to achieve your goals. You are prone to giving up at the first hurdle.
	You are here to learn to come to terms with limitation — both the limitations that are externally imposed on you and the limitations

	that you impose upon yourself.
	You are here to look at your wounded or problematic relationships and work through the feelings of lack and pain they have brought to you. All experiences have lessons embedded within them
	Avoid social isolation by socialising regularly in familiar groups and with likeminded friends.

Your Life Path and Birthday Number Eight (8)

You have chosen to incarnate to learn the lessons of the 8 life path energy because when speaking to your spirit guide before this life, you highlighted that you needed to learn the lessons of the 8 energy. You are here to work with difficulties relating to emotional and financial abundance, power, and recognition and to apply your success and power in service of the common good. You need to experience inner emotional and material abundance, but not make money your God, rather use it as a tool to help others. You must achieve business success in a balanced way and enforce a healthy work/life balance. You may either avoid achievement and struggle to support yourself or become an over achiever and a workaholic, who is money rich but love poor. Learning to balance your personal power, not to overpower or be powerless is also important for you as you are here to learn to be a world class leader.

At your highest vibration, you are a balanced achiever, teacher, and an intuitive, charismatic authority figure. You like to be in charge, you work very well in business, and you are good at organising workflow by informing everyone what their responsibilities are. At your best, you will transcend issues of abundance and power by dedicating these qualities to a higher purpose. You could live richly or modestly, be known and powerful or unknown and powerless but what is important is you do not care, you no longer have emotional attachments to these things. You are grateful for what you have, and you are a philanthropist that likes to share to help others reach abundance.

Your challenges are that you can get tunnel vision, only seeing what you want to see. You may want to control others and gain status via showing off expensive material possessions, but you never really feel satisfied. When you are at a low vibration, you feel strong drives toward money worship, power hunger, recognition, and control. Or you may feel unable to earn money because of strong fears and an aversion to money and success. Overly submissive or unable to assert yourself. A potential aversion or obsession with worldly achievement could be because of your potentially negative attitude to money. Negative feelings around money could make you resentful of the wealthy, or guilty for your own wealth because you feel you don't deserve it. Many 8's wrongly attach poor ethics to financial wealth, but it is important that you understand that affluence is not incompatible with ethics, money is just energy that can be used as a tool for positivity and negativity. In this paradigm it is essential for us to make money but making money selfishly or dishonestly without motivation to serve others will feel like something is missing in your life. You can either abuse your power or be powerless, crave recognition or hide in the wings.

The 8 energy is considered a difficult number because of the 2's and the 4's that are in it, for success, great effort is needed. You need to develop a burning desire to work hard, succeed and gain material reward, but with a healthy work/life balance. You are here to develop inner and outer financial and emotional abundance, balanced inner power, inner confidence, and authority. Possessing inner abundance is knowing that you have enough both emotionally and materially. But as a life path 8, you may struggle to feel abundant, worry about or focus on lack. As a result, you often work too hard to compensate for your fears. You must work towards abundant feelings, be grateful for what you have, feel blessed in your circumstances, and share your resulting abundance with others.

You need to attain, use positively, but not be attached to, money, material gain, power, or status. You need to be determined to achieve but in a balanced way. You may be overdetermined and focus on your financial success to the exclusion of everything else, neglecting your family and your health. Or on the opposite polarity, you could be achievement averted and struggle to enter the working world on any level. Your issues with power can be powerlessness or being overpowering. You need to develop the assertiveness to say and do what you intuitively feel is best to say and do. To 'know' when to stand your ground and when to give way, but also extend that same freedom of choice to others.

The challenges of your 8 energy could see you as wealthy, surrounded by material symbols but devoid of abundance in other areas of life or homeless on the streets, unable to support yourself financially. You must have a balanced attitude to achievement, maintain a healthy work life balance and ensure that you give equal attention to your family and your close relationships.

You are here to learn the secrets of financial success, be an excellent practical business person and a skilled, confident, charismatic leader. You may find this task difficult, but you are meant to work through your difficulties in business or your career, set goals and make things happen.

To overcome difficulties and make things happen you need to be realistic, toughen up and develop resilience as the business world is very cut throat and takes no prisoners. You need to be strong and brave enough to take intuitive, calculated risks to succeed and speculate to accumulate realistically. Work on your spiritual side too, listen to and follow your intuition to help you make sound financial and leadership decisions in the real world.

You may struggle to achieve the balanced personal power needed to be a skilled, confident, and charismatic leader. You could be over dominant, power hungry and even tyrannical, ruling by fear and aggression. Or on the other polarity, you may be overly submissive and allow other people to walk all over you. You must listen to, trust, and confidently act on your intuition to gain inner confidence, inner authority, and charisma. When you trust your intuition, you exude an energy of self-assurance and confidence in your abilities but also of compassion, ethics and fair play. When you are confident in yourself, you are charismatic, others will be confident in you and choose to follow you.

Your 8 energy is concerned with developing a healthy, balanced attitude to money. If you are struggling for money, you may feel jealousy or associate wealth with poor ethics, considering wealthy people as unethical. If you have financial abundance, you could feel guilty about having abundance and wonder if you are a bad person. Strive to be ethical in everything you do, consider the consequences of your actions on other people, and use your financial abundance as a tool to help others to achieve the same success.

You need to use the abundance that you create as a tool to help others. However, you like to have the best of everything and to enjoy the luxuries of life, designer labels, fast cars, status, and prestige. You may be driven to use these status symbols and the limelight as a prop for your confidence and to raise your status in the eyes of others. Status symbols and fame are not an adequate support for your confidence, as they are transient. But you are here to transcend the need for material status and gain satisfaction from using your wealth as a tool to help others. You could become a successful business person and philanthropist, an investor in small start-up companies that need a leg up to get started or a teacher and adviser. You have the potential to be a world class leader that functions for the good of everyone.

With power and influence comes great responsibility, it is important for you to live life honestly and positively to help you to transcend the lessons of this path and vibrate highly. Your ethics will be constantly tested.

You must always act with integrity and positive ethics, which is considering the impact of your actions and policies on other people and the environment around you. You need to be social with strong intuitive confidence and charisma, you must organise and not shy away from speaking your mind.

Your ability to attract and manifest powerfully means that it is important you have a positive mindset to manifest positively. You are a powerful manifester of what you think about, negativity will manifest negativity.

How others see you is especially important to you, but your drive for recognition can detach you from others, as an unbalanced workaholic. You can be a nag, keeping on and on, wearing others down until you get what you want. Or on the flip side, you can be timid, not have the guts to say what you want to say or under motivated and lazy because of fear of failure.

An obsessive need for recognition may also make you selfish and self-serving, you may climb over others and/or take the glory for someone else's work. Eventually, you must learn that it is not what you achieve or who you know, it is who you are and how you treat others that matters. You can be a little lacking in imagination, you find it difficult to show your emotions and you may come across rude without even realising it.

You have it within you to be a ruthless dictator, who abuses your power and will stop at nothing to get what you want, selfishly, without heed to the common good. You can be aggressive, controlling and extremely over powering, which can be difficult for the more sensitive among us to deal with. Or you can be the complete opposite of this, hiding away, never asserting yourself or achieving anything.

You must also take care not to make money your God, living in a perpetual fight to make more and more money. Your 8 path will teach you that money and power alone will not bring you the happiness that you strive for. You may have a negative attitude to money and wealth, equating wealth to poor ethics. This could cause you to feel guilty if you have money or think you are a bad person. You may staunchly avoid money and success, resent others that have money or have fears surrounding wealth and power. You need to find balance between the material and relationships which develops your spiritual side. You can be domineering or a pushover, known or ignored, rich or poor, depending on the attitude and beliefs that you manifest.

Careers that will support your life path:

Business owner, sales, finance, banking & investments, Managers, CEO's Supervisors, legal, politics, property, Working with new technology, the military, glamour, beauty, and fashion.

Key Attributes – original, imaginative, and decisive

Socially – Sociable, Organised, Leader.

Colour – Orange

Subtle body – Sacral Chakra

Day – Saturday

Astrologically – Saturn, zodiac Capricorn

Life Path 8 with Birthday Number 1

Life Path Number 8 (90% Focus)	Birthday Number 1 (10% Focus)
You are both spiritual and worldly. But you are here to learn the secrets of worldly financial success. You seek the freedom that comes from financial success. But freedom brings responsibility, your ethics will be tested multiple times.	You are here to learn to connect to source energy to download / channel unique new ideas. You often hide your ideas due to low confidence. You are here to learn to be happy in the limelight expressing new ideas for an audience.
You are here to learn to use your financial success as a tool to help others achieve the same financial success. You often spend your abundance on materialistic status symbols rather than helping others	You are here to learn to be the ideas person, but you struggle to bring your unique ideas to reality because you lose interest quickly after the initial idea.
You are here to develop a healthy attitude towards money. You may resent or hate wealthy people, or you may feel guilty about your own wealth. You must understand that financial wealth does not equate to poor ethics	You are here to learn to be confident in your uniqueness because unique people have unique ground-breaking ideas. It is important that you are not craving validation from others.
You are here to develop balanced determination for achievement but with integrity and for the good of others. You can be either obsessed with achievement or fearful of achievement from low self-esteem. It is important that you develop a positive mindset because you attract what you think about.	You need to be a practical initiator, a doer, action orientated that learns by experience. Only action makes the difference.
You are here to develop inner confidence and balanced personal power. You can swing from over dominance or misuse of power to hiding away or submission to others	You need to learn to trust your intuitive voice within. You must achieve balanced confidence in yourself & your abilities, fed by strong connection & trust in your intuition. You bring your ideas without fear.

	You must not seek validation from others or base your confidence on what others say.
You are here to develop skilled leadership, which consists of subject competence coupled with excellent social skills and charisma.	You need to bring unique, new ideas that break barriers, or challenge others comfort zones, you must learn to be brave, confident and be willing to take risks
You are here to work hard as an excellent practical businessperson, but you must ensure that you do not work too hard, you need time out and time for your family	You are here to learn to be interdependent, not so independent that you push others away and refuse to delegate. You cannot do everything alone. Independence is an illusion; we are all interconnected
You are here to be worldly, strong, resilient, disciplined, and realistic. To be successful you need to be strong, tough, and able to cope with the ups and downs of the world	You need to be determined to succeed. Constant self-discovery and development is key for you to develop complete trust in the skills you have learned and mastered to serve as a kind of "security blanket" for you when you are feeling insecure
You are here to develop bravery and the courage to take risks to progress. Success comes from having the bravery to take risks	You need to learn to be a powerful leader, be dominant and assertive. You must lead others to the fruition of your ideas, but with balanced personal power
You are here to develop organisation and management skills, resolve to making things happen and to define and meet your goals.	Your power causes ripples, both positive and negative, you must remember that great power brings great responsibility. You must ensure that your intentions are good

Life Path 8 with Birthday Number 2

Life Path Number 8 (90% Focus)	Birthday Number 2 (10% Focus)
You are both spiritual and worldly. But you are here to learn the secrets of worldly financial success. You seek the freedom that comes from financial success. But freedom brings responsibility, your ethics will be tested multiple times	You are here to learn to be responsible to others and the team. You can be too responsible and do too much. You are irresponsible if you feel undervalued and resentful
You are here to learn to use your financial success as a tool to help others achieve the same financial success. You often spend your abundance on materialistic status symbols rather than helping others	You must learn to improve your social skills, focus on widening and deepening your relationships and make decisions subjectively. It is important that you deepen your relationships and connect 121
You are here to develop a healthy attitude towards money. You may resent or hate wealthy people, or you may feel guilty about your own wealth. You must understand that financial wealth does not equate to poor ethics	You must learn not to smother your loved ones or have expectations that can never be met. OR you may back away from wanting love because it hurts too badly. You need to balance your intense need for love
You are here to develop balanced determination for achievement but with integrity and for the good of others. You can be either obsessed with achievement or fearful of achievement from low self-esteem. It is important that you develop a positive mindset because you attract what you think about.	You are here to learn to be intuitive and sensitive to the needs of others. You are here to be of service to others, the development of intuition will aid you in this journey
You are here to develop inner confidence and balanced personal power. You can swing from over dominance or misuse of power to	You are here to learn to be a cooperative team player to get the job done as part of a cohesive team. You can be a disruptive,

hiding away or submission to others	uncooperative drama queen.
You are here to develop skilled leadership, which consists of subject competence coupled with excellent social skills and charisma	You must develop the assertiveness to demand boundaries to being overworked, walked all over, taken advantage of, and/or taken for granted. You must not be a "shape shifter" who changes who you are in order to please others or keep the peace.
You are here to work hard as an excellent practical businessperson, but you must ensure that you do not work too hard, you need time out and time for your family	You are here to serve the leader, the team, the task and be dependable. You can always be counted upon to keep the cogs turning behind the scenes
You are here to be worldly, strong, resilient, disciplined, and realistic. To be successful you need to be strong, tough, and able to cope with The ups and downs of the world	You are here to be the tactful mediator of the team, helping to resolve conflicts fairly and for the good of the team. You hate conflict and often run and hide until it is over
You are here to develop bravery and the courage to take risks to progress. Success comes from having the bravery to take risks	You are here to learn to plan the next steps after the initial idea & build a team to achieve it. The energy of the two is the nurturer of ideas and a builder of teams
You are here to develop organisation and management skills, resolve to making things happen and to define and meet your goals.	You must learn to give yourself your own kudos. Oftentimes you judge yourself on what everyone else says or thinks about you. You need to develop your internal compass and turn inward for validation, do what you think you should do

Life Path 8 with Birthday Number 3

Life Path Number 8 (90% Focus)	Birthday Number 3 (10% Focus)
You are both spiritual and worldly. But you are here to learn the secrets of worldly financial success. You seek the freedom that comes from financial success. But freedom brings responsibility, your ethics will be tested multiple times	You are here to learn to express yourself verbally to inspire, inform and delight. You may struggle in some way verbally, chronic shyness, speech delay, stutter or struggling to find the words
You are here to learn to use your financial success as a tool to help others achieve the same financial success. You often spend your abundance on materialistic status symbols rather than helping others	You are here to learn to express yourself creatively to inspire, inform and delight. But you may struggle to progress, execute, and finish creative projects, due to lack of self-belief
You are here to develop a healthy attitude towards money. You may resent or hate wealthy people, or you may feel guilty about your own wealth. You must understand that financial wealth does not equate to poor ethics	You must learn to be dynamic, take risks and be confident to enjoy the attention and limelight of an audience. You can be shy, under confident and feel unable to take risks.
You are here to develop balanced determination for achievement but with integrity and for the good of others. You can be either obsessed with achievement or fearful of achievement from low self-esteem. It is important that you develop a positive mindset because you attract what you think about.	You need to develop as an entrepreneur who is able to promote, network and make money creatively. But you may procrastinate and fail to stay focused and work inconsistently.
You are here to develop inner confidence and balanced personal power. You can swing from over dominance or misuse of power to hiding away or submission to others	You are here to learn to express your emotions positively. You can be extremely sensitive to criticism and other people's emotions, causing you to express emotions negatively

You are here to develop skilled leadership, which consists of subject competence coupled with excellent social skills and charisma

You are here to develop the habit of acting, be a doer and executer of ideas. When low, you can struggle with apathy, laziness and lack of focus and direction

You are here to work hard as an excellent practical businessperson, but you must ensure that you do not work too hard, you need time out and time for your family and rest

You are here to learn to be social, talkative, the life of the party and bringer of fun & positivity. You need to be the networker, communicating an emotional message. You can be quiet and struggle to speak

You are here to be worldly, strong, resilient, disciplined, and realistic. To be successful you need to be strong, tough, and able to cope with the ups and downs of the world.

You must develop interdependence, life path 3's like to be looked after and can be prone to avoiding work or anything needing routine and commitment

You are here to develop bravery and the courage to take risks to progress. Success comes from having the bravery to take risks

You are here to be opportunistic, to network, make useful connections and snap up opportunities to spread the word and progress ideas and projects

You are here to develop organisation and management skills, resolve to making things happen and to define and meet your goals.

You must learn to take responsibility and listen to guidance; you can be irresponsible. You must think before you act, and take full responsibility for what you do

Life Path 8 with Birthday Number 4

Life Path Number 8 (90% Focus)	Birthday Number 4 (10% Focus)
You are both spiritual and worldly. But you are here to learn the secrets of worldly financial success. You seek the freedom that comes from financial success. But freedom brings responsibility, your ethics will be tested multiple times	You are here to learn to commit to a person and/or place, so that you can put down roots and dig the foundations for security. You can be uncommitted and therefore unable to build stability and security
You are here to learn to use your financial success as a tool to help others achieve the same financial success. You often spend your abundance on materialistic status symbols rather than helping others	You are here to learn to set and achieve goals to take you on your journey towards inner and outer stability and security. Foundations, structures, families, and business empires are built 1 goal at a time.
You are here to develop a healthy attitude towards money. You may resent or hate wealthy people, or you may feel guilty about your own wealth. You must understand that financial wealth does not equate to poor ethics	You are here to learn to plan, create a process and/or procedure to ensure the achievement of your goals. You can be directionless, lazy and block your own progression
You are here to develop balanced determination for achievement but with integrity and for the good of others. You can be either obsessed with achievement or fearful of achievement from low self-esteem. It is important that you develop a positive mindset because you attract what you think about.	You are here to develop deep meticulous focus on achieving stability, like a stable home, business or income and building your inner security. You can be scattered
You are here to develop inner confidence and balanced personal power. You can swing from over dominance or misuse of power to hiding away or submission to others	You are here to learn to be detail orientated, analytical, organised, and accurate to ensure your plans and processes are watertight. You can be disorganised and miss steps in the plan

You are here to develop skilled leadership, which consists of subject competence coupled with excellent social skills and charisma

You are here to develop a work ethic, to work hard and develop enjoyment of routine work and tasks. When low you can be lazy and stuck in 1 place, without progression

You are here to work hard as an excellent practical businessperson, but you must ensure that you do not work too hard, you need time out and time for your family

You are here to develop patient perseverance, so that every step in the process towards your goals for your stable foundation are taken. You are prone to impatience and missing steps

You are here to be worldly, strong, resilient, disciplined, and realistic. To be successful you need to be strong, tough, and able to cope with

The ups and downs of the world

You are here to learn to come to terms with limitation — both the limitations that are externally imposed on you and the limitations that you impose upon yourself.

You are here to develop bravery and the courage to take risks to progress. Success comes from having the bravery to take risks

You are here to look at your wounded or problematic relationships and work through the feelings of lack and pain they have brought to you.

You are here to develop organisation and management skills, resolve to making things happen and to define and meet your goals.

You are prone to choosing social isolation, avoiding social situations due to social anxiety. It is important that you socialise regularly in familiar groups and with likeminded friends.

Life Path 8 with Birthday Number 5

Life Path Number 8 (90% Focus)	Birthday Number 5 (10% Focus)
You are both spiritual and worldly. But you are here to learn the secrets of worldly financial success. You seek the freedom that comes from financial success. But freedom brings responsibility, your ethics will be tested multiple times	You are easily bored and want to look at or study lots of topics. Initial varied experience is needed in order to choose a specialism, you are here to learn to be disciplined, to continue with a topic or activity beyond the boredom of the detail, towards mastery and specialism.
You are here to learn to use your financial success as a tool to help others achieve the same financial success. You often spend your abundance on materialistic status symbols rather than helping others	You are here to develop the ability to balance variety, change and adventure with the stability of family and skill mastery. You can be totally spontaneous and take risks, jumping from one experience to another, but never settling or progressing
You are here to develop a healthy attitude towards money. You may resent or hate wealthy people, or you may feel guilty about your own wealth. You must understand that financial wealth does not equate to poor ethics	You need to learn to be extremely intuitive and access your intuitive wisdom when making decisions, assessing people and situations.
You are here to develop balanced determination for achievement but with integrity and for the good of others. You can be either obsessed with achievement or fearful of achievement from low self-esteem. It is important that you develop a positive mindset because you attract what you think about.	You are here to develop your ability to attain inner freedom and outer freedom by doing things you might not want to do. Doing what you want is not necessarily freedom, you can become a slave to your desires. Freedom and discipline are inherently linked.
You are here to develop inner confidence and balanced personal	You are here to learn to develop your verbal and written

242

power. You can swing from over dominance or misuse of power to hiding away or submission to others

communication skills towards charismatic sharing of ideas and stories related to your specialism. You have the potential to be a great communicator

You are here to develop skilled leadership, which consists of subject competence coupled with excellent social skills and charisma

You are here to learn to be committed, dependable, to do what you say you are going to do. You often forget what you promise because you are so chaotic, scattered, and changeable, looking for the next new experience

You are here to work hard as an excellent practical businessperson, but you must ensure that you do not work too hard, you need time out and time for your family

You are here to develop your social skills and charisma, to have the potential to be fun loving, positive, and optimistic. You can be uptight and argumentative

You are here to be worldly, strong, resilient, disciplined, and realistic. To be successful you need to be strong, tough, and able to cope with

The ups and downs of the world

You are here to develop consistent independence. You can swing from independence to dependence and back again. Risky behaviour and 'get rich quick' schemes can bring on dependence

You are here to develop bravery and the courage to take risks to progress. Success comes from having the bravery to take risks

You are here to learn to develop fearlessness and help others to live fearlessly. You can be fearful of many things, restriction, and boredom, to name but a few. You need to challenge yourself and others past your own comfort zone

You are here to develop organisation and management skills, resolve to making things happen and to define and meet your goals.

You are here to learn to make good use of your energy and drive, if you feel restricted and under confident, you will be restless, and you may turn into a drama queen. Use your energy for experience and adventure, be courageous

243

Life Path 8 with Birthday Number 6

Life Path Number 8 (90% Focus)	Birthday Number 6 (10% Focus)
You are both spiritual and worldly. But you are here to learn the secrets of worldly financial success. You seek the freedom that comes from financial success. But freedom brings responsibility, your ethics will be tested multiple times	You are here to be a visionary of the ideal, the dreamer of a utopian world. You must act to create a better world with your ideals.
You are here to learn to use your financial success as a tool to help others achieve the same financial success. You often spend your abundance on materialistic status symbols rather than helping others	You are here to learn to not use your ideals as a benchmark for your happiness. You must not base your emotional wellbeing on the achievement of your ideals. You often judge yourself and others for not hitting perfection, causing you great unhappiness
You are here to develop a healthy attitude towards money. You may resent or hate wealthy people, or you may feel guilty about your own wealth. You must understand that financial wealth does not equate to poor ethics	Your perfectionism can make you an over achiever due to your constant self-judgement. You never meet your own standards. You must keep your big picture in mind and not get stuck in petty detail. You can often judge small imperfections and ruin or miss your successes.
You are here to develop balanced determination for achievement but with integrity and for the good of others. You can be either obsessed with achievement or fearful of achievement from low self-esteem. It is important that you develop a positive mindset because you attract what you think about.	You are here to learn to be a nurturer, compassionate caring and giving, especially to those that are vulnerable or struggling within your close relationships, your community, and the wider world. Your judgemental nature can make you cruel and neglectful.
You are here to develop inner confidence and balanced personal power. You can swing from over	You are here to develop boundaries to ensure your mental and physical health. You do a lot for others,

dominance or misuse of power to hiding away or submission to others	sometimes too much, which can make you feel undervalued, unappreciated, and ill with exhaustion. You may force unsolicited advice and meddle in other affairs.
You are here to develop skilled leadership, which consists of subject competence coupled with excellent social skills and charisma	You are here to develop your social skills and be a team player. You must break through low self-esteem to be talkative, fun loving and relaxed around others. You can be shy and hide in the background.
You are here to work hard as an excellent practical businessperson, but you must ensure that you do not work too hard, you need time out and time for your family	You are here to create a stable, nurturing, tranquil home to maintain your security and well-being. Then nurture a family in an environment of stability and love. When low you can be a selfish, neglectful drama queen.
You are here to be worldly, strong, resilient, disciplined, and realistic. To be successful you need to be strong, tough, and able to cope with The ups and downs of the world	You are here to learn to be responsible and do good for those you care for. People naturally put you in positions of responsibility, but you often resent always being the 'responsible one.' Have boundaries on your responsibility so that you do not do too much.
You are here to develop bravery and the courage to take risks to progress. Success comes from having the bravery to take risks	You are here to learn to develop and use your artistic and aesthetic potential. Artistic, enhancing make up, great art and home designs. You have great musical potential that you may not develop.
You are here to develop organisation and management skills, resolve to making things happen and to define and meet your goals.	

Life Path 8 with Birthday Number 7

Life Path Number 8 (90% Focus)	Birthday Number 7 (10% Focus)
You are both spiritual and worldly. But you are here to learn the secrets of worldly financial success. You seek the freedom that comes from financial success. But freedom brings responsibility, your ethics will be tested multiple times.	You are here to learn to have faith that you are an immortal soul that has experience from previous lives. You must trust the soul within you by listening to and following your intuition without over thinking and applying logic. Listen to and follow your inner voice and feel safe enough to communicate your soul wisdom to the world without fear of ridicule
You are here to learn to use your financial success as a tool to help others achieve the same financial success. You often spend your abundance on materialistic status symbols rather than helping others	You are here to trust that the world is not against you. The universe is everything existing in perfect balance, it is like a cosmic library of all knowledge and experience. We must experience it all to learn and evolve
You are here to develop a healthy attitude towards money. You may resent or hate wealthy people, or you may feel guilty about your own wealth. You must understand that financial wealth does not equate to poor ethics	Your focus for this lifetime must be Inner development rather than outer development and success. You must develop yourself constantly with self-discovery and spiritual wisdom. Meditation and time in nature is imperative for you
You are here to develop balanced determination for achievement but with integrity and for the good of others. You can be either obsessed with achievement or fearful of achievement from low self-esteem. It is important that you develop a positive mindset because you attract what you think about.	You are here to learn to be a problem solver, thinker, a studier of the metaphysical and the big questions. You need to research, learn, and analyse theories to accrue wisdom.
You are here to develop inner	You are here to learn to filter your

246

confidence and balanced personal power. You can swing from over dominance or misuse of power to hiding away or submission to others

research through your intuition and use your research of other people's theories for your own needs. You can be too analytical and ignore your intuition. Or totally spiritual and ignore other theories. You must balance the two.

You are here to develop skilled leadership, which consists of subject competence coupled with excellent social skills and charisma

You are here to be a free thinker, to be less interested in popular culture and following norms of fashion and appearance. This can make you feel different and out of place and lonely

You are here to work hard as an excellent practical businessperson, but you must ensure that you do not work too hard, you need time out and time for your family

You are here to develop the ability to focus on something long enough to develop it into something useful. You can be a little scattered and struggle to focus

You are here to be worldly, strong, resilient, disciplined, and realistic. To be successful you need to be strong, tough, and able to cope with

The ups and downs of the world

You are here to develop interdependence, self-sufficiency but also a healthy dependence on other people. You like to do things for yourself but take care not to push others away

You are here to develop bravery and the courage to take risks to progress. Success comes from having the bravery to take risks

You are here to learn to deal with and reconcile your sensitive emotions. Others often think you are aloof, but you are a well of deep emotions. You need to connect emotionally, both to yourself and to other people

You are here to develop organisation and management skills, resolve to making things happen and to define and meet your goals.

You are here to learn to balance your need to be alone and work alone with social contact. You love to be alone, but you must ensure that you do not isolate yourself beyond what is healthy

Life Path 8 with Birthday Number 9

Life Path Number 8 (90% Focus)	Birthday Number 9 (10% Focus)
You are both spiritual and worldly. But you are here to learn the secrets of worldly financial success. You seek the freedom that comes from financial success. But freedom brings responsibility, your ethics will be tested multiple times	You are here to learn to follow your intuitive wisdom and live to spiritual laws, rather than worldly laws, conventions, and ideals. You tend to follow worldly laws and prejudices as an excuse for your actions. But if you had followed your intuitive spiritual wisdom, you would not have acted that way. Focus on faith over logic
You are here to learn to use your financial success as a tool to help others achieve the same financial success. You often spend your abundance on materialistic status symbols rather than helping others	You are here to learn to act with integrity for the benefit of others. You are powerful and you must use your power for the benefit of others. You can act for selfish or nefarious reasons
You are here to develop a healthy attitude towards money. You may resent or hate wealthy people, or you may feel guilty about your own wealth. You must understand that financial wealth does not equate to poor ethics	You are here to learn to lead by example, do you practise what you preach? You can be quite domineering, an adviser with all the answers. But you must let others make their own mistakes
You are here to develop balanced determination for achievement but with integrity and for the good of others. You can be either obsessed with achievement or fearful of achievement from low self-esteem. It is important that you develop a positive mindset because you attract what you think about.	You are here to make your life your teaching, you need to counsel with wisdom. You are a developed soul, the totality of all the numbers, full of cellular experience and higher knowledge
You are here to develop inner confidence and balanced personal	You are here to develop broad mindedness, meet and accept diverse

power. You can swing from over dominance or misuse of power to hiding away or submission to others	people. You must learn to be a humanitarian and make the world a better place. You need a global consciousness, as you can be narrow minded, judgemental, and even bigoted.
You are here to develop skilled leadership, which consists of subject competence coupled with excellent social skills and charisma	You are here to learn to take responsibility for your powerful choices. You sometimes run away from the consequences of your actions
You are here to work hard as an excellent practical businessperson, but you must ensure that you do not work too hard, you need time out and time for your family	You need to develop towards being a successful entrepreneur or businessperson if it is with something you feel passionate about. You must choose work that has meaning for you. You are a powerful force for change
You are here to be worldly, strong, resilient, disciplined, and realistic. To be successful you need to be strong, tough, and able to cope with The ups and downs of the world	You are here to develop excellent social skills and charisma. You could develop the skills of a powerful speaker and influencer of others. People will hang on your every word
You are here to develop bravery and the courage to take risks to progress. Success comes from having the bravery to take risks	You are here to look after the wellbeing of others. But when you are in trouble or need support, people do not notice. You must ask for what you need, you must ask for help
You are here to develop organisation and management skills, resolve to making things happen and to define and meet your goals.	You are here to wrap things up, let go and surrender. You can have a victim mentality, holding onto feelings that no longer serve you, unable to move on from perceived injustice, normally rooted in family issues.

Life Path 8 with Birthday Master 11

Life Path Number 8 (90% Focus)	Birthday Master 11 (10% Focus)
You are both spiritual and worldly. But you are here to learn the secrets of worldly financial success. You seek the freedom that comes from financial success. But freedom brings responsibility, your ethics will be tested multiple times	You are an old soul, with higher potential and higher responsibility to improve the world. You are here to learn to connect to source energy to channel unique new ideas and messages to change the world. You are here to learn to be happy in the limelight expressing new ideas for an audience. You need to develop and trust your massive intuitive potential. You often hide your ideas due to low confidence
You are here to learn to use your financial success as a tool to help others achieve the same financial success. You often spend your abundance on materialistic status symbols rather than helping others	You are here to learn to be the ideas person, but you struggle to bring your unique ideas to reality because you lose interest quickly after the initial idea of sabotage yourself due to crippling low confidence. You are an idealistic dreamer whose ideas are often not grounded in reality
You are here to develop a healthy attitude towards money. You may resent or hate wealthy people, or you may feel guilty about your own wealth. You must understand that financial wealth does not equate to poor ethics	You are here to learn to be confident in your uniqueness because unique people have unique ground-breaking ideas. It is important that you are not craving validation from others. Your validation should come from your intuition.
You are here to develop balanced determination for achievement but with integrity and for the good of others. You can be either obsessed with achievement or fearful of achievement from low self-esteem. It is important that you develop a positive mindset because you attract	You need to bring unique, new ideas that break barriers, or challenge others comfort zone. You must learn to be brave, confident and be willing to take risks

what you think about.

You are here to develop inner confidence and balanced personal power. You can swing from over dominance or misuse of power to hiding away or submission to others

You need to be a practical initiator, a doer, action orientated that learns by experience. Ideas will stay unmanifested until you act!

Only action brings change

You are here to develop skilled leadership, which consists of subject competence coupled with excellent social skills and charisma

You need to set intentions then use spiritual practice and visualisation to channel your advanced, intense master energy into initiation and action. Unchanneled or mismanaged energy can cause intense nervous energy and anxiety. You may medicate these with unhealthy substances.

You are here to work hard as an excellent practical businessperson, but you must ensure that you do not work too hard, you need time out and time for your family

You are here to learn to be interdependent, not so independent that you push others away and refuse to delegate. You cannot do everything alone. Independence is an illusion; we are all interconnected

You are here to be worldly, strong, resilient, disciplined, and realistic. To be successful you need to be strong, tough, and able to cope with

The ups and downs of the world

You need to be determined to succeed. Constant self-discovery and intuitive spiritual development is key for you to develop complete trust in the skills you have learned and mastered to serve as a kind of "security blanket" for you when you are feeling insecure

You are here to develop bravery and the courage to take risks to progress. Success comes from having the bravery to take risks

You need to learn to be a supportive, nurturing leader, be firm and assertive but also empathic and supportive. You must lead others to the fruition of your ideas, but with balanced personal power

You are here to develop organisation and management skills, resolve to

Your power causes ripples, both positive and negative, you must

251

making things happen and to define and meet your goals.	remember that great power brings great responsibility. You must ensure that your intentions are good
	You are here to learn to be responsible to others, your family, team, or group but in a balanced way. You can be too responsible and do too much. You are irresponsible if you feel undervalued, resentful, and exhausted.
	You must develop and improve your social skills, focus on widening and deepening your relationships and make decisions subjectively. It is important that you deepen your relationships and connect 121 You may struggle to maintain long term close and romantic relationships.
	You must learn not to smother your loved ones or have expectations that can never be met. OR back away from wanting love because it hurts too badly. You need to balance your intense need for love for healthy relationships.
	You are here to learn to be intuitive and sensitive to the needs of others. You are here to be of service to others, the development of intuition will aid you in this journey
	You are here to learn to be a cooperative team player to get the job done as part of a cohesive team. You can be a disruptive, uncooperative drama queen.

	You must develop the assertiveness to demand boundaries to being overworked, walked all over, taken advantage of, and/or taken for granted. You must not be a "shape shifter" who changes who you are in order to please others or keep the peace. Be you and consider yourself too.
	You are here to serve the world, help the team, the task and be dependable. You can always be relied upon to keep the cogs turning behind the scenes
	You are here to be the tactful mediator of the team/group/family, helping to resolve conflicts fairly and for the good of everyone involved. You hate conflict and often run and hide until it is over
	You are here to learn to plan the next steps after channelling your message or idea & build a team to achieve it. The energy of the 11/2 needs to be the nurturer of ideas and a builder of teams
	You must learn to give yourself your own kudos. Oftentimes you judge yourself on what everyone else says or thinks about you. You need to develop your internal compass and turn inward for validation, do what YOU think you should do

Life Path 8 with Birthday Master 22/4

Life Path Number 8 (90% Focus)	Birthday Master 22/4 (10% Focus)
You are both spiritual and worldly. But you are here to learn the secrets of worldly financial success. You seek the freedom that comes from financial success. But freedom brings responsibility, your ethics will be tested multiple times	You are an old soul, as spiritual as you are practical, here to channel and then manifest ideas in reality to build world safety, stability, and security. You must learn to handle the master builder energy and focus it to manifestation. You have a big responsibility to the team and the world to build structures (buildings, concepts, body, mind, spirit, businesses, organisations, even an empire for the purpose of world stability and security
You are here to learn to use your financial success as a tool to help others achieve the same financial success. You often spend your abundance on materialistic status symbols rather than helping others	You must develop and improve your social skills, focus on widening and deepening your relationships to assist you to manifest your big ideas. It is important that you learn to deepen your relationships and connect 121, you cannot do this alone!
You are here to develop a healthy attitude towards money. You may resent or hate wealthy people, or you may feel guilty about your own wealth. You must understand that financial wealth does not equate to poor ethics	You must learn to have balanced, healthy relationships with others that are part of your sense of security. You must learn not to smother your loved ones and your team or have expectations that can never be met. OR Your big task in this lifetime may disrupt your love relationships. You may back away from wanting love because it hurts too badly or attacks your sense of security

You are here to develop balanced determination for achievement but with integrity and for the good of others. You can be either obsessed with achievement or fearful of achievement from low self-esteem. It is important that you develop a positive mindset because you attract what you think about.

You are here to learn to listen to and follow your intuition.

Intuition is needed for you to be sensitive to the needs of others.

You are here to be of service to change the world, the development of intuition will aid you in this journey

You are here to develop inner confidence and balanced personal power. You can swing from over dominance or misuse of power to hiding away or submission to others

You are here to learn to be a cooperative team player to get the job done as part of a cohesive team.

You may fail to communicate effectively with others. You can be a hard-headed and high handed at times.

You are here to develop skilled leadership, which consists of subject competence coupled with excellent social skills and charisma

You must develop the assertiveness to demand boundaries to being overworked, walked all over, taken advantage of, and/or taken for granted. You must also develop your ability to respect other people's boundaries and not be high handed.

You are here to work hard as an excellent practical businessperson, but you must ensure that you do not work too hard, you need time out and time for your family

You are here to be of service to the world, the leader, the team, the task and be dependable.

You can always be counted upon to keep the cogs turning behind the scenes

You are here to be worldly, strong, resilient, disciplined, and realistic. To be successful you need to be strong, tough, and able to cope with

The ups and downs of the world

You are extremely sensitive, and you hate and run away from conflict.

But you are here to learn to be a tactful mediator, helping to resolve conflicts fairly and for the good of the team/family/group

You are here to develop bravery and

You are here to learn to stay focused

the courage to take risks to progress. Success comes from having the bravery to take risks	and plan the next steps after you have channelled a new idea & build a team to achieve it. The energy of the 22 needs to be the nurturer, the builder of ideas and teams.
You are here to develop organisation and management skills, resolve to making things happen and to define and meet your goals.	You must learn to give yourself your own kudos. Oftentimes you judge yourself on what everyone else says or thinks about you. You need to develop your internal compass and turn inward for validation, do what you think you should do
	You are here to learn to commit to a person and/or place, so that you can put down roots and dig the foundations for security. You can be uncommitted and therefore unable to build stability and security
	You are here to learn to set and achieve goals to take you on your journey towards inner and outer stability and security. Foundations, structures, families, and business empires are built 1 goal at a time.
	You are here to learn to plan, create a process and/or procedure to ensure the achievement of your goals and bring strength and stability to dynamic ideas. You can be directionless, lazy and block your own progression.
	You are here to develop deep meticulous focus on achieving stability, like a stable home, business or income and building your inner security. You can be scattered and

miss steps in your impatience.

You are here to learn to be detail orientated, analytical, organised, and accurate to ensure your plans and processes are watertight. You can be disorganised, flaky and miss steps in your plan

Your master 22/4 Birthday means that you are an old soul and you have agreed to bring safety, stability, and security to the world. You innovate and build empires, organisations, and businesses. This involves hard work, detail focus, routine work, and tasks. You are here to develop a work ethic, to work hard and develop enjoyment of routine work and tasks

You are here to develop patient perseverance, so that every step in the process towards your goals for your stable foundation are taken. You are prone to impatience and corner cutting.

You are here to develop determination and the perseverance to keep going past obstacles to achieve your goals. You are prone to giving up at the first hurdle.

You are here to learn to come to terms with limitation — both the limitations that are externally imposed on you and the limitations that you impose upon yourself.

You are here to look at your wounded or problematic relationships and work through the feelings of lack and pain they have

	brought to you. All experiences have lessons embedded within them
	Avoid social isolation by socialising regularly in familiar groups and with likeminded friends.

Your Life Path and Birthday Number Nine (9)

You have chosen to incarnate to learn the lessons of the 9 life path energy because when speaking to your spirit guide before this life, you highlighted that you needed to learn the lessons of the 9 energy. You are here to live in accord with your highest integrity, to align to your heart's intuitive wisdom, inspire others by example, and to confront issues in the areas of integrity and wisdom.

When you are following your path well, you have found inner integrity and wisdom in your own heart, in accord with higher laws. Your life is your teaching, you move humanity in large and small ways. It's important that you do what inspires you in life, follow it and others will follow you, because when you speak, lecture, or teach, your words will be rich with spiritual force, authority, and integrity.

Your challenges are in the area of spiritual law and the higher principles of living. You must avoid running away from taking the consequences of your actions, take responsibility and learn by your mistakes. You are here to teach, lead and guide others to improve their wellbeing but sometimes you can do too much and become a 'fixer'. Fixing others' lives and getting too involved means that you are failing to respect others path, we all need to fix our own lives and learn our own lessons.

You struggle sometimes to let go of issues from the past, holding on to a negative personal history as an excuse for your behaviour and misusing your will to dominate others. You also need to learn to listen to your heart, your intuition rather than just your idealistic, logical mind. You must understand that all experience, good and bad contain embedded lessons that you must learn to achieve your purpose.

You have difficulty with cause and effect, making poor decisions and suffering the consequences. You must learn that you are extremely influential whatever you do, you are an example to others, both good and bad, this is a big responsibility.

To ensure your ethics and responsibility, you must learn to channel intuitive wisdom and spiritual laws from source energy, then form this wisdom as the basis of all your beliefs and actions. You must act on faith rather than logic, meaning faith in your soul and the wisdom it channels. If you channel your beliefs and actions from source, you will always act with selfless integrity. But you may use worldly ideals and victimhood as an excuse for nefarious action. You need to consider your relationships regularly and ponder the following questions, what example does my life provide for others? Do I live in accord with higher laws? Am I practising what I preach? And finally, does my way of life benefit others and the common good?

Your 9 purpose energy needs you to act with integrity for the wellbeing of others, fight injustice, intolerance towards other races, religions, and ways of life. You must be above small, minded bigotry, and exercise compassion with a global consciousness. When in the negative, you can be the opposite of this and become intolerant, racist and a troublemaker.

You are here to develop broadmindedness and acceptance of the diverse people in this world. You can judge others according to your worldly ideals and prejudices, but you must work on this because you are here to be non-judgemental. Your ideals are often totally impractical without real scope for practical application.

Do you listen to the worldly logic in your head or your intuitive heart? You are likely to listen to your head more than your heart, but it is important for you to start listening to your intuitive heart because that's where your heart's intuitive wisdom lays. You are here to act with integrity, but you may justify your actions with your ideals and logical thought processes, that in your mind, is justified. But you must stop and run this course of action by your heart and intuition. With this awareness, you may take a different course that will serve you and others more positively. Acting through your intuition sets a better example to those that will inevitably follow your example.

When following your intuition, you must make your life your teaching because others naturally look to you for guidance. You must learn to manifest your teachings in your way of life, the teachings that you preach to others must be demonstrated in your attitudes and actions. For example, if you preach faith in your intuition and compassion for all, you must manifest this in your life to become a teacher by example.

You are here to learn to be an ethical, influential leader, like it or not, people look to you and follow you like the original pied piper. You are here to inspire others with your words, speak with spiritual authority, brilliance, and wisdom.

You must develop towards using your immense power responsibly, to direct your power towards improving the wellbeing of other people. You need to be a powerful force for positive change, not just in your community but the world. As you develop and progress on your 9 path, you will feel and connect with a global consciousness, leading you towards the attitude of a humanitarian, desiring justice, and the irradiation of suffering.

You have the potential to be highly creative, social, and spiritual. You need to develop your innate creative artistry through words, performance, music, or artistic expression to heal and improve the wellness of others. Your life path 9 needs you to be a symbol of parental love, family, friends, community, and the world. You must develop towards being a powerful force that demands respect, an excellent leader who leads by example with charisma, drawing people in and bending them to your will. You must learn to speak with authority, brilliance, and wisdom, while being worldly and sophisticated.

The development of your 9 path will need you to develop effective social skills and spellbinding charisma in order to teach and influence others. You are passionate, emotional, and intense with a fiery temper, but you can also come across aloof and distant to hide your heart. But when you are walking your 9 life path at a high vibration, you laugh a lot, you are a humanitarian peacemaker and loyal caretaker. You are a protector, compassionately making sure everyone is okay, accepting of others, kind, empathetic, generous, nurturing, and helpful but you will not allow yourself to become vulnerable. You can fall into the trap of being a 'fixer,' giving too much and behaving like a saviour, a domineering adviser or a martyr and sacrifice your own needs for others. But you must ensure that you develop boundaries to protect your own health and wellbeing, you cannot help everyone all the time, they must learn their own lessons. You must also understand other people's boundaries and know when to step back and let others walk their path and make their own mistakes.

Remember that sometimes you need help too, do not suffer in silence, others can help you too.

You are here to learn to be a successful entrepreneur, making a living with meaningful work that matches your passions and interests, achieving the completion of a process. You could develop the ability to excel in the arts and speech by being creative, imaginative, and intuitive champions of the underdog.

You may like the strange, the exotic, the freakish and you love danger and excitement. Whatever you choose as the basis for your success, ensure that the subject, activity, and goals are in line with your passions and mean something to you.

When you are struggling, you can be arrogant, condescending, cold and apathetic. You may look back at your personal history with negativity by holding on to memories and pain, pitying yourself into a victim mentality. You may hold onto anger resulting from perceived injustices and/or perceived infringements of your ideals. This anger could, unchecked, lead to nefarious actions on your part, justified by misguided revenge. You must let go and realise that all experience is meant to teach you lessons. Instead of holding on to anger from the past, look for the lesson within that experience to gain clarity and healing.

You can struggle to be true to yourself, choosing instead to be a chameleon, distancing yourself from what you really believe and being what others want you to be to deceive. You can make others believe you are selfless and compassionate until others find out that you are not the selfless person, they thought you were.

But you can also function on the opposite extreme, give too much, and forget to consider yourself. You need to balance your own self-care with that of others and confront your obstacles in the area of integrity and wisdom.

When your actions are negative, you can struggle to take responsibility for your actions. Your 9 energy is about completion, so you need to learn to let go of ideas, beliefs, and things that no longer serve you. Letting go of anger and victimhood will help you to take responsibility, become wiser and live a happier life, free of those limitations.

If you function through your mind, you can be very devilish, ignoring spiritual laws, dominating others, and misleading them into unethical behaviour. You must learn about cause and effect, understand that your actions influence others. You need to learn to take responsibility for the consequences of your actions, you can also be very accident prone.

You must guard against holding on to injustices from your past, making you a victim and using it as an excuse for your behaviour. It is possible, however, that you could become a well-intentioned fanatic, a rebel without a cause or you could become arrogant, cold, and apathetic to protect yourself from further harm. You must also guard against being over enthusiastic and wanting to dominate too much, be argumentative and fight too hard.

Careers that will support your life path:

Humanitarian, Non-profit organisations, Activists, Environmentalism, Health, Social Worker, Counsellors, Therapists, Education, Trainers, Government, Law, Musician, Hypnotist, Spiritualist, Healer, Writer.

Key attributes – Quirky, Active, Courageous and Emotional.

Socially – Companionable, Intense and Wacky.

Colour – White

Subtle body – Crown Chakra, command of the physical and the spiritual

Day – Tuesday

Astrologically – Mars, zodiac Aries

Life Path 9 with Birthday Number 1

Life Path Number 9 (90% Focus)	Birthday Number 1 (10% Focus)
You are here to learn to follow your intuitive wisdom and live to spiritual laws, rather than worldly laws, conventions, and ideals. You tend to follow worldly laws and prejudices as an excuse for your actions. But if you had followed your intuitive spiritual wisdom, you would not have acted that way. Focus on faith over logic	You are here to learn to connect to source energy to download / channel unique new ideas. You often hide your ideas due to low confidence. You are here to learn to be happy in the limelight expressing new ideas for an audience.
You are here to learn to act with integrity for the benefit of others. You are powerful and you must use your power for the benefit of others. You can act for selfish or nefarious reasons	You are here to learn to be the ideas person, but you struggle to bring your unique ideas to reality because you lose interest quickly after the initial idea.
You are here to learn to lead by example, do you practise what you preach? You can be quite domineering, an adviser with all the answers. But you must let others make their own mistakes	You are here to learn to be confident in your uniqueness because unique people have unique ground-breaking ideas. It is important that you are not craving validation from others.
You are here to make your life your teaching, you need to counsel with wisdom. You are a developed soul, the totality of all the numbers, full of cellular experience and higher knowledge	You need to be a practical initiator, a doer, action orientated that learns by experience. Only action makes the difference.
You are here to develop broad mindedness, meet and accept diverse people. You must learn to be a humanitarian and make the world a better place. You need a global consciousness, as you can be narrow minded, judgemental, and even	You need to learn to trust your intuitive voice within. You must achieve balanced confidence in yourself & your abilities, fed by strong connection & trust in your intuition. You bring your ideas without fear. You must not seek

bigoted.	validation from others or base your confidence on what others say.
You are here to learn to take responsibility for your powerful choices. You sometimes run away from the consequences of your actions	You need to bring unique, new ideas that break barriers, or challenge others comfort zones, you must learn to be brave, confident and be willing to take risks
You need to develop towards being a successful entrepreneur or businessperson if it is with something you feel passionate about. You must choose work that has meaning for you. You are a powerful force for change	You are here to learn to be interdependent, not so independent that you push others away and refuse to delegate. You cannot do everything alone. Independence is an illusion; we are all interconnected
You are here to develop excellent social skills and charisma. You could develop the skills of a powerful speaker and influencer of others. People will hang on your every word	You need to be determined to succeed. Constant self-discovery and development is key for you to develop complete trust in the skills you have learned and mastered to serve as a kind of "security blanket" for you when you are feeling insecure
You are here to look after the wellbeing of others. But when you are in trouble or need support, people do not notice. You must ask for what you need, you must ask for help	You need to learn to be a powerful leader, be dominant and assertive. You must lead others to the fruition of your ideas, but with balanced personal power
You are here to wrap things up, let go and surrender. You can have a victim mentality, holding onto feelings that no longer serve you, unable to move on from perceived injustice, normally rooted in family issues.	Your power causes ripples, both positive and negative, you must remember that great power brings great responsibility. You must ensure that your intentions are good

Life Path 9 with Birthday Number 2

Life Path Number 9 (90% Focus)	Birthday Number 2 (10% Focus)
You are here to learn to follow your intuitive wisdom and live to spiritual laws, rather than worldly laws, conventions, and ideals. You tend to follow worldly laws and prejudices as an excuse for your actions. But if you had followed your intuitive spiritual wisdom, you would not have acted that way. Focus on faith over logic	You are here to learn to be responsible to others and the team. You can be too responsible and do too much. You are irresponsible if you feel undervalued and resentful
You are here to learn to act with integrity for the benefit of others. You are powerful and you must use your power for the benefit of others. You can act for selfish or nefarious reasons	You must learn to improve your social skills, focus on widening and deepening your relationships and make decisions subjectively. It is important that you deepen your relationships and connect 121
You are here to learn to lead by example, do you practise what you preach? You can be quite domineering, an adviser with all the answers. But you must let others make their own mistakes	You must learn not to smother your loved ones or have expectations that can never be met. OR you may back away from wanting love because it hurts too badly. You need to balance your intense need for love
You are here to make your life your teaching, you need to counsel with wisdom. You are a developed soul, the totality of all the numbers, full of cellular experience and higher knowledge	You are here to learn to be intuitive and sensitive to the needs of others. You are here to be of service to others, the development of intuition will aid you in this journey
You are here to develop broad mindedness, meet and accept diverse people. You must learn to be a humanitarian and make the world a better place. You need a global consciousness, as you can be narrow minded, judgemental, and even	You are here to learn to be a cooperative team player to get the job done as part of a cohesive team. You can be a disruptive, uncooperative drama queen.

bigoted.

You are here to learn to take responsibility for your powerful choices. You sometimes run away from the consequences of your actions

You need to develop towards being a successful entrepreneur or businessperson if it is with something you feel passionate about. You must choose work that has meaning for you. You are a powerful force for change

You are here to develop excellent social skills and charisma. You could develop the skills of a powerful speaker and influencer of others. People will hang on your every word

You are here to look after the wellbeing of others. But when you are in trouble or need support, people do not notice. You must ask for what you need, you must ask for help

You are here to wrap things up, let go and surrender. You can have a victim mentality, holding onto feelings that no longer serve you, unable to move on from perceived injustice, normally rooted in family issues.

You must develop the assertiveness to demand boundaries to being overworked, walked all over, taken advantage of, and/or taken for granted. You must not be a "shape shifter" who changes who you are in order to please others or keep the peace.

You are here to serve the leader, the team, the task and be dependable. You can always be counted upon to keep the cogs turning behind the scenes

You are here to be the tactful mediator of the team, helping to resolve conflicts fairly and for the good of the team. You hate conflict and often run and hide until it is over

You are here to learn to plan the next steps after the initial idea & build a team to achieve it. The energy of the two is the nurturer of ideas and a builder of teams

You must learn to give yourself your own kudos. Oftentimes you judge yourself on what everyone else says or thinks about you. You need to develop your internal compass and turn inward for validation, do what you think you should do

Life Path 9 with Birthday Number 3

Life Path Number 9 (90% Focus)	Birthday Number 3 (10% Focus)
You are here to learn to follow your intuitive wisdom and live to spiritual laws, rather than worldly laws, conventions, and ideals. You tend to follow worldly laws and prejudices as an excuse for your actions. But if you had followed your intuitive spiritual wisdom, you would not have acted that way. Focus on faith over logic	You are here to learn to express yourself verbally to inspire, inform and delight. You may struggle in some way verbally, chronic shyness, speech delay, stutter or struggling to find the words.
You are here to learn to act with integrity for the benefit of others. You are powerful and you must use your power for the benefit of others. You can act for selfish or nefarious reasons	You are here to learn to express yourself creatively to inspire, inform and delight. But you may struggle to progress, execute, and finish creative projects, due to lack of self-belief
You are here to learn to lead by example, do you practise what you preach? You can be quite domineering, an adviser with all the answers. But you must let others make their own mistakes	You must learn to be dynamic, take risks and be confident to enjoy the attention and limelight of an audience. You can be shy, under confident and feel unable to take risks.
You are here to make your life your teaching, you need to counsel with wisdom. You are a developed soul, the totality of all the numbers, full of cellular experience and higher knowledge	You need to develop as an entrepreneur who is able to promote, network and make money creatively. But you may procrastinate and fail to stay focused and work inconsistently.
You are here to develop broad mindedness, meet and accept diverse people. You must learn to be a humanitarian and make the world a better place. You need a global consciousness, as you can be narrow minded, judgemental, and even	You are here to learn to express your emotions positively. You can be extremely sensitive to criticism and other people's emotions, causing you to express emotions negatively

bigoted.

You are here to learn to take responsibility for your powerful choices. You sometimes run away from the consequences of your actions

You are here to develop the habit of acting, be a doer and executer of ideas. When low, you can struggle with apathy, laziness and lack of focus and direction

You need to develop towards being a successful entrepreneur or businessperson if it is with something you feel passionate about. You must choose work that has meaning for you. You are a powerful force for change

You are here to learn to be social, talkative, the life of the party and bringer of fun & positivity. You need to be the networker, communicating an emotional message. You can be quiet and struggle to speak

You are here to develop excellent social skills and charisma. You could develop the skills of a powerful speaker and influencer of others. People will hang on your every word

You must develop interdependence, life path 3's like to be looked after and can be prone to avoiding work or anything needing routine and commitment

You are here to look after the wellbeing of others. But when you are in trouble or need support, people do not notice. You must ask for what you need, you must ask for help

You are here to be opportunistic, to network, make useful connections and snap up opportunities to spread the word and progress ideas and projects

You are here to wrap things up, let go and surrender. You can have a victim mentality, holding onto feelings that no longer serve you, unable to move on from perceived injustice, normally rooted in family issues.

You must learn to take responsibility and listen to guidance; you can be irresponsible. You must think before you act, and take full responsibility for what you do

Life Path 9 with Birthday Number 4

Life Path Number 9 (90% Focus)	Birthday Number 4 (10% Focus)
You are here to learn to follow your intuitive wisdom and live to spiritual laws, rather than worldly laws, conventions, and ideals. You tend to follow worldly laws and prejudices as an excuse for your actions. But if you had followed your intuitive spiritual wisdom, you would not have acted that way. Focus on faith over logic	You are here to learn to commit to a person and/or place, so that you can put down roots and dig the foundations for security. You can be uncommitted and therefore unable to build stability and security.
You are here to learn to act with integrity for the benefit of others. You are powerful and you must use your power for the benefit of others. You can act for selfish or nefarious reasons	You are here to learn to set and achieve goals to take you on your journey towards inner and outer stability and security. Foundations, structures, families, and business empires are built 1 goal at a time.
You are here to learn to lead by example, do you practise what you preach? You can be quite domineering, an adviser with all the answers. But you must let others make their own mistakes	You are here to learn to plan, create a process and/or procedure to ensure the achievement of your goals. You can be directionless, lazy and block your own progression
You are here to make your life your teaching, you need to counsel with wisdom. You are a developed soul, the totality of all the numbers, full of cellular experience and higher knowledge	You are here to develop deep meticulous focus on achieving stability, like a stable home, business or income and building your inner security. You can be scattered
You are here to develop broad mindedness, meet and accept diverse people. You must learn to be a humanitarian and make the world a better place. You need a global consciousness, as you can be narrow minded, judgemental, and even	You are here to learn to be detail orientated, analytical, organised, and accurate to ensure your plans and processes are watertight. You can be disorganised and miss steps in the plan

bigoted.

You are here to learn to take responsibility for your powerful choices. You sometimes run away from the consequences of your actions

You need to develop towards being a successful entrepreneur or businessperson if it is with something you feel passionate about. You must choose work that has meaning for you. You are a powerful force for change

You are here to develop excellent social skills and charisma. You could develop the skills of a powerful speaker and influencer of others. People will hang on your every word

You are here to look after the wellbeing of others. But when you are in trouble or need support, people do not notice. You must ask for what you need, you must ask for help

You are here to wrap things up, let go and surrender. You can have a victim mentality, holding onto feelings that no longer serve you, unable to move on from perceived injustice, normally rooted in family issues.

You are here to develop a work ethic, to work hard and develop enjoyment of routine work and tasks. When low you can be lazy and stuck in 1 place, without progression

You are here to develop patient perseverance, so that every step in the process towards your goals for your stable foundation are taken. You are prone to impatience and missing steps

You are here to learn to come to terms with limitation — both the limitations that are externally imposed on you and the limitations that you impose upon yourself.

You are here to look at your wounded or problematic relationships and work through the feelings of lack and pain they have brought to you.

You are prone to choosing social isolation, avoiding social situations due to social anxiety. It is important that you socialise regularly in familiar groups and with likeminded friends.

Life Path 9 with Birthday Number 5

Life Path Number 9 (90% Focus)	Birthday Number 5 (10% Focus)
You are here to learn to follow your intuitive wisdom and live to spiritual laws, rather than worldly laws, conventions, and ideals. You tend to follow worldly laws and prejudices as an excuse for your actions. But if you had followed your intuitive spiritual wisdom, you would not have acted that way. Focus on faith over logic	You are easily bored and want to look at or study lots of topics. Initial varied experience is needed in order to choose a specialism, you are here to learn to be disciplined, to continue with a topic or activity beyond the boredom of the detail, towards mastery and specialism.
You are here to learn to act with integrity for the benefit of others. You are powerful and you must use your power for the benefit of others. You can act for selfish or nefarious reasons	You are here to develop the ability to balance variety, change and adventure with the stability of family and skill mastery. You can be totally spontaneous and take risks, jumping from one experience to another, but never settling or progressing
You are here to learn to lead by example, do you practise what you preach? You can be quite domineering, an adviser with all the answers. But you must let others make their own mistakes	You need to learn to be extremely intuitive and access your intuitive wisdom when making decisions, assessing people and situations.
You are here to make your life your teaching, you need to counsel with wisdom. You are a developed soul, the totality of all the numbers, full of cellular experience and higher knowledge	You are here to develop your ability to attain inner freedom and outer freedom by doing things you might not want to do. Doing what you want is not necessarily freedom, you can become a slave to your desires. Freedom and discipline are inherently linked.
You are here to develop broad mindedness, meet and accept diverse people. You must learn to be a humanitarian and make the world a	You are here to learn to develop your verbal and written communication skills towards charismatic sharing of ideas and

better place. You need a global consciousness, as you can be narrow minded, judgemental, and even bigoted.

stories related to your specialism. You have the potential to be a great communicator

You are here to learn to take responsibility for your powerful choices. You sometimes run away from the consequences of your actions

You are here to learn to be committed, dependable, to do what you say you are going to do. You often forget what you promise because you are so chaotic, scattered, and changeable, looking for the next new experience

You need to develop towards being a successful entrepreneur or businessperson if it is with something you feel passionate about. You must choose work that has meaning for you. You are a powerful force for change

You are here to develop your social skills and charisma, to have the potential to be fun loving, positive, and optimistic. You can be uptight and argumentative

You are here to develop excellent social skills and charisma. You could develop the skills of a powerful speaker and influencer of others. People will hang on your every word

You are here to develop consistent independence. You can swing from independence to dependence and back again. Risky behaviour and 'get rich quick' schemes can bring on dependence

You are here to look after the wellbeing of others. But when you are in trouble or need support, people do not notice. You must ask for what you need, you must ask for help

You are here to learn to develop fearlessness and help others to live fearlessly. You can be fearful of many things, restriction, and boredom, to name but a few. You need to challenge yourself and others past your own comfort zone

You are here to wrap things up, let go and surrender. You can have a victim mentality, holding onto feelings that no longer serve you, unable to move on from perceived injustice, normally rooted in family issues.

You are here to learn to make good use of your energy and drive, if you feel restricted and under confident, you will be restless, and you may turn into a drama queen. Use your energy for experience and adventure, be courageous

Life Path 9 with Birthday Number 6

Life Path Number 9 (90% Focus)	Birthday Number 6 (10% Focus)
You are here to learn to follow your intuitive wisdom and live to spiritual laws, rather than worldly laws, conventions, and ideals. You tend to follow worldly laws and prejudices as an excuse for your actions. But if you had followed your intuitive spiritual wisdom, you would not have acted that way. Focus on faith over logic	You are here to be a visionary of the ideal, the dreamer of a utopian world. You must act to create a better world with your ideals.
You are here to learn to act with integrity for the benefit of others. You are powerful and you must use your power for the benefit of others. You can act for selfish or nefarious reasons	You are here to learn to not use your ideals as a benchmark for your happiness. You must not base your emotional wellbeing on the achievement of your ideals. You often judge yourself and others for not hitting perfection, causing you great unhappiness
You are here to learn to lead by example, do you practise what you preach? You can be quite domineering, an adviser with all the answers. But you must let others make their own mistakes	Your perfectionism can make you an over achiever due to your constant self-judgement. You never meet your own standards. You must keep your big picture in mind and not get stuck in petty detail. You can often judge small imperfections and ruin or miss your successes.
You are here to make your life your teaching, you need to counsel with wisdom. You are a developed soul, the totality of all the numbers, full of cellular experience and higher knowledge	You are here to learn to be a nurturer, compassionate caring and giving, especially to those that are vulnerable or struggling within your close relationships, your community, and the wider world. Your judgemental nature can make you cruel and neglectful.
You are here to develop broad	You are here to develop boundaries

mindedness, meet and accept diverse people. You must learn to be a humanitarian and make the world a better place. You need a global consciousness, as you can be narrow minded, judgemental, and even bigoted.

You are here to learn to take responsibility for your powerful choices. You sometimes run away from the consequences of your actions

You need to develop towards being a successful entrepreneur or businessperson if it is with something you feel passionate about. You must choose work that has meaning for you. You are a powerful force for change

You are here to develop excellent social skills and charisma. You could develop the skills of a powerful speaker and influencer of others. People will hang on your every word

You are here to look after the wellbeing of others. But when you are in trouble or need support, people do not notice. You must ask for what you need, you must ask for help

You are here to wrap things up, let go and surrender. You can have a victim mentality, holding onto

to ensure your mental and physical health. You do a lot for others, sometimes too much, which can make you feel undervalued, unappreciated, and ill with exhaustion. You may force unsolicited advice and meddle in other people's affairs.

You are here to develop your social skills and be a team player. You must break through low self-esteem to be talkative, fun loving and relaxed around others. You can be shy and hide in the background.

You are here to create a stable, nurturing, tranquil home to maintain your security and well-being. Then nurture a family in an environment of stability and love. When low you can be a selfish, neglectful drama queen.

You are here to learn to be responsible and do good for those you care for. People naturally put you in positions of responsibility, but you often resent always being the 'responsible one.' Have boundaries on your responsibility so that you do not do too much.

You are here to learn to develop and use your artistic and aesthetic potential. Artistic, enhancing make up, great art and home designs. You have great musical potential that you may not develop.

feelings that no longer serve you, unable to move on from perceived injustice, normally rooted in family issues.	

Life Path 9 with Birthday Number 7

Life Path Number 9 (90% Focus)	Birthday Number 7 (10% Focus)
You are here to learn to follow your intuitive wisdom and live to spiritual laws, rather than worldly laws, conventions, and ideals. You tend to follow worldly laws and prejudices as an excuse for your actions. But if you had followed your intuitive spiritual wisdom, you would not have acted that way. Focus on faith over logic	You are here to learn to have faith that you are an immortal soul that has experience from previous lives. You must trust the soul within you by listening to and following your intuition without over thinking and applying logic. Listen to and follow your inner voice and feel safe enough to communicate your soul wisdom to the world without fear of ridicule
You are here to learn to act with integrity for the benefit of others. You are powerful and you must use your power for the benefit of others. You can act for selfish or nefarious reasons	You are here to trust that the world is not against you. The universe is everything existing in perfect balance, it is like a cosmic library of all knowledge and experience. We must experience it all to learn and evolve
You are here to learn to lead by example, do you practise what you preach? You can be quite domineering, an adviser with all the answers. But you must let others make their own mistakes	Your focus for this lifetime must be Inner development rather than outer development and success. You must develop yourself constantly with self-discovery and spiritual wisdom. Meditation and time in nature is imperative for you
You are here to make your life your teaching, you need to counsel with wisdom. You are a developed soul, the totality of all the numbers, full of cellular experience and higher knowledge	You are here to learn to be a problem solver, thinker, a studier of the metaphysical and the big questions. You need to research, learn, and analyse theories to accrue wisdom.
You are here to develop broad mindedness, meet and accept diverse people. You must learn to be a humanitarian and make the world	You are here to learn to filter your research through your intuition and use your research of other people's theories for your own needs. You

a better place. You need a global consciousness, as you can be narrow minded, judgemental, and even bigoted.	can be too analytical and ignore your intuition. Or totally spiritual and ignore other theories. You must balance the two.
You are here to learn to take responsibility for your powerful choices. You sometimes run away from the consequences of your actions	You are here to be a free thinker, to be less interested in popular culture and following norms of fashion and appearance. This can make you feel different and out of place and lonely
You need to develop towards being a successful entrepreneur or businessperson if it is with something you feel passionate about. You must choose work that has meaning for you. You are a powerful force for change	You are here to develop the ability to focus on something long enough to develop it into something useful. You can be a little scattered and struggle to focus
You are here to develop excellent social skills and charisma. You could develop the skills of a powerful speaker and influencer of others. People will hang on your every word	You are here to develop interdependence, self-sufficiency but also a healthy dependence on other people. You like to do things for yourself but take care not to push others away
You are here to look after the wellbeing of others. But when you are in trouble or need support, people do not notice. You must ask for what you need, you must ask for help	You are here to learn to deal with and reconcile your sensitive emotions. Others often think you are aloof, but you are a well of deep emotions. You need to connect emotionally, both to yourself and to other people
You are here to wrap things up, let go and surrender. You can have a victim mentality, holding onto feelings that no longer serve you, unable to move on from perceived injustice, normally rooted in family issues.	You are here to learn to balance your need to be alone and work alone with social contact. You love to be alone, but you must ensure that you do not isolate yourself beyond what is healthy

Life Path 9 with Birthday Number 8

Life Path Number 9 (90% focus)	Birthday Number 8 (10% Focus)
You are here to learn to follow your intuitive wisdom and live to spiritual laws, rather than worldly laws, conventions, and ideals. You tend to follow worldly laws and prejudices as an excuse for your actions. But if you had followed your intuitive spiritual wisdom, you would not have acted that way. Focus on faith over logic	You are both spiritual and worldly. But you are here to learn the secrets of worldly financial success. You seek the freedom that comes from financial success. But freedom brings responsibility, your ethics will be tested multiple times.
You are here to learn to act with integrity for the benefit of others. You are powerful and you must use your power for the benefit of others. You can act for selfish or nefarious reasons	You are here to learn to use your financial success as a tool to help others achieve the same financial success. You often spend your abundance on materialistic status symbols rather than helping others
You are here to learn to lead by example, do you practise what you preach? You can be quite domineering, an adviser with all the answers. But you must let others make their own mistakes	You are here to develop a healthy attitude towards money. You may resent or hate wealthy people, or you may feel guilty about your own wealth. You must understand that financial wealth does not equate to poor ethics
You are here to make your life your teaching, you need to counsel with wisdom. You are a developed soul, the totality of all the numbers, full of cellular experience and higher knowledge	You are here to develop balanced determination for achievement but with integrity and for the good of others. You can be either obsessed with achievement or fearful of achievement from low self-esteem. It is important that you develop a positive mindset because you attract what you think about.
You are here to develop broad mindedness, meet and accept diverse people. You must learn to be	You are here to develop inner confidence and balanced personal power. You can swing from over

a humanitarian and make the world a better place. You need a global consciousness, as you can be narrow minded, judgemental, and even bigoted.	dominance or misuse of power to hiding away or submission to others
You are here to learn to take responsibility for your powerful choices. You sometimes run away from the consequences of your actions	You are here to develop skilled leadership, which consists of subject competence coupled with excellent social skills and charisma
You need to develop towards being a successful entrepreneur or businessperson if it is with something you feel passionate about. You must choose work that has meaning for you. You are a powerful force for change	You are here to work hard as an excellent practical businessperson, but you must ensure that you do not work too hard, you need time out and time for your family
You are here to develop excellent social skills and charisma. You could develop the skills of a powerful speaker and influencer of others. People will hang on your every word	You are here to be worldly, strong, resilient, disciplined, and realistic. To be successful you need to be strong, tough, and able to cope with The ups and downs of the world
You are here to look after the wellbeing of others. But when you are in trouble or need support, people do not notice. You must ask for what you need, you must ask for help	You are here to develop bravery and the courage to take risks to progress. Success comes from having the bravery to take risks
You are here to wrap things up, let go and surrender. You can have a victim mentality, holding onto feelings that no longer serve you, unable to move on from perceived injustice, normally rooted in family issues.	You are here to develop organisation and management skills, resolve to making things happen and to define and meet your goals.

Life Path 9 with Birthday Master 11

Life Path Number 9 (90% Focus)	Birthday Master 11 (10% Focus)
You are here to learn to follow your intuitive wisdom and live to spiritual laws, rather than worldly laws, conventions, and ideals. You tend to follow worldly laws and prejudices as an excuse for your actions. But if you had followed your intuitive spiritual wisdom, you would not have acted that way. Focus on faith over logic	You are an old soul, with higher potential and higher responsibility to improve the world. You are here to learn to connect to source energy to channel unique new ideas and messages to change the world. You are here to learn to be happy in the limelight expressing new ideas for an audience. You need to develop and trust your massive intuitive potential. You often hide your ideas due to low confidence
You are here to learn to act with integrity for the benefit of others. You are powerful and you must use your power for the benefit of others. You can act for selfish or nefarious reasons	You are here to learn to be the ideas person, but you struggle to bring your unique ideas to reality because you lose interest quickly after the initial idea of sabotage yourself due to crippling low confidence. You are an idealistic dreamer whose ideas are often not grounded in reality
You are here to learn to lead by example, do you practise what you preach? You can be quite domineering, an adviser with all the answers. But you must let others make their own mistakes	You are here to learn to be confident in your uniqueness because unique people have unique ground-breaking ideas. It is important that you are not craving validation from others. Your validation should come from your intuition.
You are here to make your life your teaching, you need to counsel with wisdom. You are a developed soul, the totality of all the numbers, full of cellular experience and higher knowledge	You need to bring unique, new ideas that break barriers, or challenge others comfort zone. You must learn to be brave, confident and be willing to take risks
You are here to develop broad mindedness, meet and accept	You need to be a practical initiator, a doer, action orientated that learns by

diverse people. You must learn to be a humanitarian and make the world a better place. You need a global consciousness, as you can be narrow minded, judgemental, and even bigoted.	experience. Ideas will stay unmanifested until you act! Only action brings change
You are here to learn to take responsibility for your powerful choices. You sometimes run away from the consequences of your actions	You need to set intentions then use spiritual practice and visualisation to channel your advanced, intense master energy into initiation and action. Unchanneled or mismanaged energy can cause intense nervous energy and anxiety. You may medicate these with unhealthy substances.
You need to develop towards being a successful entrepreneur or businessperson if it is with something you feel passionate about. You must choose work that has meaning for you. You are a powerful force for change	You are here to learn to be interdependent, not so independent that you push others away and refuse to delegate. You cannot do everything alone. Independence is an illusion; we are all interconnected
You are here to develop excellent social skills and charisma. You could develop the skills of a powerful speaker and influencer of others. People will hang on your every word	You need to be determined to succeed. Constant self-discovery and intuitive spiritual development is key for you to develop complete trust in the skills you have learned and mastered to serve as a kind of "security blanket" for you when you are feeling insecure
You are here to look after the wellbeing of others. But when you are in trouble or need support, people do not notice. You must ask for what you need, you must ask for help	You need to learn to be a supportive, nurturing leader, be firm and assertive but also empathic and supportive. You must lead others to the fruition of your ideas, but with balanced personal power
You are here to wrap things up, let go and surrender. You can have a	Your power causes ripples, both positive and negative, you must

victim mentality, holding onto feelings that no longer serve you, unable to move on from perceived injustice, normally rooted in family issues.	remember that great power brings great responsibility. You must ensure that your intentions are good
	You are here to learn to be responsible to others, your family, team, or group but in a balanced way. You can be too responsible and do too much. You are irresponsible if you feel undervalued, resentful, and exhausted.
	You must develop and improve your social skills, focus on widening and deepening your relationships and make decisions subjectively. It is important that you deepen your relationships and connect 121
	You may struggle to maintain long term close and romantic relationships.
	You must learn not to smother your loved ones or have expectations that can never be met. OR back away from wanting love because it hurts too badly. You need to balance your intense need for love for healthy relationships.
	You are here to learn to be intuitive and sensitive to the needs of others. You are here to be of service to others, the development of intuition will aid you in this journey
	You are here to learn to be a cooperative team player to get the job done as part of a cohesive team. You can be a disruptive,

	uncooperative drama queen.
	You must develop the assertiveness to demand boundaries to being overworked, walked all over, taken advantage of, and/or taken for granted. You must not be a "shape shifter" who changes who you are in order to please others or keep the peace. Be you and consider yourself too.
	You are here to serve the world, help the team, the task and be dependable. You can always be relied upon to keep the cogs turning behind the scenes
	You are here to be the tactful mediator of the team/group/family, helping to resolve conflicts fairly and for the good of everyone involved. You hate conflict and often run and hide until it is over
	You are here to learn to plan the next steps after channelling your message or idea & build a team to achieve it. The energy of the 11/2 needs to be the nurturer of ideas and a builder of teams
	You must learn to give yourself your own kudos. Oftentimes you judge yourself on what everyone else says or thinks about you. You need to develop your internal compass and turn inward for validation, do what YOU think you should do

Life Path 9 with Birthday Master 22/4

Life Path Number 9 (90% Focus)	Birthday Master 22/4 (10% Focus)
You are here to learn to follow your intuitive wisdom and live to spiritual laws, rather than worldly laws, conventions, and ideals. You tend to follow worldly laws and prejudices as an excuse for your actions. But if you had followed your intuitive spiritual wisdom, you would not have acted that way. Focus on faith over logic	You are an old soul, as spiritual as you are practical, here to channel and then manifest ideas in reality to build world safety, stability, and security. You must learn to handle the master builder energy and focus it to manifestation. You have a big responsibility to the team and the world to build structures (buildings, concepts, body, mind, spirit, businesses, organisations, even an empire for the purpose of world stability and security
You are here to learn to act with integrity for the benefit of others. You are powerful and you must use your power for the benefit of others. You can act for selfish or nefarious reasons	You must develop and improve your social skills, focus on widening and deepening your relationships to assist you to manifest your big ideas. It is important that you learn to deepen your relationships and connect 121, you cannot do this alone!
You are here to learn to lead by example, do you practise what you preach? You can be quite domineering, an adviser with all the answers. But you must let others make their own mistakes	You must learn to have balanced, healthy relationships with others that are part of your sense of security. You must learn not to smother your loved ones and your team or have expectations that can never be met. OR Your big task in this lifetime may disrupt your love relationships. You may back away from wanting love because it hurts too badly or attacks

	your sense of security
You are here to make your life your teaching, you need to counsel with wisdom. You are a developed soul, the totality of all the numbers, full of cellular experience and higher knowledge	You are here to learn to listen to and follow your intuition. Intuition is needed for you to be sensitive to the needs of others. You are here to be of service to change the world, the development of intuition will aid you in this journey
You are here to develop broad mindedness, meet and accept diverse people. You must learn to be a humanitarian and make the world a better place. You need a global consciousness, as you can be narrow minded, judgemental, and even bigoted.	You are here to learn to be a cooperative team player to get the job done as part of a cohesive team. You may fail to communicate effectively with others. You can be a hard-headed and high handed at times.
You are here to learn to take responsibility for your powerful choices. You sometimes run away from the consequences of your actions	You must develop the assertiveness to demand boundaries to being overworked, walked all over, taken advantage of, and/or taken for granted. You must also develop your ability to respect other people's boundaries and not be high handed.
You need to develop towards being a successful entrepreneur or businessperson if it is with something you feel passionate about. You must choose work that has meaning for you. You are a powerful force for change	You are here to be of service to the world, the leader, the team, the task and be dependable. You can always be counted upon to keep the cogs turning behind the scenes
You are here to develop excellent social skills and charisma. You could develop the skills of a powerful speaker and influencer of others. People will hang on your every word	You are extremely sensitive, and you hate and run away from conflict. But you are here to learn to be a tactful mediator, helping to resolve conflicts fairly and for the good of

	the team/family/group
You are here to look after the wellbeing of others. But when you are in trouble or need support, people do not notice. You must ask for what you need, you must ask for help	You are here to learn to stay focused and plan the next steps after you have channelled a new idea & build a team to achieve it. The energy of the 22 needs to be the nurturer, the builder of ideas and teams.
You are here to wrap things up, let go and surrender. You can have a victim mentality, holding onto feelings that no longer serve you, unable to move on from perceived injustice, normally rooted in family issues.	You must learn to give yourself your own kudos. Oftentimes you judge yourself on what everyone else says or thinks about you. You need to develop your internal compass and turn inward for validation, do what you think you should do
	You are here to learn to commit to a person and/or place, so that you can put down roots and dig the foundations for security. You can be uncommitted and therefore unable to build stability and security
	You are here to learn to set and achieve goals to take you on your journey towards inner and outer stability and security. Foundations, structures, families, and business empires are built 1 goal at a time.
	You are here to learn to plan, create a process and/or procedure to ensure the achievement of your goals and bring strength and stability to dynamic ideas. You can be directionless, lazy and block your own progression.
	You are here to develop deep meticulous focus on achieving stability, like a stable home, business

	or income and building your inner security. You can be scattered and miss steps in your impatience.
	You are here to learn to be detail orientated, analytical, organised, and accurate to ensure your plans and processes are watertight. You can be disorganised, flaky and miss steps in your plan
	Your master 22/4 Birthday means that you are an old soul and you have agreed to bring safety, stability, and security to the world. You innovate and build empires, organisations, and businesses. This involves hard work, detail focus, routine work, and tasks. You are here to develop a work ethic, to work hard and develop enjoyment of routine work and tasks
	You are here to develop patient perseverance, so that every step in the process towards your goals for your stable foundation are taken. You are prone to impatience and corner cutting.
	You are here to develop determination and the perseverance to keep going past obstacles to achieve your goals. You are prone to giving up at the first hurdle.
	You are here to learn to come to terms with limitation — both the limitations that are externally imposed on you and the limitations that you impose upon yourself.
	You are here to look at your

	wounded or problematic relationships and work through the feelings of lack and pain they have brought to you. All experiences have lessons embedded within them
	Avoid social isolation by socialising regularly in familiar groups and with likeminded friends.

Your Life Path and Birthday Number Master Eleven (11)

You have chosen to incarnate to learn the lessons of the master 11 life path energy because when speaking to your spirit guide before this life, you highlighted that you needed to learn the lessons of the 1 energy at double intensity. You are studying for a 'spiritual master's degree' in the 1 energy with double the potential but double the challenge too, it's not an easy path. You have ascended to this important path of development because you are an old soul that has accumulated much wisdom. In this incarnation you are working towards mastery of the 1 energy and advanced Spiritual Teaching as an 'illuminator'.

You are here to learn to connect to source energy to channel healing new ideas and messages to bring change. You need to learn to be intuitive, to act and make decisions from your own intuitive wisdom and not be dependent on validation from others. Spiritual practise like relaxation, meditation and musing are needed to help you develop your connection to your soul and source energy.

Your 11 energy vibrates at a higher octave of the lower 2 energy, with the need for you to realise our profound oneness. As a Master 11 energy, you also need to master the 2 energy. Mastery of the 2 energy is the profound realisation that we are all one and interconnected. What you do to others you do to yourself. Full realisation of this wisdom will mean that you will not need appreciation from others for your service.

You have strong potential for self-mastery. Developing self-understanding is vital, as you need to teach this strategy, wisdom and self-understanding to others. You must learn to take responsibility for the role you play in your own life and live by higher intuitive ideals, like respect and honesty.

As an old soul developing your master energy, you have very intense energy from source bombarding you all the time. You are here to learn to manage this intense energy, harness it and channel it into healing ideas, confidence, expression, and courage. Mismanaged energy may cause anxiety and severe nervous tension which left unchecked, could exacerbate your low confidence, and possible progression into substance abuse and/or addictions. Your intense energy means that you are always creating, both positively and negatively, whether you control it or not.

As a master 11 life path, you have lots to achieve in this world, you are constantly pushed and pulled to be better because others unconsciously sense your higher energy and expect much more from you. But your expectations of yourself are just as high because you 'know' from previous life experience, that you should have done better. You are here to develop yourself constantly to help you to channel world changing, healing messages and wisdom. You need to use your gifts of heightened sensitivity and intuition to help others as an inspired leader, healer, artistic force, and spiritual catalyst.

When you are working on the 11 life path, you have double the need to bring unique new ideas to this world, to channel ideas wisdom and messages that illuminate and heal the world. But your life path 11 suggests that you struggle with low confidence, you may feel that others are better than you because your sensitivity and uniqueness are judged by others as weird. You may then spend much energy burying your uniqueness to fit in and gain validation from others. But hiding your uniqueness is not your path, you are here to be unique because the unique is what you are here to channel into this world in order to raise the world's vibration.

To channel unique new ideas, healing messages, wisdom, and intuition, you must develop your connection to source energy and be intuitively confident enough to take risks. Remember, you are not here to be conventional, you are here to take the road less travelled and bring positive creative energy into this world. This takes courage as new messages that challenge other people's comfort zone or core beliefs can sometimes spark others hostility. You need to learn to trust your connection to source and intuition to such an extent that you are confident and brave enough to surge ahead despite potential hostility.

You are here to develop a balanced and flexible sense of independence by intuitively knowing that we are all fundamentally interconnected and interdependent. Sometimes we are independent, sometimes dependent, but we are always interdependent and connected. We all need and influence each other.

Your life path 11 suggests that you struggle in your relationships, you tend to push other people away and go off to do your own thing. You may go to great lengths to avoid dealing with issues and potential team or family conflict, you run away and hide. This leaves issues to bubble, fester and explode in unhelpful ways, potentially damaging your relationships. To achieve your life path 11, you must learn not to push other people away, especially those you love. You must develop your ability to face issues and potential conflict head on with tact and diplomacy. To learn to cooperate, be of service, dependable and nurture others supportively to maintain harmony. You have the potential to be an excellent supportive, caring leader and parent, that skilfully manages conflict rather than running away from it. You have the potential to develop your skills and intuition as a tactful mediator to create and maintain harmony. However, you must also be self-aware and assertive enough to know your own and other people's boundaries and express them appropriately. You can be very dependable, but you must also take care of yourself.

Your 11 energy needs you to lead using double the energy of the 1 whilst blending the contrasting attributes of the 2 energy. The path you are here to travel needs you to stand out, to be doubly innovative, doubly unique, doubly confident and inspire people with your unique message like a 1 at double the intensity. But you also need to master the 2 with a path of service to others rooted in your sense of our profound interconnectedness. To assist you in this, you are endowed with the added perceptions, awareness, and increased capabilities of an old soul. The veil between a master energy like you and source energy is thinner. You are potentially psychic and empathic.

As an 11, you have the potential to be a supportive leader who is willing to roll up your sleeves, cooperate, support, and serve when the occasion calls for it. Your ability to cooperate and support will give you the strength to finish what you start and form great relationships with others. You must learn to develop and deepen your relationships, work, and play well with others. You must learn to lead like a compassionate prophet, who is not as harsh and strong as a single 1 energy because of your contrasting gentler 2 energy. Your potential 2 energy makes you more of a nurturing, supportive leader, service orientated, more of a relationship builder and team worker than a 1 energy alone would be.

Your old soul traits provide you with much potential in the spiritual and intuitive. You are extremely sensitive to the energy in your environment, and you pick up on everyone else's feelings. The negative energy of conflict, negativity, and stress are especially bad for you, so you promote peace at all costs, subordinating your own needs and desires. You must learn, using spiritual practice to manage your sensitivity to avoid people pleasing, anxiety and substance abuse. Managing your sensitivity will help you to use your sensitivity to your advantage, to help you to heal and be of service to others. You are potentially diplomatic, tactful, patient, cooperative and self-reflective, preferring a quiet, harmonious, and positive environment.

You must bravely channel, express and manifest your unique, ground-breaking ideas, messages, and intuition with confidence, and with the support of others. You must be a doer, an initiator who learns by experience. You need to be determined to succeed, responsibly and ethically. You have a strong internal compass that underpins and initiates your actions and your personal learning. However, you are an idealistic dreamer, so not all of your ideas are grounded in reality and your hesitancy to act, due to fear or low confidence, could stop you in your tracks. All of the above are challenges that you will strive to achieve and maintain your whole life, so you will have inevitable barriers that will get in your way, but that it's your path to keep trying and learning.

Your 11 energy is concerned with spiritual illumination and the instinctive understanding of the metaphysical. You are a potential channel from the higher realms, using your intuition and psychic abilities to illuminate and heal. You need to be very exploratory, get out into the world, seek wisdom and experience to learn and then teach, to develop humanity. Self-discovery and spiritual development will strengthen your link to the Spirit World, God, Buddha, Allah, the universe or whatever else you call the higher power.

Your Master 11 energy development needs you to tap into the realms of the unseen, the psychic, the spiritual and the astrological. You must seek to understand how spirit and human life overlap, to be deeply explorative in the realms of the metaphysical. Explore psychic development, spiritual healing, astrology, tarot and numerology, anything that has an element of mysticism, your number 11 energy is a deeply mystic number.

Your 11 life path makes you potentially charismatic and philanthropic, tending to gain notoriety and fame, just by being who you naturally are. This is one of the reasons that you are not supposed to use the master number vibrations for selfish or nefarious purposes, because your intentions and actions are powerful, causing ripples, both good and bad.

Your philanthropy is about helping people, it is about going out into the world, building things, energising things, and making things happen to serve humanity. Funding things, to become realities, taking ideas and concepts, and making them real, making them tangible, making them yield results. Your path is about opening up and channelling from source, pouring your resources, both inner and outer into something in order to make it grow and have a positive global impact.

When your 11 energy expresses at your highest vibration, creative ideas, projects and energy flow like a stream and your confidence, not based on the approval of others, is established, and used to project unique new ideas that you manifest powerfully. You have the leadership, assertiveness, and bravery to be an independent warrior with your bright, demeanour. You have a massive energy field, you are joyful, passionate, full of personal magnetism and very productive. You stand for unity, cooperation, caring, nurturing, and parental protection. You take complete responsibility for your life, balancing yours and others needs equally. You assure the success of great undertakings and achievements with your drive to serve, help, instruct, guide, assist and support. A big hearted person who can be counted on for anything for the common good. But you are not conscious of this ability because you have transcended cooperation, you see others as part of your larger self, and you have become a source of loving service to all.

Your challenges are primarily in the realms of confidence and responsible creativity. Your creativity will always manifest even if it is in bad or destructive ways. You need to channel your creativity positively and come to terms with your responsibilities and the power of your choices. For example, planning a crime may not be the best choice to manifest your creativity.

You can sometimes feel different, out of place or somehow inferior. Your need for approval from others can repress your creativity until it bursts out through substance abuse, food, or sex. When you are like this, your reproductive and lower areas of your torso can cause you problems.

You must rely on your own intuitive voice and base your confidence in your trusted intuition and not validation from others.

Your potential in the 2 energy can cause problems, in that, your need to be helpful can cause you to subordinate your own needs and enter servitude. Perpetually ignoring your own feelings and needs and doing what you 'should' do will bring on exhaustion and stress related conditions. You can feel responsible for others happiness, have trouble saying no, over commit and ignore your limits. Forgetting your own limits will cause you exhaustion and resentment leading to drama queen outbursts and irresponsibility. You must act on what you truly feel, or you will swing from give give give to stubborn resistance and conflict. When in resentful stubborn resistance, you can be the opposite of parental, prone to co-dependent substance abuse, disruptive and fearful.

As an 11, you may be a late bloomer, because of the intensity of your master 11 energy and the sheer weight of things that you need to learn first. As a master energy, you have more to achieve in this life time. This means that having a master energy as your life path is not going to be easy. You may have difficulty coping with the intensity of your master energy, leading to anxiety and even substance abuse. The key to improving your health is improved energy management via meditation and spiritual practice. You need to set intensions for each day then use visualisation and spiritual practice to focus your intense energy into your intentions.

You were a quiet, sensitive, shy child, who struggled with the noise and chaos of other children your own age. This is because you were such an old soul, an experienced adult in a child's body. You can be lonely, because your master 11 makes you unique, causing you to feel quite misunderstood. In fact, you often feel 'not of this world', you may even feel homesick and want to get in a spaceship and get the hell out of here! However, you are independent, and you can do well as a loner.

You can be resentful, especially when you give too much, you can also be narrow minded, childish, self-centred, and manipulative. When you are not engaging in spiritual practice and managing your energy, you are oversensitive, anxious and at risk of self-medicating with addictions. You are an idealistic dreamer and you channel world changing messages and ideas but sometimes those ideas are totally impractical.

However, by far your biggest nemesis is lack of confidence. 1's and double 1's especially, suffer from crippling self-doubt, constantly comparing yourself to others when you should be creating something new and breaking new ground. You are not here to compete, live to standards or live up to someone else's expectations, you're here to illuminate, enlighten, shake things up and raise the world's vibration.

Your low self-esteem means that you hide your uniqueness and perceive others as 'better' than you. You must learn to see your uniqueness as a gift that helps you to illuminate and bring positive world change. You are here to channel unique messages from source energy, messages that are not of this 'work, buy, consume, die' paradigm, messages that cannot be replicated by anyone else. This path can make you feel 'out of place' like you do not fit in, and you can often desire to get on a space ship and get the hell out of here! Accept that you are an old soul with a unique potential to heal the world, you have an amazing gift, embrace it!

You are very vulnerable to stress related conditions, especially when working in a negative environment. You need a tranquil environment and calm energy, or you can feel exhausted, hopeless, and even slip into depression. It is important that you work in a calm, compassionate and accepting environment, but this can often be difficult to achieve in the working world.

Careers that will help you achieve your life path:

Astrologer, Numerologist, Sharman, Psychic, Healer, Charity worker, Musician, Professor, Psychologist, Pioneer, Politician, Spiritual Teacher, Energy worker, Hypnotherapist, Fantasy writer, Healer, Monk, Nun, and an Inventor.

Life Path Master 11 with Birthday Number 1

Life Path Master 11 (90% Focus)	Birthday Number 1 (10% Focus)
You are an old soul, with higher potential and higher responsibility to improve the world. You are here to learn to connect to source energy to channel unique new ideas and messages to change the world. You are here to learn to be happy in the limelight expressing new ideas for an audience. You need to develop and trust your massive intuitive potential. You often hide your ideas due to low confidence	You are here to learn to connect to source energy to download / channel unique new ideas. You often hide your ideas due to low confidence. You are here to learn to be happy in the limelight expressing new ideas for an audience.
You are here to learn to be the ideas person, but you struggle to bring your unique ideas to reality because you lose interest quickly after the initial idea of sabotage yourself due to crippling low confidence. You are an idealistic dreamer whose ideas are often not grounded in reality	You are here to learn to be the ideas person, but you struggle to bring your unique ideas to reality because you lose interest quickly after the initial idea.
You are here to learn to be confident in your uniqueness because unique people have unique ground-breaking ideas. It is important that you are not craving validation from others. Your validation should come from your intuition.	You are here to learn to be confident in your uniqueness because unique people have unique ground-breaking ideas. It is important that you are not craving validation from others.
You need to bring unique, new ideas that break barriers, or challenge others comfort zone. You must learn to be brave, confident and be willing to take risks	You need to be a practical initiator, a doer, action orientated that learns by experience. Only action makes the difference.
You need to be a practical initiator, a doer, action orientated that learns by experience. Ideas will stay	You need to learn to trust your intuitive voice within. You must achieve balanced confidence in

unmanifested until you act! Only action brings change	yourself & your abilities, fed by strong connection & trust in your intuition. You bring your ideas without fear. You must not seek validation from others or base your confidence on what others say.
You need to set intentions then use spiritual practice and visualisation to channel your advanced, intense master energy into initiation and action. Unchanneled or mismanaged energy can cause intense nervous energy and anxiety. You may medicate these with unhealthy substances.	You need to bring unique, new ideas that break barriers, or challenge others comfort zones, you must learn to be brave, confident and be willing to take risks
You are here to learn to be interdependent, not so independent that you push others away and refuse to delegate. You cannot do everything alone. Independence is an illusion; we are all interconnected	You are here to learn to be interdependent, not so independent that you push others away and refuse to delegate. You cannot do everything alone. Independence is an illusion; we are all interconnected
You need to be determined to succeed. Constant self-discovery and intuitive spiritual development is key for you to develop complete trust in the skills you have learned and mastered to serve as a kind of "security blanket" for you when you are feeling insecure	You need to be determined to succeed. Constant self-discovery and development is key for you to develop complete trust in the skills you have learned and mastered to serve as a kind of "security blanket" for you when you are feeling insecure
You need to learn to be a supportive, nurturing leader, be firm and assertive but also empathic and supportive. You must lead others to the fruition of your ideas, but with balanced personal power	You need to learn to be a powerful leader, be dominant and assertive. You must lead others to the fruition of your ideas, but with balanced personal power
Your power causes ripples, both positive and negative, you must remember that great power brings	Your power causes ripples, both positive and negative, you must remember that great power brings

great responsibility. You must ensure that your intentions are good	great responsibility. You must ensure that your intentions are good
You are here to learn to be responsible to others, your family, team, or group but in a balanced way. You can be too responsible and do too much. You are irresponsible if you feel undervalued, resentful, and exhausted.	
You must develop and improve your social skills, focus on widening and deepening your relationships and make decisions subjectively. It is important that you deepen your relationships and connect 121 You may struggle to maintain long term close and romantic relationships.	
You must learn not to smother your loved ones or have expectations that can never be met. OR back away from wanting love because it hurts too badly. You need to balance your intense need for love for healthy relationships.	
You are here to learn to be intuitive and sensitive to the needs of others. You are here to be of service to others, the development of intuition will aid you in this journey	
You are here to learn to be a cooperative team player to get the job done as part of a cohesive team. You can be a disruptive, uncooperative drama queen.	
You must develop the assertiveness to demand boundaries to being	

overworked, walked all over, taken advantage of, and/or taken for granted. You must not be a "shape shifter" who changes who you are in order to please others or keep the peace. Be you and consider yourself too.	
You are here to serve the world, help the team, the task and be dependable. You can always be relied upon to keep the cogs turning behind the scenes	
You are here to be the tactful mediator of the team/group/family, helping to resolve conflicts fairly and for the good of everyone involved. You hate conflict and often run and hide until it is over	
You are here to learn to plan the next steps after channelling your message or idea & build a team to achieve it. The energy of the 11/2 needs to be the nurturer of ideas and a builder of teams	
You must learn to give yourself your own kudos. Oftentimes you judge yourself on what everyone else says or thinks about you. You need to develop your internal compass and turn inward for validation, do what YOU think you should do	

Life Path Master 11 with Birthday Number 2

Life Path Master 11 (90% Focus)	Birthday Number 2 (10% Focus)
You are an old soul, with higher potential and higher responsibility to improve the world. You are here to learn to connect to source energy to channel unique new ideas and messages to change the world. You are here to learn to be happy in the limelight expressing new ideas for an audience. You need to develop and trust your massive intuitive potential. You often hide your ideas due to low confidence	You are here to learn to be responsible to others and the team. You can be too responsible and do too much. You are irresponsible if you feel undervalued and resentful.
You are here to learn to be the ideas person, but you struggle to bring your unique ideas to reality because you lose interest quickly after the initial idea of sabotage yourself due to crippling low confidence. You are an idealistic dreamer whose ideas are often not grounded in reality	You must learn to improve your social skills, focus on widening and deepening your relationships and make decisions subjectively. It is important that you deepen your relationships and connect 121
You are here to learn to be confident in your uniqueness because unique people have unique ground-breaking ideas. It is important that you are not craving validation from others. Your validation should come from your intuition.	You must learn not to smother your loved ones or have expectations that can never be met. OR you may back away from wanting love because it hurts too badly. You need to balance your intense need for love
You need to bring unique, new ideas that break barriers, or challenge others comfort zone. You must learn to be brave, confident and be willing to take risks	You are here to learn to be intuitive and sensitive to the needs of others. You are here to be of service to others, the development of intuition will aid you in this journey
You need to be a practical initiator, a doer, action orientated that learns by experience. Ideas will stay	You are here to learn to be a cooperative team player to get the job done as part of a cohesive team.

unmanifested until you act!	You can be a disruptive, uncooperative drama queen.
Only action brings change	
You need to set intentions then use spiritual practice and visualisation to channel your advanced, intense master energy into initiation and action. Unchanneled or mismanaged energy can cause intense nervous energy and anxiety. You may medicate these with unhealthy substances.	You must develop the assertiveness to demand boundaries to being overworked, walked all over, taken advantage of, and/or taken for granted. You must not be a "shape shifter" who changes who you are in order to please others or keep the peace.
You are here to learn to be interdependent, not so independent that you push others away and refuse to delegate. You cannot do everything alone. Independence is an illusion; we are all interconnected	You are here to serve the leader, the team, the task and be dependable. You can always be counted upon to keep the cogs turning behind the scenes
You need to be determined to succeed. Constant self-discovery and intuitive spiritual development is key for you to develop complete trust in the skills you have learned and mastered to serve as a kind of "security blanket" for you when you are feeling insecure	You are here to be the tactful mediator of the team, helping to resolve conflicts fairly and for the good of the team. You hate conflict and often run and hide until it is over
You need to learn to be a supportive, nurturing leader, be firm and assertive but also empathic and supportive. You must lead others to the fruition of your ideas, but with balanced personal power	You are here to learn to plan the next steps after the initial idea & build a team to achieve it. The energy of the two is the nurturer of ideas and a builder of teams
Your power causes ripples, both positive and negative, you must remember that great power brings great responsibility. You must ensure that your intentions are good	You must learn to give yourself your own kudos. Oftentimes you judge yourself on what everyone else says or thinks about you. You need to develop your internal compass and turn inward for validation, do what

	you think you should do
You are here to learn to be responsible to others, your family, team, or group but in a balanced way. You can be too responsible and do too much. You are irresponsible if you feel undervalued, resentful, and exhausted.	
You must develop and improve your social skills, focus on widening and deepening your relationships and make decisions subjectively. It is important that you deepen your relationships and connect 121 You may struggle to maintain long term close and romantic relationships.	
You must learn not to smother your loved ones or have expectations that can never be met. OR back away from wanting love because it hurts too badly. You need to balance your intense need for love for healthy relationships.	
You are here to learn to be intuitive and sensitive to the needs of others. You are here to be of service to others, the development of intuition will aid you in this journey	
You are here to learn to be a cooperative team player to get the job done as part of a cohesive team. You can be a disruptive, uncooperative drama queen.	
You must develop the assertiveness to demand boundaries to being overworked, walked all over, taken	

advantage of, and/or taken for granted. You must not be a "shape shifter" who changes who you are in order to please others or keep the peace. Be you and consider yourself too.	
You are here to serve the world, help the team, the task and be dependable. You can always be relied upon to keep the cogs turning behind the scenes	
You are here to be the tactful mediator of the team/group/family, helping to resolve conflicts fairly and for the good of everyone involved. You hate conflict and often run and hide until it is over	
You are here to learn to plan the next steps after channelling your message or idea & build a team to achieve it. The energy of the 11/2 needs to be the nurturer of ideas and a builder of teams	
You must learn to give yourself your own kudos. Oftentimes you judge yourself on what everyone else says or thinks about you. You need to develop your internal compass and turn inward for validation, do what YOU think you should do	

Life Path Master 11 with Birthday Number 3

Life Path Master 11 (90% Focus)	Birthday Number 3 (10% Focus)
You are an old soul, with higher potential and higher responsibility to improve the world. You are here to learn to connect to source energy to channel unique new ideas and messages to change the world. You are here to learn to be happy in the limelight expressing new ideas for an audience. You need to develop and trust your massive intuitive potential. You often hide your ideas due to low confidence	You are here to learn to express yourself verbally to inspire, inform and delight. You may struggle in some way verbally, chronic shyness, speech delay, stutter or struggling to find the words.
You are here to learn to be the ideas person, but you struggle to bring your unique ideas to reality because you lose interest quickly after the initial idea of sabotage yourself due to crippling low confidence. You are an idealistic dreamer whose ideas are often not grounded in reality	You are here to learn to express yourself creatively to inspire, inform and delight. But you may struggle to progress, execute, and finish creative projects, due to lack of self-belief
You are here to learn to be confident in your uniqueness because unique people have unique ground-breaking ideas. It is important that you are not craving validation from others. Your validation should come from your intuition.	You must learn to be dynamic, take risks and be confident to enjoy the attention and limelight of an audience. You can be shy, under confident and feel unable to take risks.
You need to bring unique, new ideas that break barriers, or challenge others comfort zone. You must learn to be brave, confident and be willing to take risks	You need to develop as an entrepreneur who is able to promote, network and make money creatively. But you may procrastinate and fail to stay focused and work inconsistently.
You need to be a practical initiator, a doer, action orientated that learns	You are here to learn to express your emotions positively. You can

by experience. Ideas will stay unmanifested until you act! Only action brings change	be extremely sensitive to criticism and other people's emotions, causing you to express emotions negatively
You need to set intentions then use spiritual practice and visualisation to channel your advanced, intense master energy into initiation and action. Unchanneled or mismanaged energy can cause intense nervous energy and anxiety. You may medicate these with unhealthy substances.	You are here to develop the habit of acting, be a doer and executer of ideas. When low, you can struggle with apathy, laziness and lack of focus and direction
You are here to learn to be interdependent, not so independent that you push others away and refuse to delegate. You cannot do everything alone. Independence is an illusion; we are all interconnected	You are here to learn to be social, talkative, the life of the party and bringer of fun & positivity. You need to be the networker, communicating an emotional message. You can be quiet and struggle to speak
You need to be determined to succeed. Constant self-discovery and intuitive spiritual development is key for you to develop complete trust in the skills you have learned and mastered to serve as a kind of "security blanket" for you when you are feeling insecure	You must develop interdependence, life path 3's like to be looked after and can be prone to avoiding work or anything needing routine and commitment
You need to learn to be a supportive, nurturing leader, be firm and assertive but also empathic and supportive. You must lead others to the fruition of your ideas, but with balanced personal power	You are here to be opportunistic, to network, make useful connections and snap up opportunities to spread the word and progress ideas and projects
Your power causes ripples, both positive and negative, you must remember that great power brings great responsibility. You must	You must learn to take responsibility and listen to guidance; you can be irresponsible. You must think before you act, and

ensure that your intentions are good	take full responsibility for what you do
You are here to learn to be responsible to others, your family, team, or group but in a balanced way. You can be too responsible and do too much. You are irresponsible if you feel undervalued, resentful, and exhausted.	
You must develop and improve your social skills, focus on widening and deepening your relationships and make decisions subjectively. It is important that you deepen your relationships and connect 121 You may struggle to maintain long term close and romantic relationships.	
You must learn not to smother your loved ones or have expectations that can never be met. OR back away from wanting love because it hurts too badly. You need to balance your intense need for love for healthy relationships.	
You are here to learn to be intuitive and sensitive to the needs of others. You are here to be of service to others, the development of intuition will aid you in this journey	
You are here to learn to be a cooperative team player to get the job done as part of a cohesive team. You can be a disruptive, uncooperative drama queen.	
You must develop the assertiveness to demand boundaries to being	

overworked, walked all over, taken advantage of, and/or taken for granted. You must not be a "shape shifter" who changes who you are in order to please others or keep the peace. Be you and consider yourself too.	
You are here to serve the world, help the team, the task and be dependable. You can always be relied upon to keep the cogs turning behind the scenes	
You are here to be the tactful mediator of the team/group/family, helping to resolve conflicts fairly and for the good of everyone involved. You hate conflict and often run and hide until it is over	
You are here to learn to plan the next steps after channelling your message or idea & build a team to achieve it. The energy of the 11/2 needs to be the nurturer of ideas and a builder of teams	
You must learn to give yourself your own kudos. Oftentimes you judge yourself on what everyone else says or thinks about you. You need to develop your internal compass and turn inward for validation, do what YOU think you should do	

Life Path Master 11 with Birthday Number 4

Life Path Master 11 (90% Focus)	Birthday Number 4 (10% Focus)
You are an old soul, with higher potential and higher responsibility to improve the world. You are here to learn to connect to source energy to channel unique new ideas and messages to change the world. You are here to learn to be happy in the limelight expressing new ideas for an audience. You need to develop and trust your massive intuitive potential. You often hide your ideas due to low confidence	You are here to learn to commit to a person and/or place, so that you can put down roots and dig the foundations for security. You can be uncommitted and therefore unable to build stability and security.
You are here to learn to be the ideas person, but you struggle to bring your unique ideas to reality because you lose interest quickly after the initial idea of sabotage yourself due to crippling low confidence. You are an idealistic dreamer whose ideas are often not grounded in reality	You are here to learn to set and achieve goals to take you on your journey towards inner and outer stability and security. Foundations, structures, families, and business empires are built 1 goal at a time.
You are here to learn to be confident in your uniqueness because unique people have unique ground-breaking ideas. It is important that you are not craving validation from others. Your validation should come from your intuition.	You are here to learn to plan, create a process and/or procedure to ensure the achievement of your goals. You can be directionless, lazy and block your own progression
You need to bring unique, new ideas that break barriers, or challenge others comfort zone. You must learn to be brave, confident and be willing to take risks	You are here to develop deep meticulous focus on achieving stability, like a stable home, business or income and building your inner security. You can be scattered
You need to be a practical initiator, a doer, action orientated that learns by experience. Ideas will stay	You are here to learn to be detail orientated, analytical, organised, and accurate to ensure your plans and

unmanifested until you act! Only action brings change	processes are watertight. You can be disorganised and miss steps in the plan
You need to set intentions then use spiritual practice and visualisation to channel your advanced, intense master energy into initiation and action. Unchanneled or mismanaged energy can cause intense nervous energy and anxiety. You may medicate these with unhealthy substances.	You are here to develop a work ethic, to work hard and develop enjoyment of routine work and tasks. When low you can be lazy and stuck in 1 place, without progression
You are here to learn to be interdependent, not so independent that you push others away and refuse to delegate. You cannot do everything alone. Independence is an illusion; we are all interconnected	You are here to develop patient perseverance, so that every step in the process towards your goals for your stable foundation are taken. You are prone to impatience and missing steps
You need to be determined to succeed. Constant self-discovery and intuitive spiritual development is key for you to develop complete trust in the skills you have learned and mastered to serve as a kind of "security blanket" for you when you are feeling insecure	You are here to learn to come to terms with limitation — both the limitations that are externally imposed on you and the limitations that you impose upon yourself.
You need to learn to be a supportive, nurturing leader, be firm and assertive but also empathic and supportive. You must lead others to the fruition of your ideas, but with balanced personal power	You are here to look at your wounded or problematic relationships and work through the feelings of lack and pain they have brought to you.
Your power causes ripples, both positive and negative, you must remember that great power brings great responsibility. You must ensure that your intentions are good	You are prone to choosing social isolation, avoiding social situations due to social anxiety. It is important that you socialise regularly in familiar groups and with likeminded

friends.

You are here to learn to be responsible to others, your family, team, or group but in a balanced way. You can be too responsible and do too much. You are irresponsible if you feel undervalued, resentful, and exhausted.

You must develop and improve your social skills, focus on widening and deepening your relationships and make decisions subjectively. It is important that you deepen your relationships and connect 121

You may struggle to maintain long term close and romantic relationships.

You must learn not to smother your loved ones or have expectations that can never be met. OR back away from wanting love because it hurts too badly. You need to balance your intense need for love for healthy relationships.

You are here to learn to be intuitive and sensitive to the needs of others. You are here to be of service to others, the development of intuition will aid you in this journey

You are here to learn to be a cooperative team player to get the job done as part of a cohesive team. You can be a disruptive, uncooperative drama queen.

You must develop the assertiveness to demand boundaries to being overworked, walked all over, taken

advantage of, and/or taken for granted. You must not be a "shape shifter" who changes who you are in order to please others or keep the peace. Be you and consider yourself too.	
You are here to serve the world, help the team, the task and be dependable. You can always be relied upon to keep the cogs turning behind the scenes	
You are here to be the tactful mediator of the team/group/family, helping to resolve conflicts fairly and for the good of everyone involved. You hate conflict and often run and hide until it is over	
You are here to learn to plan the next steps after channelling your message or idea & build a team to achieve it. The energy of the 11/2 needs to be the nurturer of ideas and a builder of teams	
You must learn to give yourself your own kudos. Oftentimes you judge yourself on what everyone else says or thinks about you. You need to develop your internal compass and turn inward for validation, do what YOU think you should do	

Life Path Master 11 with Birthday Number 5

Life Path Master 11 (90% Focus)	Birthday Number 5 (10% Focus)
You are an old soul, with higher potential and higher responsibility to improve the world. You are here to learn to connect to source energy to channel unique new ideas and messages to change the world. You are here to learn to be happy in the limelight expressing new ideas for an audience. You need to develop and trust your massive intuitive potential. You often hide your ideas due to low confidence	You are easily bored and want to look at or study lots of topics. Initial varied experience is needed in order to choose a specialism, you are here to learn to be disciplined, to continue with a topic or activity beyond the boredom of the detail, towards mastery and specialism.
You are here to learn to be the ideas person, but you struggle to bring your unique ideas to reality because you lose interest quickly after the initial idea of sabotage yourself due to crippling low confidence. You are an idealistic dreamer whose ideas are often not grounded in reality	You are here to develop the ability to balance variety, change and adventure with the stability of family and skill mastery. You can be totally spontaneous and take risks, jumping from one experience to another, but never settling or progressing
You are here to learn to be confident in your uniqueness because unique people have unique ground-breaking ideas. It is important that you are not craving validation from others. Your validation should come from your intuition.	You need to learn to be extremely intuitive and access your intuitive wisdom when making decisions, assessing people and situations.
You need to bring unique, new ideas that break barriers, or challenge others comfort zone. You must learn to be brave, confident and be willing to take risks	You are here to develop your ability to attain inner freedom and outer freedom by doing things you might not want to do. Doing what you want is not necessarily freedom, you can become a slave to your desires. Freedom and discipline are inherently linked.

You need to be a practical initiator, a doer, action orientated that learns by experience. Ideas will stay unmanifested until you act!

Only action brings change

You are here to learn to develop your verbal and written communication skills towards charismatic sharing of ideas and stories related to your specialism. You have the potential to be a great communicator

You need to set intentions then use spiritual practice and visualisation to channel your advanced, intense master energy into initiation and action. Unchanneled or mismanaged energy can cause intense nervous energy and anxiety. You may medicate these with unhealthy substances.

You are here to learn to be committed, dependable, to do what you say you are going to do. You often forget what you promise because you are so chaotic, scattered, and changeable, looking for the next new experience

You are here to learn to be interdependent, not so independent that you push others away and refuse to delegate. You cannot do everything alone. Independence is an illusion; we are all interconnected

You are here to develop your social skills and charisma, to have the potential to be fun loving, positive, and optimistic. You can be uptight and argumentative

You need to be determined to succeed. Constant self-discovery and intuitive spiritual development is key for you to develop complete trust in the skills you have learned and mastered to serve as a kind of "security blanket" for you when you are feeling insecure

You are here to develop consistent independence. You can swing from independence to dependence and back again. Risky behaviour and 'get rich quick' schemes can bring on dependence

You need to learn to be a supportive, nurturing leader, be firm and assertive but also empathic and supportive. You must lead others to the fruition of your ideas, but with balanced personal power

You are here to learn to develop fearlessness and help others to live fearlessly. You can be fearful of many things, restriction, and boredom, to name but a few. You need to challenge yourself and others past your own comfort zone

Your power causes ripples, both positive and negative, you must remember that great power brings great responsibility. You must ensure that your intentions are good

You are here to learn to make good use of your energy and drive, if you feel restricted and under confident, you will be restless, and you may turn into a drama queen. Use your energy for experience and adventure, be courageous

You are here to learn to be responsible to others, your family, team, or group but in a balanced way. You can be too responsible and do too much. You are irresponsible if you feel undervalued, resentful, and exhausted.

You must develop and improve your social skills, focus on widening and deepening your relationships and make decisions subjectively. It is important that you deepen your relationships and connect 121

You may struggle to maintain long term close and romantic relationships.

You must learn not to smother your loved ones or have expectations that can never be met. OR back away from wanting love because it hurts too badly. You need to balance your intense need for love for healthy relationships.

You are here to learn to be intuitive and sensitive to the needs of others. You are here to be of service to others, the development of intuition will aid you in this journey

You are here to learn to be a cooperative team player to get the

job done as part of a cohesive team. You can be a disruptive, uncooperative drama queen.	
You must develop the assertiveness to demand boundaries to being overworked, walked all over, taken advantage of, and/or taken for granted. You must not be a "shape shifter" who changes who you are in order to please others or keep the peace. Be you and consider yourself too.	
You are here to serve the world, help the team, the task and be dependable. You can always be relied upon to keep the cogs turning behind the scenes	
You are here to be the tactful mediator of the team/group/family, helping to resolve conflicts fairly and for the good of everyone involved. You hate conflict and often run and hide until it is over	
You are here to learn to plan the next steps after channelling your message or idea & build a team to achieve it. The energy of the 11/2 needs to be the nurturer of ideas and a builder of teams	
You must learn to give yourself your own kudos. Oftentimes you judge yourself on what everyone else says or thinks about you. You need to develop your internal compass and turn inward for validation, do what YOU think you should do	

Life Path Master 11 with Birthday Number 6

Life Path Master 11 (90% Focus)	Birthday Number 6 (10% Focus)
You are an old soul, with higher potential and higher responsibility to improve the world. You are here to learn to connect to source energy to channel unique new ideas and messages to change the world. You are here to learn to be happy in the limelight expressing new ideas for an audience. You need to develop and trust your massive intuitive potential. You often hide your ideas due to low confidence	You are here to be a visionary of the ideal, the dreamer of a utopian world. You must act to create a better world with your ideals.
You are here to learn to be the ideas person, but you struggle to bring your unique ideas to reality because you lose interest quickly after the initial idea of sabotage yourself due to crippling low confidence. You are an idealistic dreamer whose ideas are often not grounded in reality	You are here to learn to not use your ideals as a benchmark for your happiness. You must not base your emotional wellbeing on the achievement of your ideals. You often judge yourself and others for not hitting perfection, causing you great unhappiness
You are here to learn to be confident in your uniqueness because unique people have unique ground-breaking ideas. It is important that you are not craving validation from others. Your validation should come from your intuition.	Your perfectionism can make you an over achiever due to your constant self-judgement. You never meet your own standards. You must keep your big picture in mind and not get stuck in petty detail. You can often judge small imperfections and ruin or miss your successes.
You need to bring unique, new ideas that break barriers, or challenge others comfort zone. You must learn to be brave, confident and be willing to take risks	You are here to learn to be a nurturer, compassionate caring and giving, especially to those that are vulnerable or struggling within your close relationships, your community, and the wider world. Your judgemental nature can make

	you cruel and neglectful.
You need to be a practical initiator, a doer, action orientated that learns by experience. Ideas will stay unmanifested until you act! Only action brings change	You are here to develop boundaries to ensure your mental and physical health. You do a lot for others, sometimes too much, which can make you feel undervalued, unappreciated, and ill with exhaustion. You may force unsolicited advice and meddle in other people's affairs.
You need to set intentions then use spiritual practice and visualisation to channel your advanced, intense master energy into initiation and action. Unchanneled or mismanaged energy can cause intense nervous energy and anxiety. You may medicate these with unhealthy substances.	You are here to develop your social skills and be a team player. You must break through low self-esteem to be talkative, fun loving and relaxed around others. You can be shy and hide in the background.
You are here to learn to be interdependent, not so independent that you push others away and refuse to delegate. You cannot do everything alone. Independence is an illusion; we are all interconnected	You are here to create a stable, nurturing, tranquil home to maintain your security and well-being. Then nurture a family in an environment of stability and love. When low you can be a selfish, neglectful drama queen.
You need to be determined to succeed. Constant self-discovery and intuitive spiritual development is key for you to develop complete trust in the skills you have learned and mastered to serve as a kind of "security blanket" for you when you are feeling insecure	You are here to learn to be responsible and do good for those you care for. People naturally put you in positions of responsibility, but you often resent always being the 'responsible one.' Have boundaries on your responsibility so that you do not do too much.
You need to learn to be a supportive, nurturing leader, be firm and assertive but also empathic and supportive. You must lead others to the fruition of your ideas, but with balanced	You are here to learn to develop and use your artistic and aesthetic potential. Artistic, enhancing make up, great art and home designs. You have great musical potential

personal power	that you may not develop.
Your power causes ripples, both positive and negative, you must remember that great power brings great responsibility. You must ensure that your intentions are good	
You are here to learn to be responsible to others, your family, team, or group but in a balanced way. You can be too responsible and do too much. You are irresponsible if you feel undervalued, resentful, and exhausted.	
You must develop and improve your social skills, focus on widening and deepening your relationships and make decisions subjectively. It is important that you deepen your relationships and connect 121 You may struggle to maintain long term close and romantic relationships.	
You must learn not to smother your loved ones or have expectations that can never be met. OR back away from wanting love because it hurts too badly. You need to balance your intense need for love for healthy relationships.	
You are here to learn to be intuitive and sensitive to the needs of others. You are here to be of service to others, the development of intuition will aid you in this journey	
You are here to learn to be a cooperative team player to get the job done as part of a cohesive team. You can be a disruptive, uncooperative	

drama queen.	
You must develop the assertiveness to demand boundaries to being overworked, walked all over, taken advantage of, and/or taken for granted. You must not be a "shape shifter" who changes who you are in order to please others or keep the peace. Be you and consider yourself too.	
You are here to serve the world, help the team, the task and be dependable. You can always be relied upon to keep the cogs turning behind the scenes	
You are here to be the tactful mediator of the team/group/family, helping to resolve conflicts fairly and for the good of everyone involved. You hate conflict and often run and hide until it is over	
You are here to learn to plan the next steps after channelling your message or idea & build a team to achieve it. The energy of the 11/2 needs to be the nurturer of ideas and a builder of teams	
You must learn to give yourself your own kudos. Oftentimes you judge yourself on what everyone else says or thinks about you. You need to develop your internal compass and turn inward for validation, do what YOU think you should do	

Life Path Master 11 with Birthday Number 7

Life Path Master 11 (90% Focus)	Birthday Number 7 (10% Focus)
You are an old soul, with higher potential and higher responsibility to improve the world. You are here to learn to connect to source energy to channel unique new ideas and messages to change the world. You are here to learn to be happy in the limelight expressing new ideas for an audience. You need to develop and trust your massive intuitive potential. You often hide your ideas due to low confidence	You are here to learn to have faith that you are an immortal soul that has experience from previous lives. You must trust the soul within you by listening to and following your intuition without over thinking and applying logic. Listen to and follow your inner voice and feel safe enough to communicate your soul wisdom to the world without fear of ridicule
You are here to learn to be the ideas person, but you struggle to bring your unique ideas to reality because you lose interest quickly after the initial idea of sabotage yourself due to crippling low confidence. You are an idealistic dreamer whose ideas are often not grounded in reality	You are here to trust that the world is not against you. The universe is everything existing in perfect balance, it is like a cosmic library of all knowledge and experience. We must experience it all to learn and evolve
You are here to learn to be confident in your uniqueness because unique people have unique ground-breaking ideas. It is important that you are not craving validation from others. Your validation should come from your intuition.	Your focus for this lifetime must be Inner development rather than outer development and success. You must develop yourself constantly with self-discovery and spiritual wisdom. Meditation and time in nature is imperative for you
You need to bring unique, new ideas that break barriers, or challenge others comfort zone. You must learn to be brave, confident and be willing to take risks	You are here to learn to be a problem solver, thinker, a studier of the metaphysical and the big questions. You need to research, learn, and analyse theories to accrue wisdom.
You need to be a practical initiator, a doer, action orientated that learns	You are here to learn to filter your research through your intuition

by experience. Ideas will stay unmanifested until you act!

Only action brings change

and use your research of other people's theories for your own needs. You can be too analytical and ignore your intuition. Or totally spiritual and ignore other theories. You must balance the two.

You need to set intentions then use spiritual practice and visualisation to channel your advanced, intense master energy into initiation and action. Unchanneled or mismanaged energy can cause intense nervous energy and anxiety. You may medicate these with unhealthy substances.

You are here to be a free thinker, to be less interested in popular culture and following norms of fashion and appearance. This can make you feel different and out of place and lonely

You are here to learn to be interdependent, not so independent that you push others away and refuse to delegate. You cannot do everything alone. Independence is an illusion; we are all interconnected

You are here to develop the ability to focus on something long enough to develop it into something useful. You can be a little scattered and struggle to focus

You need to be determined to succeed. Constant self-discovery and intuitive spiritual development is key for you to develop complete trust in the skills you have learned and mastered to serve as a kind of "security blanket" for you when you are feeling insecure

You are here to develop interdependence, self-sufficiency but also a healthy dependence on other people. You like to do things for yourself but take care not to push others away

You need to learn to be a supportive, nurturing leader, be firm and assertive but also empathic and supportive. You must lead others to the fruition of your ideas, but with balanced personal power

You are here to learn to deal with and reconcile your sensitive emotions. Others often think you are aloof, but you are a well of deep emotions. You need to connect emotionally, both to yourself and to other people

Your power causes ripples, both positive and negative, you must remember that great power brings great responsibility. You must ensure that your intentions are good

You are here to learn to balance your need to be alone and work alone with social contact. You love to be alone, but you must ensure that you do not isolate yourself beyond what is healthy

You are here to learn to be responsible to others, your family, team, or group but in a balanced way. You can be too responsible and do too much. You are irresponsible if you feel undervalued, resentful, and exhausted.

You must develop and improve your social skills, focus on widening and deepening your relationships and make decisions subjectively. It is important that you deepen your relationships and connect 121

You may struggle to maintain long term close and romantic relationships.

You must learn not to smother your loved ones or have expectations that can never be met. OR back away from wanting love because it hurts too badly. You need to balance your intense need for love for healthy relationships.

You are here to learn to be intuitive and sensitive to the needs of others. You are here to be of service to others, the development of intuition will aid you in this journey

You are here to learn to be a cooperative team player to get the job done as part of a cohesive team.

You can be a disruptive, uncooperative drama queen.	
You must develop the assertiveness to demand boundaries to being overworked, walked all over, taken advantage of, and/or taken for granted. You must not be a "shape shifter" who changes who you are in order to please others or keep the peace. Be you and consider yourself too.	
You are here to serve the world, help the team, the task and be dependable. You can always be relied upon to keep the cogs turning behind the scenes	
You are here to be the tactful mediator of the team/group/family, helping to resolve conflicts fairly and for the good of everyone involved. You hate conflict and often run and hide until it is over	
You are here to learn to plan the next steps after channelling your message or idea & build a team to achieve it. The energy of the 11/2 needs to be the nurturer of ideas and a builder of teams	
You must learn to give yourself your own kudos. Oftentimes you judge yourself on what everyone else says or thinks about you. You need to develop your internal compass and turn inward for validation, do what YOU think you should do	

Life Path Master 11 with Birthday Number 8

Life Path Master 11 (90% Focus)	Birthday Number 8 (10% Focus)
You are an old soul, with higher potential and higher responsibility to improve the world. You are here to learn to connect to source energy to channel unique new ideas and messages to change the world. You are here to learn to be happy in the limelight expressing new ideas for an audience. You need to develop and trust your massive intuitive potential. You often hide your ideas due to low confidence	You are both spiritual and worldly. But you are here to learn the secrets of worldly financial success. You seek the freedom that comes from financial success. But freedom brings responsibility, your ethics will be tested multiple times.
You are here to learn to be the ideas person, but you struggle to bring your unique ideas to reality because you lose interest quickly after the initial idea of sabotage yourself due to crippling low confidence. You are an idealistic dreamer whose ideas are often not grounded in reality	You are here to learn to use your financial success as a tool to help others achieve the same financial success. You often spend your abundance on materialistic status symbols rather than helping others.
You are here to learn to be confident in your uniqueness because unique people have unique ground-breaking ideas. It is important that you are not craving validation from others. Your validation should come from your intuition.	You are here to develop a healthy attitude towards money. You may resent or hate wealthy people, or you may feel guilty about your own wealth. You must understand that financial wealth does not equate to poor ethics.
You need to bring unique, new ideas that break barriers, or challenge others comfort zone. You must learn to be brave, confident and be willing to take risks	You are here to develop balanced determination for achievement but with integrity and for the good of others. You can be either obsessed with achievement or fearful of achievement from low self-esteem. It is important that you develop a positive mindset because you attract

	what you think about.
You need to be a practical initiator, a doer, action orientated that learns by experience. Ideas will stay unmanifested until you act!

Only action brings change | You are here to develop inner confidence and balanced personal power. You can swing from over dominance or misuse of power to hiding away or submission to others. |
| You need to set intentions then use spiritual practice and visualisation to channel your advanced, intense master energy into initiation and action. Unchanneled or mismanaged energy can cause intense nervous energy and anxiety. You may medicate these with unhealthy substances. | You are here to develop skilled leadership, which consists of subject competence coupled with excellent social skills and charisma. |
| You are here to learn to be interdependent, not so independent that you push others away and refuse to delegate. You cannot do everything alone. Independence is an illusion; we are all interconnected | You are here to work hard as an excellent practical businessperson, but you must ensure that you do not work too hard, you need time out and time for your family. |
| You need to be determined to succeed. Constant self-discovery and intuitive spiritual development is key for you to develop complete trust in the skills you have learned and mastered to serve as a kind of "security blanket" for you when you are feeling insecure | You are here to be worldly, strong, resilient, disciplined, and realistic. To be successful you need to be strong, tough, and able to cope with

The ups and downs of the world. |
| You need to learn to be a supportive, nurturing leader, be firm and assertive but also empathic and supportive. You must lead others to the fruition of your ideas, but with balanced personal power | You are here to develop bravery and the courage to take risks to progress. Success comes from having the bravery to take risks. |
| Your power causes ripples, both positive and negative, you must | You are here to develop organisation and management skills, resolve to |

remember that great power brings great responsibility. You must ensure that your intentions are good

making things happen and to define and meet your goals.

You are here to learn to be responsible to others, your family, team, or group but in a balanced way. You can be too responsible and do too much. You are irresponsible if you feel undervalued, resentful, and exhausted.

You must develop and improve your social skills, focus on widening and deepening your relationships and make decisions subjectively. It is important that you deepen your relationships and connect 121

You may struggle to maintain long term close and romantic relationships.

You must learn not to smother your loved ones or have expectations that can never be met. OR back away from wanting love because it hurts too badly. You need to balance your intense need for love for healthy relationships.

You are here to learn to be intuitive and sensitive to the needs of others. You are here to be of service to others, the development of intuition will aid you in this journey

You are here to learn to be a cooperative team player to get the job done as part of a cohesive team. You can be a disruptive, uncooperative drama queen.

You must develop the assertiveness to demand boundaries to being overworked, walked all over, taken advantage of, and/or taken for granted. You must not be a "shape shifter" who changes who you are in order to please others or keep the peace. Be you and consider yourself too.	
You are here to serve the world, help the team, the task and be dependable. You can always be relied upon to keep the cogs turning behind the scenes	
You are here to be the tactful mediator of the team/group/family, helping to resolve conflicts fairly and for the good of everyone involved. You hate conflict and often run and hide until it is over	
You are here to learn to plan the next steps after channelling your message or idea & build a team to achieve it. The energy of the 11/2 needs to be the nurturer of ideas and a builder of teams	
You must learn to give yourself your own kudos. Oftentimes you judge yourself on what everyone else says or thinks about you. You need to develop your internal compass and turn inward for validation, do what YOU think you should do	

Life Path Master 11 with Birthday Number 9

Life Path Master 11 (90% Focus)	Birthday Number 9 (10% Focus)
You are an old soul, with higher potential and higher responsibility to improve the world. You are here to learn to connect to source energy to channel unique new ideas and messages to change the world. You are here to learn to be happy in the limelight expressing new ideas for an audience. You need to develop and trust your massive intuitive potential. You often hide your ideas due to low confidence	You are here to learn to follow your intuitive wisdom and live to spiritual laws, rather than worldly laws, conventions, and ideals. You tend to follow worldly laws and prejudices as an excuse for your actions. But if you had followed your intuitive spiritual wisdom, you would not have acted that way. Focus on faith over logic
You are here to learn to be the ideas person, but you struggle to bring your unique ideas to reality because you lose interest quickly after the initial idea of sabotage yourself due to crippling low confidence. You are an idealistic dreamer whose ideas are often not grounded in reality	You are here to learn to act with integrity for the benefit of others. You are powerful and you must use your power for the benefit of others. You can act for selfish or nefarious reasons
You are here to learn to be confident in your uniqueness because unique people have unique ground-breaking ideas. It is important that you are not craving validation from others. Your validation should come from your intuition.	You are here to learn to lead by example, do you practise what you preach? You can be quite domineering, an adviser with all the answers. But you must let others make their own mistakes
You need to bring unique, new ideas that break barriers, or challenge others comfort zone. You must learn to be brave, confident and be willing to take risks	You are here to make your life your teaching, you need to counsel with wisdom. You are a developed soul, the totality of all the numbers, full of cellular experience and higher knowledge
You need to be a practical initiator, a doer, action orientated that learns	You are here to develop broad mindedness, meet and accept

by experience. Ideas will stay unmanifested until you act! Only action brings change	diverse people. You must learn to be a humanitarian and make the world a better place. You need a global consciousness, as you can be narrow minded, judgemental, and even bigoted.
You need to set intentions then use spiritual practice and visualisation to channel your advanced, intense master energy into initiation and action. Unchanneled or mismanaged energy can cause intense nervous energy and anxiety. You may medicate these with unhealthy substances.	You are here to learn to take responsibility for your powerful choices. You sometimes run away from the consequences of your actions
You are here to learn to be interdependent, not so independent that you push others away and refuse to delegate. You cannot do everything alone. Independence is an illusion; we are all interconnected	You need to develop towards being a successful entrepreneur or businessperson if it is with something you feel passionate about. You must choose work that has meaning for you. You are a powerful force for change
You need to be determined to succeed. Constant self-discovery and intuitive spiritual development is key for you to develop complete trust in the skills you have learned and mastered to serve as a kind of "security blanket" for you when you are feeling insecure	You are here to develop excellent social skills and charisma. You could develop the skills of a powerful speaker and influencer of others. People will hang on your every word
You need to learn to be a supportive, nurturing leader, be firm and assertive but also empathic and supportive. You must lead others to the fruition of your ideas, but with balanced personal power	You are here to look after the wellbeing of others. But when you are in trouble or need support, people do not notice. You must ask for what you need, you must ask for help
Your power causes ripples, both positive and negative, you must	You are here to wrap things up, let go and surrender. You can have a

remember that great power brings great responsibility. You must ensure that your intentions are good

victim mentality, holding onto feelings that no longer serve you, unable to move on from perceived injustice, normally rooted in family issues.

You are here to learn to be responsible to others, your family, team, or group but in a balanced way. You can be too responsible and do too much. You are irresponsible if you feel undervalued, resentful, and exhausted.

You must develop and improve your social skills, focus on widening and deepening your relationships and make decisions subjectively. It is important that you deepen your relationships and connect 121

You may struggle to maintain long term close and romantic relationships.

You must learn not to smother your loved ones or have expectations that can never be met. OR back away from wanting love because it hurts too badly. You need to balance your intense need for love for healthy relationships.

You are here to learn to be intuitive and sensitive to the needs of others. You are here to be of service to others, the development of intuition will aid you in this journey

You are here to learn to be a cooperative team player to get the job done as part of a cohesive team. You can be a disruptive,

uncooperative drama queen.	
You must develop the assertiveness to demand boundaries to being overworked, walked all over, taken advantage of, and/or taken for granted. You must not be a "shape shifter" who changes who you are in order to please others or keep the peace. Be you and consider yourself too.	
You are here to serve the world, help the team, the task and be dependable. You can always be relied upon to keep the cogs turning behind the scenes	
You are here to be the tactful mediator of the team/group/family, helping to resolve conflicts fairly and for the good of everyone involved. You hate conflict and often run and hide until it is over	
You are here to learn to plan the next steps after channelling your message or idea & build a team to achieve it. The energy of the 11/2 needs to be the nurturer of ideas and a builder of teams	
You must learn to give yourself your own kudos. Oftentimes you judge yourself on what everyone else says or thinks about you. You need to develop your internal compass and turn inward for validation, do what YOU think you should do	

Life Path Master 11 with Birthday Master 22/4

Life Path Master 11 (90% Focus)	Birthday Master 22/4 (10% Focus)
You are an old soul, with higher potential and higher responsibility to improve the world. You are here to learn to connect to source energy to channel unique new ideas and messages to change the world. You are here to learn to be happy in the limelight expressing new ideas for an audience. You need to develop and trust your massive intuitive potential. You often hide your ideas due to low confidence	You are an old soul, as spiritual as you are practical, here to channel and then manifest ideas in reality to build world safety, stability, and security. You must learn to handle the master builder energy and focus it to manifestation. You have a big responsibility to the team and the world to build structures (buildings, concepts, body, mind, spirit, businesses, organisations, even an empire for the purpose of world stability and security
You are here to learn to be the ideas person, but you struggle to bring your unique ideas to reality because you lose interest quickly after the initial idea of sabotage yourself due to crippling low confidence. You are an idealistic dreamer whose ideas are often not grounded in reality	You must develop and improve your social skills, focus on widening and deepening your relationships to assist you to manifest your big ideas. It is important that you learn to deepen your relationships and connect 121, you cannot do this alone!
You are here to learn to be confident in your uniqueness because unique people have unique ground-breaking ideas. It is important that you are not craving validation from others. Your validation should come from your intuition.	You must learn to have balanced, healthy relationships with others that are part of your sense of security. You must learn not to smother your loved ones and your team or have expectations that can never be met. OR Your big task in this lifetime may disrupt your love relationships. You may back away from wanting love because it hurts too badly or attacks

	your sense of security
You need to bring unique, new ideas that break barriers, or challenge others comfort zone. You must learn to be brave, confident and be willing to take risks	You are here to learn to listen to and follow your intuition. Intuition is needed for you to be sensitive to the needs of others. You are here to be of service to change the world, the development of intuition will aid you in this journey
You need to be a practical initiator, a doer, action orientated that learns by experience. Ideas will stay unmanifested until you act! Only action brings change	You are here to learn to be a cooperative team player to get the job done as part of a cohesive team. You may fail to communicate effectively with others. You can be a hard-headed and high handed at times.
You need to set intentions then use spiritual practice and visualisation to channel your advanced, intense master energy into initiation and action. Unchanneled or mismanaged energy can cause intense nervous energy and anxiety. You may medicate these with unhealthy substances.	You must develop the assertiveness to demand boundaries to being overworked, walked all over, taken advantage of, and/or taken for granted. You must also develop your ability to respect other people's boundaries and not be high handed.
You are here to learn to be interdependent, not so independent that you push others away and refuse to delegate. You cannot do everything alone. Independence is an illusion; we are all interconnected	You are here to be of service to the world, the leader, the team, the task and be dependable. You can always be counted upon to keep the cogs turning behind the scenes
You need to be determined to succeed. Constant self-discovery and intuitive spiritual development is key for you to develop complete trust in the skills you have learned and	You are extremely sensitive, and you hate and run away from conflict. But you are here to learn to be a tactful mediator, helping to resolve conflicts fairly and for the good of

mastered to serve as a kind of "security blanket" for you when you are feeling insecure	the team/family/group
You need to learn to be a supportive, nurturing leader, be firm and assertive but also empathic and supportive. You must lead others to the fruition of your ideas, but with balanced personal power	You are here to learn to stay focused and plan the next steps after you have channelled a new idea & build a team to achieve it. The energy of the 22 needs to be the nurturer, the builder of ideas and teams.
Your power causes ripples, both positive and negative, you must remember that great power brings great responsibility. You must ensure that your intentions are good	You must learn to give yourself your own kudos. Oftentimes you judge yourself on what everyone else says or thinks about you. You need to develop your internal compass and turn inward for validation, do what you think you should do
You are here to learn to be responsible to others, your family, team, or group but in a balanced way. You can be too responsible and do too much. You are irresponsible if you feel undervalued, resentful, and exhausted.	You are here to learn to commit to a person and/or place, so that you can put down roots and dig the foundations for security. You can be uncommitted and therefore unable to build stability and security
You must develop and improve your social skills, focus on widening and deepening your relationships and make decisions subjectively. It is important that you deepen your relationships and connect 121 You may struggle to maintain long term close and romantic relationships.	You are here to learn to set and achieve goals to take you on your journey towards inner and outer stability and security. Foundations, structures, families, and business empires are built 1 goal at a time.
You must learn not to smother your loved ones or have expectations that can never be met. OR back away from wanting love because it hurts too badly. You need to balance your	You are here to learn to plan, create a process and/or procedure to ensure the achievement of your goals and bring strength and stability to dynamic ideas. You can be

intense need for love for healthy relationships.	directionless, lazy and block your own progression.
You are here to learn to be intuitive and sensitive to the needs of others. You are here to be of service to others, the development of intuition will aid you in this journey	You are here to develop deep meticulous focus on achieving stability, like a stable home, business or income and building your inner security. You can be scattered and miss steps in your impatience.
You are here to learn to be a cooperative team player to get the job done as part of a cohesive team. You can be a disruptive, uncooperative drama queen.	You are here to learn to be detail orientated, analytical, organised, and accurate to ensure your plans and processes are watertight. You can be disorganised, flaky and miss steps in your plan
You must develop the assertiveness to demand boundaries to being overworked, walked all over, taken advantage of, and/or taken for granted. You must not be a "shape shifter" who changes who you are in order to please others or keep the peace. Be you and consider yourself too.	Your master 22/4 Birthday means that you are an old soul and you have agreed to bring safety, stability, and security to the world. You innovate and build empires, organisations, and businesses. This involves hard work, detail focus, routine work, and tasks. You are here to develop a work ethic, to work hard and develop enjoyment of routine work and tasks
You are here to serve the world, help the team, the task and be dependable. You can always be relied upon to keep the cogs turning behind the scenes	You are here to develop patient perseverance, so that every step in the process towards your goals for your stable foundation are taken. You are prone to impatience and corner cutting.
You are here to be the tactful mediator of the team/group/family, helping to resolve conflicts fairly and for the good of everyone involved. You hate conflict and often run and hide until it is over	You are here to develop determination and the perseverance to keep going past obstacles to achieve your goals. You are prone to giving up at the first hurdle.

You are here to learn to plan the next steps after channelling your message or idea & build a team to achieve it. The energy of the 11/2 needs to be the nurturer of ideas and a builder of teams

You are here to learn to come to terms with limitation — both the limitations that are externally imposed on you and the limitations that you impose upon yourself.

You must learn to give yourself your own kudos. Oftentimes you judge yourself on what everyone else says or thinks about you. You need to develop your internal compass and turn inward for validation, do what YOU think you should do

You are here to look at your wounded or problematic relationships and work through the feelings of lack and pain they have brought to you. All experiences have lessons embedded within them

Avoid social isolation by socialising regularly in familiar groups and with likeminded friends.

Your Life Path and Birthday Number Master Twenty Two (22)

You have chosen to incarnate to learn the lessons of the master 22/4 Life Path energy because when speaking to your spirit guide before this life, you highlighted that you needed to learn the lessons of the master number 22/4 energy. You have this path because you are an old soul that has accumulated much wisdom, strongly connected to source energy due to your soul's advanced development. Your experience of many lives means that you have experienced many energies, so now you are working towards being a master vibration. You need to master, double cooperation, double balance and you have double the need to make a difference in the world through service. Be an unsung hero, driven to serve and help others. You need to clarify the boundaries of your responsibility and learn to work with others in a spirit of harmony, balance, and mutual support.

Your 22/4 energy vibrates at a higher octave of the lower 4 energy. You must realise that the world is abundant with more than enough to go around, you don't need to worry about lack. Focus your master builder energy into building security, safety and stability for yourself and the world. You need to develop your potential for self-mastery and worldly success, with the achievement of goals via planning, meticulous focus, and hard work, all to bring about positive world change. You are here to learn to be a Master Builder, a builder of structures, both physical and theoretical, from making individuals feel strong and safe to channelling environmental, political, financial, or social innovation for world strength and security. You could build a safe and secure home or place of work and build strong, secure businesses, organisations, even empires.

To be the best Master Builder you can be, you must first ensure that you have committed to a person, place, or idea. Then from there, you can ground your ideas in reality. To ground your ideas securely, you need to develop meticulous focus, perseverance, and attention to detail to ensure that the foundations of your security are strong, stand the test of time and overcome obstacles.

When you are walking this difficult path at your highest vibration, you stand for unity, cooperation, caring, nurturing, and parental protection. You take complete responsibility for your life, balancing yours and others needs equally and creating a secure foundation for your life. You are highly perceptive and intuitive due to the volume of cell memories within you from your many previous lives. You can connect extremely easily with spirit because the veil between experienced master souls and source is thinner. You assure the success of great undertakings and achievements with your drive to serve, help, instruct, guide, assist and support. You are a big hearted person who can be counted on for anything for the common good. But you are not conscious of this ability because you have transcended cooperation. You see others as part of you, you know that we are all one and you have become a source of loving service to all. However, this is your life path, so it will take your whole life for you to develop to this level.

At your absolute best, you are a Master Builder, you draw creative, innovative ideas from spirit and then endeavour to bring those ideas into reality to bring safety, security, and stability to humanity. You can channel a world changing idea from source and then create a solid foundation for the idea, structure, business, organisation or undertaking. You are organised, honest, and appreciative of structure and stability. You take responsibility, make clear plans, broken into steps and you commit to a step by step process which achieves any goal. You do this with strength, vigour, ambition, and perseverance.

You are here to learn to analyse the path from where you are to your goal, break it down into steps and act, you could teach others to do the same. You always prepare well, commit, and follow through step by step. However, this is a difficult life path to develop, so it may take most of your life for you to reach your master vibration.

Your challenges are that you receive extraordinarily strong energy from source. This intense master energy can be extremely overwhelming and cause you nervous tension and anxiety, which if not handled properly, can draw you into substance abuse to medicate. You must channel your intense master energy by setting intentions, then via meditation, visualisation, and spiritual practice, focus your intense energy into action. Channelling your intense master energy in productive directions will stop your intense energy from overwhelming you.

Your attitude of service and need to be helpful can cause you to subordinate your own needs and enter servitude, ignoring your own feelings and doing what you 'should' do. You can feel responsible for others happiness, have trouble saying no, over commit and ignore your limits, causing you to feel resentment and exhaustion. You must act on what you truly feel, or you will swing from give give to stubborn resistance and conflict. When in resentful stubborn resistance, you can be the opposite of parental, prone to co-dependent substance abuse, disruptive and fearful.

You can be competitive, rigid, and opinionated and yet you are insecure about the validity of your beliefs and ideas. You may argue a point that you are not even sure that you subscribe too, just to see what others will argue back with. You may experience psychological rigidity, manifesting stubborn self-deception or tunnel vision. You do not listen to others advice and just hope that things will just work themselves out without you going through the steps to make sure. You will be called upon to deal with difficult trials and experiences that will test your stability, safety, and security. For example, your worries surrounding not having enough resources could turn you into a workaholic who misses out on quality time with the family you are trying to make secure.

You may have difficulties with planning and process, you need to learn the necessity of preparation and not skipping steps. But when you do formulate a sound process, you can use that process elsewhere in your life as it's all part of your master builder development.

The immense energy of the Master Builder 22/4 energy can be hard to deal with. Master numbers are only given to old souls that have experienced and progressed enough to attempt to handle the master energy. Your master energy can be overwhelming if you do not manage and direct the energy in productive ways. Your master energy hits you like a torrent of water, causing nervous issues and sometimes an inability to cope with everyday life. Meditation and musing in isolation or walking in nature can be used to help you capture and funnel all that master energy into goals that will make the world a safer and more secure place to be.

As you learn to develop your master energy potential, you will often find that you just know things, you won't know how you know, you just know. You unconsciously exude a powerful master energy that causes people to unconsciously expect more from you. Your parents may have expected more from you than your siblings, which could have put added pressure on you. Additionally, your own extensive previous experience will make you expect more from yourself. You have experienced similar situations before, and you berate yourself if you feel that you are not using your previous experience effectively. Other people's expectations and the unreachable standards that you put onto yourself can cause low mood and low self-esteem, especially if you think you have failed. Keep in mind that life is a journey of up's and downs all for your learning and evolution. Instead of feeling that you have failed, be happy that you have learnt, now you have the opportunity to develop yourself further and do things better next time.

You are here to learn to be both spiritual and practical and link them skilfully. You have the potential to channel ideas and intuition from source energy and then utilise your practical potential to bring those ideas to the real world. Your 22/4 master energy actualised has one foot in the spiritual and the other in the practical real world. To help the achievement of your 22/4 life path, you can help yourself and other people by developing your spiritual, intuitive potential. Learn to hear and feel your intuition, trust it, and then act on it to make decisions and assess world need. It is important that you listen to and trust your feelings and inner voice when manifesting your ideas. Your intuition should inform and guide your own inner compass, you know what you need to do, you need to use your practical potential to do it.

You must learn to improve your socials skills and express a healthy need for love and connection. You need to widen and deepen your relationships and have balanced healthy relationships. One of your struggles within relationships is your sensitivity, causing an inability to deal with conflict or be a part of the mediation and resolution process. You are extremely sensitive and easily hurt, so sometimes instead of dealing with a situation tactfully, you either run away and brush it under the carpet or you become a drama queen and disrupt the groups cohesion and effectiveness. Dealt with properly, conflict and resolution can serve to further deepen your relationship, as facing deep truths together can help you both to develop more connection and trust.

As a master 22/4 life path, you have big responsibilities! You have double the task to learn to play nice, to be patient, to be balanced, tactful, to cooperate and nurture to be of service to mankind. But you must ensure that you develop the assertiveness to demand healthy boundaries for your own wellbeing, balancing your wellbeing with the wellbeing and development of other souls.

You need to develop towards being able to build an effective team to get things done and then be able to cooperate as part of that team. You struggle with impatience; you can be a little high handed and you can fail to communicate your desires and intentions effectively. The team cannot always depend on you to get the job done, especially if you are feeling exhausted, resentful, or unappreciated. You may fail to communicate your requirements clearly, so you must work through issues surrounding your cooperative efforts. For example, defining yours and other people's responsibilities, communicating clearly and compassionately and learning that it takes great patience and determination to achieve your goals.

As a 22/4 life path, your double 2 energy can suggest that you have difficulty dealing with giving and receiving love in a balanced way. You may either be smothering or totally rejecting of love. Your 22/4 life path means that you have a big job to do in this life time. This big responsibility could exacerbate your tendency to push love away, as you end up spending most of your time trying to be that hard working, world changing master builder that you came here to be. You need some balance in your relationships so that you give and receive love in a healthy way. You may be obsessively immersed in your love relationships or totally rejecting of love. It is important that you find balance, so that you can pursue happy, balanced, and healthy love relationships.

To be the master builder that you are here to be, you must start by committing to a person, place, and an idea, so that you can dig the foundations for your own stability and security. You struggle to commit to anything long enough to develop it into something secure enough for you to depend on. You must set goals that lead to your safety and security, have a detailed, meticulous plan and a strict, water tight process to achieve them. You must achieve your goals with determination, perseverance, and a strong work ethic to help you get the job done and your goals achieved. You struggle with lack of commitment, apathy, a weak will, lack of direction and laziness. Any or all of these will hinder your ability to build great things until you overcome them.

You are here to learn the importance of focus, stability, perseverance, and process. You must focus on the detail in any situation to ensure that nothing is missed, and no steps have been omitted or done incorrectly. This kind of deep focus demands great patience and perseverance which can be a struggle for you. You can be a little slap dash because of impatience, and you may give up easily when the going gets tough. Blaming other people for issues or past perceived injustices that you have not dealt with properly is not healthy for you. You need to look for the lessons in all your experiences to help you to move forward stronger. Bad, even horrific experience provides you with a huge opportunity to learn, develop and progress. It should not be an excuse for emotional limitation and victimhood that stops you from progressing. You may blame others for your short comings and impose limitations on yourself that will stop you in your tracks if you let them. You are here to channel ideas and get things done for the security, safety and stability of the team, family, and the world. You must ensure that goals and tasks are planned and executed with accuracy to keep the cogs turning and achieve goals behind the scenes.

You must develop towards and endeavour to always be reliable, good with routine, a steadfast collaborator of the universe and a true self explorer. For you, developing organisation skills is key for everything, as you aspire to collaborate, coach, and facilitate to achieve your goals. It is important that you harmonise your inner life with what you want before you try to control your environment. When you know who you are and what you want, you can be methodical. When you are methodical, you can achieve anything. You can be a real hard head, ignoring other suggestions and opinions but if you develop a little adaptability, let go of your rigidity, and collaborate clearly, you can really succeed.

Take care that you do not swing towards workaholism because you constantly worry that you do not have enough. You worry about lack, that nagging feeling that there might not be enough and that you could lose what you have built if you do not work hard enough. You worry too much because you focus too much on the negative, you are always saying, I do not have enough. Instead of focusing on what you do not have, focus on what you do have. You have the potential to set lofty, world changing goals, to plan, focus and take each step to achieve great success, slow and steady wins the race! When imbalanced, you can be uncommitted, lazy, dependent, and directionless to the point where you achieve nothing and make decisions that are not for your good. You can be set in your ways, controlling, unmovable and rigid, even if proved wrong. So, if things go wrong, you often stay rigid, blame everyone else and miss the lesson that you were meant to learn.

Life Path Master 22/4 with Birthday Number 2

Life Path Master 22/4 (90% Focus)	Birthday Number 2 (10% Focus)
You are an old soul, as spiritual as you are practical, here to channel and then manifest ideas in reality to build world safety, stability, and security. You must learn to handle the master builder energy and focus it to manifestation. You have a big responsibility to the team and the world to build structures (buildings, concepts, body, mind, spirit, businesses, organisations, even an empire for the purpose of world stability and security	You are here to learn to be responsible to others and the team. You can be too responsible and do too much. You are irresponsible if you feel undervalued and resentful
You must develop and improve your social skills, focus on widening and deepening your relationships to assist you to manifest your big ideas. It is important that you learn to deepen your relationships and connect 121, you cannot do this alone!	You must learn to improve your social skills, focus on widening and deepening your relationships and make decisions subjectively. It is important that you deepen your relationships and connect 121
You must learn to have balanced, healthy relationships with others that are part of your sense of security. You must learn not to smother your loved ones and your team or have expectations that can never be met. OR Your big task in this lifetime may disrupt your love relationships. You may back away from wanting love because it hurts too badly or attacks	You must learn not to smother your loved ones or have expectations that can never be met. OR you may back away from wanting love because it hurts too badly. You need to balance your intense need for love

your sense of security	
You are here to learn to listen to and follow your intuition. Intuition is needed for you to be sensitive to the needs of others. You are here to be of service to change the world, the development of intuition will aid you in this journey	You are here to learn to be intuitive and sensitive to the needs of others. You are here to be of service to others, the development of intuition will aid you in this journey
You are here to learn to be a cooperative team player to get the job done as part of a cohesive team. You may fail to communicate effectively with others. You can be a hard-headed and high handed at times.	You are here to learn to be a cooperative team player to get the job done as part of a cohesive team. You can be a disruptive, uncooperative drama queen.
You must develop the assertiveness to demand boundaries to being overworked, walked all over, taken advantage of, and/or taken for granted. You must also develop your ability to respect other people's boundaries and not be high handed.	You must develop the assertiveness to demand boundaries to being overworked, walked all over, taken advantage of, and/or taken for granted. You must not be a "shape shifter" who changes who you are in order to please others or keep the peace.
You are here to be of service to the world, the leader, the team, the task and be dependable. You can always be counted upon to keep the cogs turning behind the scenes	You are here to serve the leader, the team, the task and be dependable. You can always be counted upon to keep the cogs turning behind the scenes
You are extremely sensitive, and you hate and run away from conflict. But you are here to learn to be a tactful mediator, helping to resolve conflicts fairly and for the good of the team/family/group	You are here to be the tactful mediator of the team, helping to resolve conflicts fairly and for the good of the team. You hate conflict and often run and hide until it is over

You are here to learn to stay focused and plan the next steps after you have channelled a new idea & build a team to achieve it. The energy of the 22 needs to be the nurturer, the builder of ideas and teams.	You are here to learn to plan the next steps after the initial idea & build a team to achieve it. The energy of the two is the nurturer of ideas and a builder of teams
You must learn to give yourself your own kudos. Oftentimes you judge yourself on what everyone else says or thinks about you. You need to develop your internal compass and turn inward for validation, do what you think you should do	You must learn to give yourself your own kudos. Oftentimes you judge yourself on what everyone else says or thinks about you. You need to develop your internal compass and turn inward for validation, do what you think you should do
You are here to learn to commit to a person and/or place, so that you can put down roots and dig the foundations for security. You can be uncommitted and therefore unable to build stability and security	.
You are here to learn to set and achieve goals to take you on your journey towards inner and outer stability and security. Foundations, structures, families, and business empires are built 1 goal at a time.	
You are here to learn to plan, create a process and/or procedure to ensure the achievement of your goals and bring strength and stability to dynamic ideas. You can be directionless, lazy and block your own progression.	
You are here to develop deep meticulous focus on achieving stability, like a stable home, business or income and building your inner	

security. You can be scattered and miss steps in your impatience.

You are here to learn to be detail orientated, analytical, organised, and accurate to ensure your plans and processes are watertight. You can be disorganised, flaky and miss steps in your plan

Your master life path 22/4 means that you are an old soul and you have agreed to bring safety, stability, and security to the world. You innovate and build empires, organisations, and businesses. This involves hard work, detail focus, routine work, and tasks. You are here to develop a work ethic, to work hard and develop enjoyment of routine work and tasks

You are here to develop patient perseverance, so that every step in the process towards your goals for your stable foundation are taken. You are prone to impatience and corner cutting.

You are here to develop determination and the perseverance to keep going past obstacles to achieve your goals. You are prone to giving up at the first hurdle.

You are here to learn to come to terms with limitation — both the limitations that are externally imposed on you and the limitations that you impose upon yourself.

You are here to look at your wounded or problematic

relationships and work through the feelings of lack and pain they have brought to you. All experiences have lessons embedded within them	
Avoid social isolation by socialising regularly in familiar groups and with likeminded friends.	

Life Path Master 22/4 with Birthday Number 3

Life Path Master 22/4 (90% Focus)	Birthday Number 3 (10% Focus)
You are an old soul, as spiritual as you are practical, here to channel and then manifest ideas in reality to build world safety, stability, and security. You must learn to handle the master builder energy and focus it to manifestation. You have a big responsibility to the team and the world to build structures (buildings, concepts, body, mind, spirit, businesses, organisations, even an empire for the purpose of world stability and security	You are here to learn to express yourself verbally to inspire, inform and delight. You may struggle in some way verbally, chronic shyness, speech delay, stutter or struggling to find the words.
You must develop and improve your social skills, focus on widening and deepening your relationships to assist you to manifest your big ideas. It is important that you learn to deepen your relationships and connect 121, you cannot do this alone!	You are here to learn to express yourself creatively to inspire, inform and delight. But you may struggle to progress, execute, and finish creative projects, due to lack of self-belief
You must learn to have balanced, healthy relationships with others that are part of your sense of security. You must learn not to smother your loved ones and your team or have expectations that can never be met. OR Your big task in this lifetime may disrupt your love relationships. You may back away from wanting love because it hurts too badly or attacks	You must learn to be dynamic, take risks and be confident to enjoy the attention and limelight of an audience. You can be shy, under confident and feel unable to take risks.

your sense of security	
You are here to learn to listen to and follow your intuition. Intuition is needed for you to be sensitive to the needs of others. You are here to be of service to change the world, the development of intuition will aid you in this journey	You need to develop as an entrepreneur who is able to promote, network and make money creatively. But you may procrastinate and fail to stay focused and work inconsistently.
You are here to learn to be a cooperative team player to get the job done as part of a cohesive team. You may fail to communicate effectively with others. You can be a hard-headed and high handed at times.	You are here to learn to express your emotions positively. You can be extremely sensitive to criticism and other people's emotions, causing you to express emotions negatively
You must develop the assertiveness to demand boundaries to being overworked, walked all over, taken advantage of, and/or taken for granted. You must also develop your ability to respect other people's boundaries and not be high handed.	You are here to develop the habit of acting, be a doer and executer of ideas. When low, you can struggle with apathy, laziness and lack of focus and direction
You are here to be of service to the world, the leader, the team, the task and be dependable. You can always be counted upon to keep the cogs turning behind the scenes	You are here to learn to be social, talkative, the life of the party and bringer of fun & positivity. You need to be the networker, communicating an emotional message. You can be quiet and struggle to speak
You are extremely sensitive, and you hate and run away from conflict. But you are here to learn to be a tactful mediator, helping to resolve conflicts fairly and for the good of the team/family/group	You must develop interdependence, life path 3's like to be looked after and can be prone to avoiding work or anything needing routine and commitment

You are here to learn to stay focused and plan the next steps after you have channelled a new idea & build a team to achieve it. The energy of the 22 needs to be the nurturer, the builder of ideas and teams.

You are here to be opportunistic, to network, make useful connections and snap up opportunities to spread the word and progress ideas and projects

You must learn to give yourself your own kudos. Oftentimes you judge yourself on what everyone else says or thinks about you. You need to develop your internal compass and turn inward for validation, do what you think you should do

You must learn to take responsibility and listen to guidance; you can be irresponsible. You must think before you act, and take full responsibility for what you do

You are here to learn to commit to a person and/or place, so that you can put down roots and dig the foundations for security. You can be uncommitted and therefore unable to build stability and security

You are here to learn to set and achieve goals to take you on your journey towards inner and outer stability and security.

Foundations, structures, families, and business empires are built 1 goal at a time.

You are here to learn to plan, create a process and/or procedure to ensure the achievement of your goals and bring strength and stability to dynamic ideas. You can be directionless, lazy and block your own progression.

You are here to develop deep meticulous focus on achieving stability, like a stable home, business or income and building your inner

security. You can be scattered and miss steps in your impatience.

You are here to learn to be detail orientated, analytical, organised, and accurate to ensure your plans and processes are watertight. You can be disorganised, flaky and miss steps in your plan

Your master life path 22/4 means that you are an old soul and you have agreed to bring safety, stability, and security to the world. You innovate and build empires, organisations, and businesses. This involves hard work, detail focus, routine work, and tasks. You are here to develop a work ethic, to work hard and develop enjoyment of routine work and tasks

You are here to develop patient perseverance, so that every step in the process towards your goals for your stable foundation are taken. You are prone to impatience and corner cutting.

You are here to develop determination and the perseverance to keep going past obstacles to achieve your goals. You are prone to giving up at the first hurdle.

You are here to learn to come to terms with limitation — both the limitations that are externally imposed on you and the limitations that you impose upon yourself.

You are here to look at your wounded or problematic

relationships and work through the feelings of lack and pain they have brought to you. All experiences have lessons embedded within them	
Avoid social isolation by socialising regularly in familiar groups and with likeminded friends.	

Life Path Master 22/4 with Birthday Number 4

Life Path Master 22/4 (90% Focus)	Birthday Number 4 (10% Focus)
You are an old soul, as spiritual as you are practical, here to channel and then manifest ideas in reality to build world safety, stability, and security. You must learn to handle the master builder energy and focus it to manifestation. You have a big responsibility to the team and the world to build structures (buildings, concepts, body, mind, spirit, businesses, organisations, even an empire for the purpose of world stability and security	You are here to learn to commit to a person and/or place, so that you can put down roots and dig the foundations for security. You can be uncommitted and therefore unable to build stability and security.
You must develop and improve your social skills, focus on widening and deepening your relationships to assist you to manifest your big ideas. It is important that you learn to deepen your relationships and connect 121, you cannot do this alone!	You are here to learn to set and achieve goals to take you on your journey towards inner and outer stability and security. Foundations, structures, families, and business empires are built 1 goal at a time.
You must learn to have balanced, healthy relationships with others that are part of your sense of security. You must learn not to smother your loved ones and your team or have expectations that can never be met. OR Your big task in this lifetime may disrupt your love relationships. You may back away from wanting love because it hurts too badly or attacks	You are here to learn to plan, create a process and/or procedure to ensure the achievement of your goals. You can be directionless, lazy and block your own progression

your sense of security

You are here to learn to listen to and follow your intuition.

Intuition is needed for you to be sensitive to the needs of others.

You are here to be of service to change the world, the development of intuition will aid you in this journey

You are here to develop deep meticulous focus on achieving stability, like a stable home, business or income and building your inner security. You can be scattered

You are here to learn to be a cooperative team player to get the job done as part of a cohesive team.

You may fail to communicate effectively with others. You can be a hard-headed and high handed at times.

You are here to learn to be detail orientated, analytical, organised, and accurate to ensure your plans and processes are watertight. You can be disorganised and miss steps in the plan

You must develop the assertiveness to demand boundaries to being overworked, walked all over, taken advantage of, and/or taken for granted. You must also develop your ability to respect other people's boundaries and not be high handed.

You are here to develop a work ethic, to work hard and develop enjoyment of routine work and tasks. When low you can be lazy and stuck in 1 place, without progression

You are here to be of service to the world, the leader, the team, the task and be dependable.

You can always be counted upon to keep the cogs turning behind the scenes

You are here to develop patient perseverance, so that every step in the process towards your goals for your stable foundation are taken. You are prone to impatience and missing steps

You are extremely sensitive, and you hate and run away from conflict.

But you are here to learn to be a tactful mediator, helping to resolve conflicts fairly and for the good of the team/family/group

You are here to learn to come to terms with limitation — both the limitations that are externally imposed on you and the limitations that you impose upon yourself.

You are here to learn to stay focused and plan the next steps after you have channelled a new idea & build a team to achieve it. The energy of the 22 needs to be the nurturer, the builder of ideas and teams.	You are here to look at your wounded or problematic relationships and work through the feelings of lack and pain they have brought to you.
You must learn to give yourself your own kudos. Oftentimes you judge yourself on what everyone else says or thinks about you. You need to develop your internal compass and turn inward for validation, do what you think you should do	You are prone to choosing social isolation, avoiding social situations due to social anxiety. It is important that you socialise regularly in familiar groups and with likeminded friends.
You are here to learn to commit to a person and/or place, so that you can put down roots and dig the foundations for security. You can be uncommitted and therefore unable to build stability and security	
You are here to learn to set and achieve goals to take you on your journey towards inner and outer stability and security. Foundations, structures, families, and business empires are built 1 goal at a time.	
You are here to learn to plan, create a process and/or procedure to ensure the achievement of your goals and bring strength and stability to dynamic ideas. You can be directionless, lazy and block your own progression.	
You are here to develop deep meticulous focus on achieving stability, like a stable home, business or income and building your inner	

security. You can be scattered and miss steps in your impatience.

You are here to learn to be detail orientated, analytical, organised, and accurate to ensure your plans and processes are watertight. You can be disorganised, flaky and miss steps in your plan

Your master life path 22/4 means that you are an old soul and you have agreed to bring safety, stability, and security to the world. You innovate and build empires, organisations, and businesses. This involves hard work, detail focus, routine work, and tasks. You are here to develop a work ethic, to work hard and develop enjoyment of routine work and tasks

You are here to develop patient perseverance, so that every step in the process towards your goals for your stable foundation are taken. You are prone to impatience and corner cutting.

You are here to develop determination and the perseverance to keep going past obstacles to achieve your goals. You are prone to giving up at the first hurdle.

You are here to learn to come to terms with limitation — both the limitations that are externally imposed on you and the limitations that you impose upon yourself.

You are here to look at your wounded or problematic

relationships and work through the feelings of lack and pain they have brought to you. All experiences have lessons embedded within them	
Avoid social isolation by socialising regularly in familiar groups and with likeminded friends.	

Life Path Master 22/4 with Birthday Number 5

Life Path Master 22/4 (90% Focus)	Birthday Number 5 (10% Focus)
You are an old soul, as spiritual as you are practical, here to channel and then manifest ideas in reality to build world safety, stability, and security.	You are easily bored and want to look at or study lots of topics. Initial varied experience is needed in order to choose a specialism, you are here to learn to be disciplined, to continue with a topic or activity beyond the boredom of the detail, towards mastery and specialism.
You must learn to handle the master builder energy and focus it to manifestation.	
You have a big responsibility to the team and the world to build structures (buildings, concepts, body, mind, spirit, businesses, organisations, even an empire for the purpose of world stability and security	
You must develop and improve your social skills, focus on widening and deepening your relationships to assist you to manifest your big ideas. It is important that you learn to deepen your relationships and connect 121, you cannot do this alone!	You are here to develop the ability to balance variety, change and adventure with the stability of family and skill mastery. You can be totally spontaneous and take risks, jumping from one experience to another, but never settling or progressing
You must learn to have balanced, healthy relationships with others that are part of your sense of security. You must learn not to smother your loved ones and your team or have expectations that can never be met.	You need to learn to be extremely intuitive and access your intuitive wisdom when making decisions, assessing people and situations.
OR Your big task in this lifetime may disrupt your love relationships. You may back away from wanting love because it hurts too badly or attacks	

your sense of security	
You are here to learn to listen to and follow your intuition. Intuition is needed for you to be sensitive to the needs of others. You are here to be of service to change the world, the development of intuition will aid you in this journey	You are here to develop your ability to attain inner freedom and outer freedom by doing things you might not want to do. Doing what you want is not necessarily freedom, you can become a slave to your desires. Freedom and discipline are inherently linked.
You are here to learn to be a cooperative team player to get the job done as part of a cohesive team. You may fail to communicate effectively with others. You can be a hard-headed and high handed at times.	You are here to learn to develop your verbal and written communication skills towards charismatic sharing of ideas and stories related to your specialism. You have the potential to be a great communicator
You must develop the assertiveness to demand boundaries to being overworked, walked all over, taken advantage of, and/or taken for granted. You must also develop your ability to respect other people's boundaries and not be high handed.	You are here to learn to be committed, dependable, to do what you say you are going to do. You often forget what you promise because you are so chaotic, scattered, and changeable, looking for the next new experience
You are here to be of service to the world, the leader, the team, the task and be dependable. You can always be counted upon to keep the cogs turning behind the scenes	You are here to develop your social skills and charisma, to have the potential to be fun loving, positive, and optimistic. You can be uptight and argumentative
You are extremely sensitive, and you hate and run away from conflict. But you are here to learn to be a tactful mediator, helping to resolve conflicts fairly and for the good of the team/family/group	You are here to develop consistent independence. You can swing from independence to dependence and back again. Risky behaviour and 'get rich quick' schemes can bring on dependence

You are here to learn to stay focused and plan the next steps after you have channelled a new idea & build a team to achieve it. The energy of the 22 needs to be the nurturer, the builder of ideas and teams.

You must learn to give yourself your own kudos. Oftentimes you judge yourself on what everyone else says or thinks about you. You need to develop your internal compass and turn inward for validation, do what you think you should do

You are here to learn to commit to a person and/or place, so that you can put down roots and dig the foundations for security. You can be uncommitted and therefore unable to build stability and security

You are here to learn to set and achieve goals to take you on your journey towards inner and outer stability and security.

Foundations, structures, families, and business empires are built 1 goal at a time.

You are here to learn to plan, create a process and/or procedure to ensure the achievement of your goals and bring strength and stability to dynamic ideas. You can be directionless, lazy and block your own progression.

You are here to develop deep meticulous focus on achieving stability, like a stable home, business

You are here to learn to develop fearlessness and help others to live fearlessly. You can be fearful of many things, restriction, and boredom, to name but a few. You need to challenge yourself and others past your own comfort zone

You are here to learn to make good use of your energy and drive, if you feel restricted and under confident, you will be restless, and you may turn into a drama queen. Use your energy for experience and adventure, be courageous

or income and building your inner security. You can be scattered and miss steps in your impatience.	
You are here to learn to be detail orientated, analytical, organised, and accurate to ensure your plans and processes are watertight. You can be disorganised, flaky and miss steps in your plan	
Your master life path 22/4 means that you are an old soul and you have agreed to bring safety, stability, and security to the world. You innovate and build empires, organisations, and businesses. This involves hard work, detail focus, routine work, and tasks. You are here to develop a work ethic, to work hard and develop enjoyment of routine work and tasks	
You are here to develop patient perseverance, so that every step in the process towards your goals for your stable foundation are taken. You are prone to impatience and corner cutting.	
You are here to develop determination and the perseverance to keep going past obstacles to achieve your goals. You are prone to giving up at the first hurdle.	
You are here to learn to come to terms with limitation — both the limitations that are externally imposed on you and the limitations that you impose upon yourself.	
You are here to look at your	

wounded or problematic relationships and work through the feelings of lack and pain they have brought to you. All experiences have lessons embedded within them	
Avoid social isolation by socialising regularly in familiar groups and with likeminded friends.	

Life Path Master 22/4 with Birthday Number 6

Life Path Master 22/4 (90% Focus)	Birthday Number 6 (10% Focus)
You are an old soul, as spiritual as you are practical, here to channel and then manifest ideas in reality to build world safety, stability, and security. You must learn to handle the master builder energy and focus it to manifestation. You have a big responsibility to the team and the world to build structures (buildings, concepts, body, mind, spirit, businesses, organisations, even an empire for the purpose of world stability and security	You are here to be a visionary of the ideal, the dreamer of a utopian world. You must act to create a better world with your ideals.
You must develop and improve your social skills, focus on widening and deepening your relationships to assist you to manifest your big ideas. It is important that you learn to deepen your relationships and connect 121, you cannot do this alone!	You are here to learn to not use your ideals as a benchmark for your happiness. You must not base your emotional wellbeing on the achievement of your ideals. You often judge yourself and others for not hitting perfection, causing you great unhappiness
You must learn to have balanced, healthy relationships with others that are part of your sense of security. You must learn not to smother your loved ones and your team or have expectations that can never be met. OR Your big task in this lifetime may disrupt your love relationships. You may back away from wanting love because it hurts too badly or attacks	Your perfectionism can make you an over achiever due to your constant self-judgement. You never meet your own standards. You must keep your big picture in mind and not get stuck in petty detail. You can often judge small imperfections and ruin or miss your successes.

your sense of security

You are here to learn to listen to and follow your intuition.

Intuition is needed for you to be sensitive to the needs of others.

You are here to be of service to change the world, the development of intuition will aid you in this journey

You are here to learn to be a cooperative team player to get the job done as part of a cohesive team.

You may fail to communicate effectively with others. You can be a hard-headed and high handed at times.

You must develop the assertiveness to demand boundaries to being overworked, walked all over, taken advantage of, and/or taken for granted. You must also develop your ability to respect other people's boundaries and not be high handed.

You are here to be of service to the world, the leader, the team, the task and be dependable.

You can always be counted upon to keep the cogs turning behind the scenes

You are extremely sensitive, and you hate and run away from conflict.

But you are here to learn to be a tactful mediator, helping to resolve conflicts fairly and for the good of

You are here to learn to be a nurturer, compassionate caring and giving, especially to those that are vulnerable or struggling within your close relationships, your community, and the wider world. Your judgemental nature can make you cruel and neglectful.

You are here to develop boundaries to ensure your mental and physical health. You do a lot for others, sometimes too much, which can make you feel undervalued, unappreciated, and ill with exhaustion. You may force unsolicited advice and meddle in other people's affairs.

You are here to develop your social skills and be a team player. You must break through low self-esteem to be talkative, fun loving and relaxed around others. You can be shy and hide in the background.

You are here to create a stable, nurturing, tranquil home to maintain your security and well-being. Then nurture a family in an environment of stability and love. When low you can be a selfish, neglectful drama queen.

You are here to learn to be responsible and do good for those you care for. People naturally put you in positions of responsibility, but you often resent always being

the team/family/group	the 'responsible one.' Have boundaries on your responsibility so that you do not do too much.
You are here to learn to stay focused and plan the next steps after you have channelled a new idea & build a team to achieve it. The energy of the 22 needs to be the nurturer, the builder of ideas and teams.	You are here to learn to develop and use your artistic and aesthetic potential. Artistic, enhancing make up, great art and home designs. You have great musical potential that you may not develop.
You must learn to give yourself your own kudos. Oftentimes you judge yourself on what everyone else says or thinks about you. You need to develop your internal compass and turn inward for validation, do what you think you should do	
You are here to learn to commit to a person and/or place, so that you can put down roots and dig the foundations for security. You can be uncommitted and therefore unable to build stability and security	
You are here to learn to set and achieve goals to take you on your journey towards inner and outer stability and security. Foundations, structures, families, and business empires are built 1 goal at a time.	
You are here to learn to plan, create a process and/or procedure to ensure the achievement of your goals and bring strength and stability to dynamic ideas. You can be directionless, lazy and block your own progression.	

You are here to develop deep meticulous focus on achieving stability, like a stable home, business or income and building your inner security. You can be scattered and miss steps in your impatience.

You are here to learn to be detail orientated, analytical, organised, and accurate to ensure your plans and processes are watertight. You can be disorganised, flaky and miss steps in your plan

Your master life path 22/4 means that you are an old soul and you have agreed to bring safety, stability, and security to the world. You innovate and build empires, organisations, and businesses. This involves hard work, detail focus, routine work, and tasks. You are here to develop a work ethic, to work hard and develop enjoyment of routine work and tasks

You are here to develop patient perseverance, so that every step in the process towards your goals for your stable foundation are taken. You are prone to impatience and corner cutting.

You are here to develop determination and the perseverance to keep going past obstacles to achieve your goals. You are prone to giving up at the first hurdle.

You are here to learn to come to terms with limitation — both the limitations that are externally

imposed on you and the limitations that you impose upon yourself.	
You are here to look at your wounded or problematic relationships and work through the feelings of lack and pain they have brought to you. All experiences have lessons embedded within them	
Avoid social isolation by socialising regularly in familiar groups and with likeminded friends.	

Life Path Master 22/4 with Birthday Number 7

Life Path Master 22/4 (90% Focus)	Birthday Number 7 (10% Focus)
You are an old soul, as spiritual as you are practical, here to channel and then manifest ideas in reality to build world safety, stability, and security. You must learn to handle the master builder energy and focus it to manifestation. You have a big responsibility to the team and the world to build structures (buildings, concepts, body, mind, spirit, businesses, organisations, even an empire for the purpose of world stability and security	You are here to learn to have faith that you are an immortal soul that has experience from previous lives. You must trust the soul within you by listening to and following your intuition without over thinking and applying logic. Listen to and follow your inner voice and feel safe enough to communicate your soul wisdom to the world without fear of ridicule.
You must develop and improve your social skills, focus on widening and deepening your relationships to assist you to manifest your big ideas. It is important that you learn to deepen your relationships and connect 121, you cannot do this alone!	You are here to trust that the world is not against you. The universe is everything existing in perfect balance, it is like a cosmic library of all knowledge and experience. We must experience it all to learn and evolve
You must learn to have balanced, healthy relationships with others that are part of your sense of security. You must learn not to smother your loved ones and your team or have expectations that can never be met. OR Your big task in this lifetime may disrupt your love relationships. You may back away from wanting love because it hurts too badly or attacks	Your focus for this lifetime must be Inner development rather than outer development and success. You must develop yourself constantly with self-discovery and spiritual wisdom. Meditation and time in nature is imperative for you

your sense of security	
You are here to learn to listen to and follow your intuition. Intuition is needed for you to be sensitive to the needs of others. You are here to be of service to change the world, the development of intuition will aid you in this journey	You are here to learn to be a problem solver, thinker, a studier of the metaphysical and the big questions. You need to research, learn, and analyse theories to accrue wisdom.
You are here to learn to be a cooperative team player to get the job done as part of a cohesive team. You may fail to communicate effectively with others. You can be a hard-headed and high handed at times.	You are here to learn to filter your research through your intuition and use your research of other people's theories for your own needs. You can be too analytical and ignore your intuition. Or totally spiritual and ignore other theories. You must balance the two.
You must develop the assertiveness to demand boundaries to being overworked, walked all over, taken advantage of, and/or taken for granted. You must also develop your ability to respect other people's boundaries and not be high handed.	You are here to be a free thinker, to be less interested in popular culture and following norms of fashion and appearance. This can make you feel different and out of place and lonely
You are here to be of service to the world, the leader, the team, the task and be dependable. You can always be counted upon to keep the cogs turning behind the scenes	You are here to develop the ability to focus on something long enough to develop it into something useful. You can be a little scattered and struggle to focus
You are extremely sensitive, and you hate and run away from conflict. But you are here to learn to be a tactful mediator, helping to resolve conflicts fairly and for the good of the team/family/group	You are here to develop interdependence, self-sufficiency but also a healthy dependence on other people. You like to do things for yourself but take care not to push others away

You are here to learn to stay focused and plan the next steps after you have channelled a new idea & build a team to achieve it. The energy of the 22 needs to be the nurturer, the builder of ideas and teams.

You are here to learn to deal with and reconcile your sensitive emotions. Others often think you are aloof, but you are a well of deep emotions. You need to connect emotionally, both to yourself and to other people

You must learn to give yourself your own kudos. Oftentimes you judge yourself on what everyone else says or thinks about you. You need to develop your internal compass and turn inward for validation, do what you think you should do

You are here to learn to balance your need to be alone and work alone with social contact. You love to be alone, but you must ensure that you do not isolate yourself beyond what is healthy

You are here to learn to commit to a person and/or place, so that you can put down roots and dig the foundations for security. You can be uncommitted and therefore unable to build stability and security

You are here to learn to set and achieve goals to take you on your journey towards inner and outer stability and security.

Foundations, structures, families, and business empires are built 1 goal at a time.

You are here to learn to plan, create a process and/or procedure to ensure the achievement of your goals and bring strength and stability to dynamic ideas. You can be directionless, lazy and block your own progression.

You are here to develop deep meticulous focus on achieving stability, like a stable home, business

or income and building your inner security. You can be scattered and miss steps in your impatience.	
You are here to learn to be detail orientated, analytical, organised, and accurate to ensure your plans and processes are watertight. You can be disorganised, flaky and miss steps in your plan	
Your master life path 22/4 means that you are an old soul and you have agreed to bring safety, stability, and security to the world. You innovate and build empires, organisations, and businesses. This involves hard work, detail focus, routine work, and tasks. You are here to develop a work ethic, to work hard and develop enjoyment of routine work and tasks	
You are here to develop patient perseverance, so that every step in the process towards your goals for your stable foundation are taken. You are prone to impatience and corner cutting.	
You are here to develop determination and the perseverance to keep going past obstacles to achieve your goals. You are prone to giving up at the first hurdle.	
You are here to learn to come to terms with limitation — both the limitations that are externally imposed on you and the limitations that you impose upon yourself.	
You are here to look at your	

wounded or problematic relationships and work through the feelings of lack and pain they have brought to you. All experiences have lessons embedded within them	
Avoid social isolation by socialising regularly in familiar groups and with likeminded friends.	

Life Path Master 22/4 with Birthday Number 8

Life Path Master 22/4 (90% Focus)	Birthday Number 8 (10% Focus)
You are an old soul, as spiritual as you are practical, here to channel and then manifest ideas in reality to build world safety, stability, and security. You must learn to handle the master builder energy and focus it to manifestation. You have a big responsibility to the team and the world to build structures (buildings, concepts, body, mind, spirit, businesses, organisations, even an empire for the purpose of world stability and security	You are both spiritual and worldly. But you are here to learn the secrets of worldly financial success. You seek the freedom that comes from financial success. But freedom brings responsibility, your ethics will be tested multiple times.
You must develop and improve your social skills, focus on widening and deepening your relationships to assist you to manifest your big ideas. It is important that you learn to deepen your relationships and connect 121, you cannot do this alone!	You are here to learn to use your financial success as a tool to help others achieve the same financial success. You often spend your abundance on materialistic status symbols rather than helping others
You must learn to have balanced, healthy relationships with others that are part of your sense of security. You must learn not to smother your loved ones and your team or have expectations that can never be met. OR Your big task in this lifetime may disrupt your love relationships. You may back away from wanting love because it hurts too badly or attacks	You are here to develop a healthy attitude towards money. You may resent or hate wealthy people, or you may feel guilty about your own wealth. You must understand that financial wealth does not equate to poor ethics

your sense of security

You are here to learn to listen to and follow your intuition.

Intuition is needed for you to be sensitive to the needs of others.

You are here to be of service to change the world, the development of intuition will aid you in this journey

You are here to learn to be a cooperative team player to get the job done as part of a cohesive team.

You may fail to communicate effectively with others. You can be a hard-headed and high handed at times.

You must develop the assertiveness to demand boundaries to being overworked, walked all over, taken advantage of, and/or taken for granted. You must also develop your ability to respect other people's boundaries and not be high handed.

You are here to be of service to the world, the leader, the team, the task and be dependable.

You can always be counted upon to keep the cogs turning behind the scenes

You are extremely sensitive, and you hate and run away from conflict.

But you are here to learn to be a tactful mediator, helping to resolve conflicts fairly and for the good of the team/family/group

You are here to develop balanced determination for achievement but with integrity and for the good of others. You can be either obsessed with achievement or fearful of achievement from low self-esteem. It is important that you develop a positive mindset because you attract what you think about.

You are here to develop inner confidence and balanced personal power. You can swing from over dominance or misuse of power to hiding away or submission to others

You are here to develop skilled leadership, which consists of subject competence coupled with excellent social skills and charisma

You are here to work hard as an excellent practical businessperson, but you must ensure that you do not work too hard, you need time out and time for your family

You are here to be worldly, strong, resilient, disciplined, and realistic. To be successful you need to be strong, tough, and able to cope with

The ups and downs of the world

You are here to learn to stay focused and plan the next steps after you have channelled a new idea & build a team to achieve it. The energy of the 22 needs to be the nurturer, the builder of ideas and teams.	You are here to develop bravery and the courage to take risks to progress. Success comes from having the bravery to take risks
You must learn to give yourself your own kudos. Oftentimes you judge yourself on what everyone else says or thinks about you. You need to develop your internal compass and turn inward for validation, do what you think you should do	You are here to develop organisation and management skills, resolve to making things happen and to define and meet your goals.
You are here to learn to commit to a person and/or place, so that you can put down roots and dig the foundations for security. You can be uncommitted and therefore unable to build stability and security	
You are here to learn to set and achieve goals to take you on your journey towards inner and outer stability and security. Foundations, structures, families, and business empires are built 1 goal at a time.	
You are here to learn to plan, create a process and/or procedure to ensure the achievement of your goals and bring strength and stability to dynamic ideas. You can be directionless, lazy and block your own progression.	
You are here to develop deep meticulous focus on achieving stability, like a stable home, business or income and building your inner	

security. You can be scattered and miss steps in your impatience.	
You are here to learn to be detail orientated, analytical, organised, and accurate to ensure your plans and processes are watertight. You can be disorganised, flaky and miss steps in your plan	
Your master life path 22/4 means that you are an old soul and you have agreed to bring safety, stability, and security to the world. You innovate and build empires, organisations, and businesses. This involves hard work, detail focus, routine work, and tasks. You are here to develop a work ethic, to work hard and develop enjoyment of routine work and tasks	
You are here to develop patient perseverance, so that every step in the process towards your goals for your stable foundation are taken. You are prone to impatience and corner cutting.	
You are here to develop determination and the perseverance to keep going past obstacles to achieve your goals. You are prone to giving up at the first hurdle.	
You are here to learn to come to terms with limitation — both the limitations that are externally imposed on you and the limitations that you impose upon yourself.	
You are here to look at your wounded or problematic	

relationships and work through the feelings of lack and pain they have brought to you. All experiences have lessons embedded within them	
Avoid social isolation by socialising regularly in familiar groups and with likeminded friends.	

Life Path Master 22/4 with Birthday Number 9

Life Path Master 22/4 (90% Focus)	Birthday Number 9 (10% Focus)
You are an old soul, as spiritual as you are practical, here to channel and then manifest ideas in reality to build world safety, stability, and security.	You are here to learn to follow your intuitive wisdom and live to spiritual laws, rather than worldly laws, conventions, and ideals. You tend to follow worldly laws and prejudices as an excuse for your actions. But if you had followed your intuitive spiritual wisdom, you would not have acted that way. Focus on faith over logic
You must learn to handle the master builder energy and focus it to manifestation.	
You have a big responsibility to the team and the world to build structures (buildings, concepts, body, mind, spirit, businesses, organisations, even an empire for the purpose of world stability and security	
You must develop and improve your social skills, focus on widening and deepening your relationships to assist you to manifest your big ideas. It is important that you learn to deepen your relationships and connect 121, you cannot do this alone!	You are here to learn to act with integrity for the benefit of others. You are powerful and you must use your power for the benefit of others. You can act for selfish or nefarious reasons
You must learn to have balanced, healthy relationships with others that are part of your sense of security. You must learn not to smother your loved ones and your team or have expectations that can never be met.	You are here to learn to lead by example, do you practise what you preach? You can be quite domineering, an adviser with all the answers. But you must let others make their own mistakes
OR Your big task in this lifetime may disrupt your love relationships. You may back away from wanting love because it hurts too badly or attacks	

your sense of security	
You are here to learn to listen to and follow your intuition. Intuition is needed for you to be sensitive to the needs of others. You are here to be of service to change the world, the development of intuition will aid you in this journey	You are here to make your life your teaching, you need to counsel with wisdom. You are a developed soul, the totality of all the numbers, full of cellular experience and higher knowledge
You are here to learn to be a cooperative team player to get the job done as part of a cohesive team. You may fail to communicate effectively with others. You can be a hard-headed and high handed at times.	You are here to develop broad mindedness, meet and accept diverse people. You must learn to be a humanitarian and make the world a better place. You need a global consciousness, as you can be narrow minded, judgemental, and even bigoted.
You must develop the assertiveness to demand boundaries to being overworked, walked all over, taken advantage of, and/or taken for granted. You must also develop your ability to respect other people's boundaries and not be high handed.	You are here to learn to take responsibility for your powerful choices. You sometimes run away from the consequences of your actions
You are here to be of service to the world, the leader, the team, the task and be dependable. You can always be counted upon to keep the cogs turning behind the scenes	You need to develop towards being a successful entrepreneur or businessperson if it is with something you feel passionate about. You must choose work that has meaning for you. You are a powerful force for change
You are extremely sensitive, and you hate and run away from conflict. But you are here to learn to be a tactful mediator, helping to resolve conflicts fairly and for the good of	You are here to develop excellent social skills and charisma. You could develop the skills of a powerful speaker and influencer of others. People will hang on your every word

the team/family/group

You are here to learn to stay focused and plan the next steps after you have channelled a new idea & build a team to achieve it. The energy of the 22 needs to be the nurturer, the builder of ideas and teams.

You are here to look after the wellbeing of others. But when you are in trouble or need support, people do not notice. You must ask for what you need, you must ask for help

You must learn to give yourself your own kudos. Oftentimes you judge yourself on what everyone else says or thinks about you. You need to develop your internal compass and turn inward for validation, do what you think you should do

You are here to wrap things up, let go and surrender. You can have a victim mentality, holding onto feelings that no longer serve you, unable to move on from perceived injustice, normally rooted in family issues.

You are here to learn to commit to a person and/or place, so that you can put down roots and dig the foundations for security. You can be uncommitted and therefore unable to build stability and security

You are here to learn to set and achieve goals to take you on your journey towards inner and outer stability and security.

Foundations, structures, families, and business empires are built 1 goal at a time.

You are here to learn to plan, create a process and/or procedure to ensure the achievement of your goals and bring strength and stability to dynamic ideas. You can be directionless, lazy and block your own progression.

You are here to develop deep meticulous focus on achieving stability, like a stable home, business

or income and building your inner security. You can be scattered and miss steps in your impatience.	
You are here to learn to be detail orientated, analytical, organised, and accurate to ensure your plans and processes are watertight. You can be disorganised, flaky and miss steps in your plan	
Your master life path 22/4 means that you are an old soul and you have agreed to bring safety, stability, and security to the world. You innovate and build empires, organisations, and businesses. This involves hard work, detail focus, routine work, and tasks. You are here to develop a work ethic, to work hard and develop enjoyment of routine work and tasks	
You are here to develop patient perseverance, so that every step in the process towards your goals for your stable foundation are taken. You are prone to impatience and corner cutting.	
You are here to develop determination and the perseverance to keep going past obstacles to achieve your goals. You are prone to giving up at the first hurdle.	
You are here to learn to come to terms with limitation — both the limitations that are externally imposed on you and the limitations that you impose upon yourself.	
You are here to look at your	

wounded or problematic relationships and work through the feelings of lack and pain they have brought to you. All experiences have lessons embedded within them	
Avoid social isolation by socialising regularly in familiar groups and with likeminded friends.	

Life Path Master 22/4 with Birthday Master 11

Life Path Master 22/4 (90% Focus)	Birthday Master 11 (10% Focus)
You are an old soul, as spiritual as you are practical, here to channel and then manifest ideas in reality to build world safety, stability, and security. You must learn to handle the master builder energy and focus it to manifestation. You have a big responsibility to the team and the world to build structures (buildings, concepts, body, mind, spirit, businesses, organisations, even an empire for the purpose of world stability and security	You are an old soul, with higher potential and higher responsibility to improve the world. You are here to learn to connect to source energy to channel unique new ideas and messages to change the world. You are here to learn to be happy in the limelight expressing new ideas for an audience. You need to develop and trust your massive intuitive potential. You often hide your ideas due to low confidence
You must develop and improve your social skills, focus on widening and deepening your relationships to assist you to manifest your big ideas. It is important that you learn to deepen your relationships and connect 121, you cannot do this alone!	You are here to learn to be the ideas person, but you struggle to bring your unique ideas to reality because you lose interest quickly after the initial idea of sabotage yourself due to crippling low confidence. You are an idealistic dreamer whose ideas are often not grounded in reality
You must learn to have balanced, healthy relationships with others that are part of your sense of security. You must learn not to smother your loved ones and your team or have expectations that can never be met. OR Your big task in this lifetime may disrupt your love relationships. You may back away from wanting love because it hurts too badly or attacks	You are here to learn to be confident in your uniqueness because unique people have unique ground-breaking ideas. It is important that you are not craving validation from others. Your validation should come from your intuition.

your sense of security

You are here to learn to listen to and follow your intuition.

Intuition is needed for you to be sensitive to the needs of others.

You are here to be of service to change the world, the development of intuition will aid you in this journey

You need to bring unique, new ideas that break barriers, or challenge others comfort zone. You must learn to be brave, confident and be willing to take risks

You are here to learn to be a cooperative team player to get the job done as part of a cohesive team.

You may fail to communicate effectively with others. You can be a hard-headed and high handed at times.

You need to be a practical initiator, a doer, action orientated that learns by experience. Ideas will stay unmanifested until you act!

Only action brings change

You must develop the assertiveness to demand boundaries to being overworked, walked all over, taken advantage of, and/or taken for granted. You must also develop your ability to respect other people's boundaries and not be high handed.

You need to set intentions then use spiritual practice and visualisation to channel your advanced, intense master energy into initiation and action. Unchanneled or mismanaged energy can cause intense nervous energy and anxiety. You may medicate these with unhealthy substances.

You are here to be of service to the world, the leader, the team, the task and be dependable.

You can always be counted upon to keep the cogs turning behind the scenes

You are here to learn to be interdependent, not so independent that you push others away and refuse to delegate. You cannot do everything alone. Independence is an illusion; we are all interconnected

You are extremely sensitive, and you hate and run away from conflict.

But you are here to learn to be a tactful mediator, helping to resolve conflicts fairly and for the good of

You need to be determined to succeed. Constant self-discovery and intuitive spiritual development is key for you to develop complete trust in the skills you have learned and

the team/family/group	mastered to serve as a kind of "security blanket" for you when you are feeling insecure
You are here to learn to stay focused and plan the next steps after you have channelled a new idea & build a team to achieve it. The energy of the 22 needs to be the nurturer, the builder of ideas and teams.	You need to learn to be a supportive, nurturing leader, be firm and assertive but also empathic and supportive. You must lead others to the fruition of your ideas, but with balanced personal power
You must learn to give yourself your own kudos. Oftentimes you judge yourself on what everyone else says or thinks about you. You need to develop your internal compass and turn inward for validation, do what you think you should do	Your power causes ripples, both positive and negative, you must remember that great power brings great responsibility. You must ensure that your intentions are good
You are here to learn to commit to a person and/or place, so that you can put down roots and dig the foundations for security. You can be uncommitted and therefore unable to build stability and security	You are here to learn to be responsible to others, your family, team, or group but in a balanced way. You can be too responsible and do too much. You are irresponsible if you feel undervalued, resentful, and exhausted.
You are here to learn to set and achieve goals to take you on your journey towards inner and outer stability and security. Foundations, structures, families, and business empires are built 1 goal at a time.	You must develop and improve your social skills, focus on widening and deepening your relationships and make decisions subjectively. It is important that you deepen your relationships and connect 121 You may struggle to maintain long term close and romantic relationships.
You are here to learn to plan, create a process and/or procedure to ensure the achievement of your goals and bring strength and stability to dynamic ideas. You can be	You must learn not to smother your loved ones or have expectations that can never be met. OR back away from wanting love because it hurts too badly. You need to balance your

directionless, lazy and block your own progression.

You are here to develop deep meticulous focus on achieving stability, like a stable home, business or income and building your inner security. You can be scattered and miss steps in your impatience.

You are here to learn to be detail orientated, analytical, organised, and accurate to ensure your plans and processes are watertight. You can be disorganised, flaky and miss steps in your plan

Your master life path 22/4 means that you are an old soul and you have agreed to bring safety, stability, and security to the world. You innovate and build empires, organisations, and businesses. This involves hard work, detail focus, routine work, and tasks. You are here to develop a work ethic, to work hard and develop enjoyment of routine work and tasks

You are here to develop patient perseverance, so that every step in the process towards your goals for your stable foundation are taken. You are prone to impatience and corner cutting.

You are here to develop determination and the perseverance to keep going past obstacles to achieve your goals. You are prone to giving up at the first hurdle.

intense need for love for healthy relationships.

You are here to learn to be intuitive and sensitive to the needs of others. You are here to be of service to others, the development of intuition will aid you in this journey

You are here to learn to be a cooperative team player to get the job done as part of a cohesive team. You can be a disruptive, uncooperative drama queen.

You must develop the assertiveness to demand boundaries to being overworked, walked all over, taken advantage of, and/or taken for granted. You must not be a "shape shifter" who changes who you are in order to please others or keep the peace. Be you and consider yourself too.

You are here to serve the world, help the team, the task and be dependable. You can always be relied upon to keep the cogs turning behind the scenes

You are here to be the tactful mediator of the team/group/family, helping to resolve conflicts fairly and for the good of everyone involved. You hate conflict and often run and hide until it is over

You are here to learn to come to terms with limitation — both the limitations that are externally imposed on you and the limitations that you impose upon yourself.	You are here to learn to plan the next steps after channelling your message or idea & build a team to achieve it. The energy of the 11/2 needs to be the nurturer of ideas and a builder of teams
You are here to look at your wounded or problematic relationships and work through the feelings of lack and pain they have brought to you. All experiences have lessons embedded within them	You must learn to give yourself your own kudos. Oftentimes you judge yourself on what everyone else says or thinks about you. You need to develop your internal compass and turn inward for validation, do what YOU think you should do
Avoid social isolation by socialising regularly in familiar groups and with likeminded friends.	

Your Life Path Number Master Thirty Three (33)

You have chosen to incarnate to learn the lessons of the master 33/6 life path energy because when speaking to your spirit guide before this life, you highlighted that you needed to learn the lessons of the energy of the master communicator energy. You are here to learn to utilise your emotional sensitivity to bring positive verbal and creative self-expression to the world to inspire, heal, nurture, and change the world.

You need to confront issues of blocked, distorted expression from emotional over sensitivity. You must also reconcile your visions of utopian ideals with practical reality and stop using your ideals to sabotage your happiness and inner peace.

At your highest vibration, you are filled with child like fun, a thrill seeker who loves novelty, new experience, and excitement. You may be involved with extreme sports or other exciting, activities. At your best you are energetic, independent, talkative, sure of yourself, optimistic and determined. Your potential for excellent, emotional verbal communication gives you the potential to be an entertainer. Confidence in your expression means that you could speak, act, or sing publicly and use carefully chosen words, spoken from the heart with the power to move people to tears or laughter and inspire action that could change the world in big or small ways. You have learned the power of positive authentic emotional expression combined with compassion, sensitivity, passion, and love, moving others to joy and inspiration. You express your feelings and needs directly and appropriately, explore self-expression like music, art, dance, acting or physical activity, confronting and moving through self-doubt.

When you are developing well on your path, you are becoming more social, friendly, outgoing, reliable, trustworthy, caring and an excellent team player. You love home, family, community, and you must keep in close contact with those close. You like home decoration and impressing others with your beautiful things. You are a practical visionary, pointing the way to an ideal world. You do this very effectively because you have accepted yourself, others, and the world as they are now, applying more realism as a pragmatic idealist. You have realised that it is who you are that matters, not how well you do or what you know. You will have released judgements that follow ideals and help all of us see our own perfection, while realising and pointing out, how problems are actually opportunities for development.

Your challenges are that you can struggle in early life with self-expression, primarily your speech. This can express as an inability to find the right words, speech delay or a stutter and in some cases selective mutism. You encounter difficulties expressing yourself, from speech difficulties to chronic shyness and you can struggle to express your emotions appropriately or positively. Negative expression via emotional explosions, whining, complaining, bad mouthing or criticizing, may be causing issues for you in relationships. Be careful not to become an emotional sponge for others negativity. At your lowest, you can also be lazy, selfish, and inconsistent, taking advantage of those around you and using them for what they can give you. You are fearful of socialising, being the centre of attention, and you may find the idea of public speaking or expressing your emotions uncomfortable or even frightening.

You can be materialistic and want lots of stuff, mistakenly thinking that stuff and fast cars will finally make you feel happy. You can also be vain, compare yourself to others and manifest jealousy, you are best to stay away from social media. You tend to see the world and other people as either perfect or flawed and you use your ideals as a benchmark for your happiness. When you meet someone, you see an idealised version of the person and do not see the signs to the contrary, leading to disappointment when reality is experienced.

On the other extreme, sometimes no one is perfect enough, you look for flaws and can get lost in petty detail, dwelling obsessively on one tiny flaw. Your perfectionism brings you self-inflicted internal pressure from your own high often unreachable standards. Your self-judgment leads to low self-esteem and judgement that you project onto others. You tend towards asthma and complaints in the chest area.

You have chosen to incarnate to learn the lessons of the master 33/6 Life Path energy because when speaking to your spirit guide before this life, you highlighted that you needed to learn the lessons of the master number 33 energy. You have this path because you are an old soul that has accumulated much wisdom, you are strongly connected to source energy due to your soul's advanced development. Your experience of many lives means that you have experienced many energies, so now you are working towards being a master vibration. You need to master, double positive emotional expression to nurture, entertain, teach, inspire laughter or action for world change.

You have double the need to make a difference in the world through service as a master communicator, driven to nurture, serve and help others. You need to balance your emotions, by realising the effect of your emotional expression on others. Dedicate yourself to using positive emotional expression to entertain, heal, teach, inspire, and nurture.

Your 33/6 energy vibrates at a higher octave of the lower 6 energy, you must reconcile your ideals with reality, safe in the knowledge that all experience both good and bad is a lesson for your evolution. It is not what happens to you, it is how you deal with it, learn, and evolve that counts. You must learn to express yourself in a positive, healing manner, verbally and creatively to bring about positive world change.

You are here to learn to be a Master Communicator, teacher, and entertainer. A creative, verbal, artistic expresser of art and information that elicits joy and positivity. To be the best Master Communicator you can be, you must learn to deal with, and channel your emotions positively, using your emotions as a tool to raise others up, rather than bringing them down.

You would be helped on your life path by being a humanitarian, focused on helping others with your passions, values and ideals. Your ideals may drive you to work or volunteer for charities or NGO's (non-governmental organisations) in order to make a difference in the world. On the flip side, when your vibration is low, you can be self-absorbed and self-centred. You may need to conquer confidence issues that block your expression and learn not to judge yourself and others by impossible ideals. Your self-imposed ideals may sabotage your own emotional happiness and inner peace.

You are an older soul with lots of experience from previous lives, you have an inner knowing, you do not know how you know, you just know. You 'know' because you have experienced situations many times before. This can be a double edged sword for you because your inner knowledge can cause you to berate yourself for not doing things better and others will unconsciously expect more from you than others because of the intensity of your energy. The weight of responsibility that you put on yourself and other people's expectations, can be overwhelming. Some master energies slip into substance abuse to help them deal with the energy, but the best medication is spiritual practice and meditation. You must resist the urge to set the bar too high for yourself and set yourself up to fail.

As a master energy, the intensity of the energy channelled to you from source can be overwhelming like gushing water that chokes you. Mismanagement of your master energy can tend you to panic attacks, anxiety, and exhaustion. You must learn to control and funnel your intense master energy into world changing tasks both big and small. Set intensions linked to your big picture and funnel your energy into these projects. Use meditation and/or time in nature to help you focus on your funnels!

You are here to master the lessons of the 3 energy, to master the art of inspired expressive verbal communication to uplift and inspire.

When you are walking your life path at your highest vibration, you heal, teach, and entertain with your words and creative artistry. Whether you inspire people with the spoken word, the written word or both, just your presence and the way you say just the right things at the right time can be enough to bring healing to the soul of others. But you are not just about learning to heal, you have the potential to be a teacher or entertainer with innovative, emotional, and creative expression of information that your students or audience cannot help but retain. But to reach this level, you must overcome communication blocks that are rooted in low self-esteem. You may battle with speech impediments, and difficulty saying what you need and want to say. You must also learn the deep impact, both positive and negative, of your words on others and commit to expressing positivity.

Words, however, are not the only way that you can authentically and emotionally express yourself, you are here to learn to express your creativity to inspire. But you may procrastinate and struggle to finish creative projects due to lack of self-belief. When you believe in yourself you have the potential to nurture others as an amazing creative artist, via music, art, beauty, and/or decorating your environment.

You may choose to emotionally express yourself using your body through singing, acting, dance, sports, and/or adrenaline activities to astound, amaze and delight. So, whether you express yourself through your words, your music, your art, or your body, you must inspire and uplift others.

You are here to develop towards being comfortably social, talkative, and joyful, to network, make useful connections and create a stable, nurturing family. You are shy when you first meet others and your sensitivity, if unmanaged, could exacerbate nervous tension and social anxiety. You need to manage your sensitivity via meditation and spending time in a relaxing, tranquil environment to help you to manage your master energy, make connections, work with and alongside others effectively. Without spiritual practice, you may medicate your anxiety and low mood with substances.

You are here to learn to work with others within a team, group, and family situation. You must learn to nurture and be more giving of your time and heart, especially to those that are the most vulnerable in our society. The creation of a stable, tranquil supportive family rooted in love within a close community will provide you with opportunities to flourish, nurture and teach others positively.

Your high responsibility life purpose will bring you into contact with the most vulnerable and broken in our society. You must live up to the responsibilities that you accept and treat others with utmost ethics and integrity.

When low, you have the potential to forget your responsibilities and express your emotions negatively to hurt and destroy. At your worst, you could take advantage of the vulnerable rather than nurture them, acting unethically and irresponsibly. When you are with vulnerable people, you are powerful, but that great power brings with it great responsibility. To ensure that you are always responsible, you must access your powerful intuition, become aware of and manage your intense emotions, and seek guidance from your spirit guide(s) and others with more experience when you need it.

You are here to be a practical doer, you must learn to act and express ideas to delight, teach, support, and nurture the world. When low you can be depressive, apathetic, lazy, and lacking in direction. You must access spirituality and develop yourself to get past this. You need to learn to be dynamic, always on the lookout for, and ready to snap up, opportunities that you can capitalise upon. This will require you to develop your confidence, commitment, and independence. You can learn to be independent and committed by completing tasks consistently, both creative and routine that link to your goals and intentions.

There are many ways to channel positivity, you could manifest your 33/6 life path and purpose by developing as an entertainer with the ability to lift the energy of any audience and the ability to handle being the centre of attention or in the limelight. If a gathering is getting bored, queue the 3, to entertain and raise everyone's spirits. You must develop towards having the confidence to be the life of the party, the conversationalist, and the joker in any social situation. You can be quiet, shy, inhibited, and depressive or aggressive and abusive. Your negative emotions could stem from mismanaged master energy, low self-esteem, self-criticism and/or being critical of others, blaming them for your own short comings.

Your 33/6 life path needs you to be a dreamer, a visionary of the utopian ideal that manifests realistic ideals daily. You have visions of a utopian world where everyone is happy, cared for and nurtured and you may have set yourself a mission to create that better world. This utopian vision is fine because it gives humanity something to aspire towards. However, you must take care not to put the responsibility for this solely on your shoulders, you are capable, but you are not a superhero. You can be extremely judgemental of yourself when you feel that you have not achieved the ideals you have envisioned which can be destructive of your happiness and self-esteem.

You can be extremely judgemental of others when they do not share your ideals or even try to achieve them. You must not set the achievement of your ideals as a benchmark for your acceptance and happiness. You must reconcile your ideals with practical reality. Like it or not, the universe is the perfect balance of all experience, both positive and negative. It is our path to go through difficulty and challenge, for the purpose of our personal learning and evolution.

You can be emotionally explosive and even abusive, the opposite of the inspired teacher and nurturer that you are here to be. You can also be high maintenance, critical, judgemental, and come across as self-righteous. However, you are actually more judgemental of yourself than you are of others. You need to lower the bar and cut yourself and others some slack, otherwise your self-esteem will suffer. You must realise that reality often doesn't live up to your idea of perfection. Stop nit picking and judging the petty detail and keep your big picture in mind. Otherwise, nothing you or anyone else does will ever be good enough for you, you will miss big picture success by judging and obsessing over the petty detail.

As a master energy with an old soul vibration, you will often feel different and out of place, like you are waiting for your people to come pick you up and take you away. You need to use your raised master vibration for service to the world, but you must also develop boundaries on how much you will do to preserve your own wellbeing, health, and self-respect.

Life Path Master 33/6 with Birthday Number 2

Life Path Master 33/6 (90% Focus)	Birthday Number 2 (10% Focus)
You are an old soul, here to spiritually channel, communicate & manifest ideas to raise the world's vibration. You are here to learn to be a master communicator, to teach and/or entertain, to emotionally nurture and heal others in a big way. You must learn to handle the energy of this big responsibility to your audience. You can be too responsible and do too much.	You are here to learn to be responsible to others and the team. You can be too responsible and do too much. You are irresponsible if you feel undervalued and resentful.
You are here to learn to express yourself verbally to inspire, inform and delight. You may struggle in some way verbally, chronic shyness, speech delay, stutter, language barriers or struggling to find the words	You must learn to improve your social skills, focus on widening and deepening your relationships and make decisions subjectively. It is important that you deepen your relationships and connect 121
You are here to learn to express yourself creatively to inspire, inform and delight. You may procrastinate and thus struggle to finish creative projects, due to lack of self-belief	You must learn not to smother your loved ones or have expectations that can never be met. OR you may back away from wanting love because it hurts too badly. You need to balance your intense need for love
You must learn to be dynamic, take risks and be confident to enjoy the attention and limelight of an audience. You can be shy, under confident and feel unable to take risks.	You are here to learn to be intuitive and sensitive to the needs of others. You are here to be of service to others, the development of intuition will aid you in this journey
You need to develop as an entrepreneur who is able to promote, network and make money	You are here to learn to be a cooperative team player to get the job done as part of a cohesive team.

creatively.	You can be a disruptive, uncooperative drama queen.
You are here to learn to express your emotions positively. You can be extremely sensitive to criticism and a sponge for other people's emotions, causing you to express emotions negatively	You must develop the assertiveness to demand boundaries to being overworked, walked all over, taken advantage of, and/or taken for granted. You must not be a "shape shifter" who changes who you are in order to please others or keep the peace.
You are here to develop the habit of acting, be a doer and executer of ideas. When low, you can struggle with apathy, laziness and lack of focus and direction	You are here to serve the leader, the team, the task and be dependable. You can always be counted upon to keep the cogs turning behind the scenes
You are here to learn to be social, talkative, the life of the party and bringer of fun & positivity. You need to be the networker, communicating an emotional message. You can be quiet and struggle to speak	You are here to be the tactful mediator of the team, helping to resolve conflicts fairly and for the good of the team. You hate conflict and often run and hide until it is over
You must develop independence; that becomes interdependence.

the 3 energy likes to be looked after and can be prone to avoiding work or anything needing routine and commitment. | You are here to learn to plan the next steps after the initial idea & build a team to achieve it. The energy of the two is the nurturer of ideas and a builder of teams |
| You are here to be opportunistic, to network and make useful connections. Confidently snap up opportunities to spread the word, progress ideas and projects. You are extremely shy, and you may even avoid social contact at all. | You must learn to give yourself your own kudos. Oftentimes you judge yourself on what everyone else says or thinks about you. You need to develop your internal compass and turn inward for validation, do what you think you should do |
| You must learn to take responsibility and listen to guidance; you can be irresponsible. You must think before | |

you act, and take full responsibility for what you do	
You are here to be a visionary of the ideal, the dreamer of a utopian world. You want to create a better world with your ideals. You may be judgemental of yourself, other people, and the world for not meeting your unreachable ideals causing disappointment and nefarious counterintuitive actions.	
You are here to learn to not use your ideals as a benchmark for your happiness. You often judge yourself and others for not hitting perfection, causing you great unhappiness	
You are here to learn to reconcile your ideals with practical reality. You must accept that the universe or source energy is everything existing in perfect balance, to fully experience love, you must fully experience hate	
Your perfectionism can make you an over achiever due to self-judgement. You never meet your own standards. You must see the big picture and not get stuck in petty detail. You can often judge small imperfections and ruin or miss your successes.	
You are here to learn to be a nurturer, compassionate caring and giving, especially to those that are vulnerable or struggling within your close relationships, your community, and the wider world. When low, you can be incredibly neglectful.	

You are here to develop boundaries to ensure your mental and physical health. You do a lot for others, sometimes too much, which can make you feel undervalued, unappreciated, resentful, and ill with exhaustion.

You are here to develop your social skills and be a team player. You must break through low self-esteem to be talkative, fun loving and relaxed around others

You are here to create a stable, nurturing, tranquil home to maintain your security and well-being. Then nurture a family in an environment of stability and love

You are here to learn to be responsible and do good for those you care for. People naturally put you in positions of responsibility, but you often resent always being the 'responsible one.'

You are here to develop your musical creative artistry and/or your artistic and aesthetic potential. You could nurture others with your musical potential and your eye for colour and aesthetics.

Life Path Master 33/6 with Birthday Number 3

Life Path Master 33/6 (90% Focus)	Birthday Number 3 (10% Focus)
You are an old soul, here to spiritually channel, communicate & manifest ideas to raise the world's vibration. You are here to learn to be a master communicator, to teach and/or entertain, to emotionally nurture and heal others in a big way. You must learn to handle the energy of this big responsibility to your audience. You can be too responsible and do too much.	You are here to learn to express yourself verbally to inspire, inform and delight. You may struggle in some way verbally, chronic shyness, speech delay, stutter or struggling to find the words.
You are here to learn to express yourself verbally to inspire, inform and delight. You may struggle in some way verbally, chronic shyness, speech delay, stutter, language barriers or struggling to find the words	You are here to learn to express yourself creatively to inspire, inform and delight. But you may struggle to progress, execute, and finish creative projects, due to lack of self-belief
You are here to learn to express yourself creatively to inspire, inform and delight. You may procrastinate and thus struggle to finish creative projects, due to lack of self-belief	You must learn to be dynamic, take risks and be confident to enjoy the attention and limelight of an audience. You can be shy, under confident and feel unable to take risks.
You must learn to be dynamic, take risks and be confident to enjoy the attention and limelight of an audience. You can be shy, under confident and feel unable to take risks.	You need to develop as an entrepreneur who is able to promote, network and make money creatively. But you may procrastinate and fail to stay focused and work inconsistently.
You need to develop as an entrepreneur who is able to promote, network and make money	You are here to learn to express your emotions positively. You can be extremely sensitive to criticism and

creatively.

other people's emotions, causing you to express emotions negatively

You are here to learn to express your emotions positively. You can be extremely sensitive to criticism and a sponge for other people's emotions, causing you to express emotions negatively

You are here to develop the habit of acting, be a doer and executer of ideas. When low, you can struggle with apathy, laziness and lack of focus and direction

You are here to develop the habit of acting, be a doer and executer of ideas. When low, you can struggle with apathy, laziness and lack of focus and direction

You are here to learn to be social, talkative, the life of the party and bringer of fun & positivity. You need to be the networker, communicating an emotional message. You can be quiet and struggle to speak

You are here to learn to be social, talkative, the life of the party and bringer of fun & positivity. You need to be the networker, communicating an emotional message. You can be quiet and struggle to speak

You must develop interdependence, life path 3's like to be looked after and can be prone to avoiding work or anything needing routine and commitment

You must develop independence; that becomes interdependence.

the 3 energy likes to be looked after and can be prone to avoiding work or anything needing routine and commitment.

You are here to be opportunistic, to network, make useful connections and snap up opportunities to spread the word and progress ideas and projects

You are here to be opportunistic, to network and make useful connections. Confidently snap up opportunities to spread the word, progress ideas and projects. You are extremely shy, and you may even avoid social contact at all.

You must learn to take responsibility and listen to guidance; you can be irresponsible. You must think before you act, and take full responsibility for what you do

You must learn to take responsibility and listen to guidance; you can be irresponsible. You must think before you act, and take full responsibility

for what you do	
You are here to be a visionary of the ideal, the dreamer of a utopian world. You want to create a better world with your ideals. You may be judgemental of yourself, other people, and the world for not meeting your unreachable ideals causing disappointment and nefarious counterintuitive actions.	
You are here to learn to not use your ideals as a benchmark for your happiness. You often judge yourself and others for not hitting perfection, causing you great unhappiness	
You are here to learn to reconcile your ideals with practical reality. You must accept that the universe or source energy is everything existing in perfect balance, to fully experience love, you must fully experience hate	
Your perfectionism can make you an over achiever due to self-judgement. You never meet your own standards. You must see the big picture and not get stuck in petty detail. You can often judge small imperfections and ruin or miss your successes.	
You are here to learn to be a nurturer, compassionate caring and giving, especially to those that are vulnerable or struggling within your close relationships, your community, and the wider world. When low, you can be incredibly neglectful.	
You are here to develop boundaries	

to ensure your mental and physical health. You do a lot for others, sometimes too much, which can make you feel undervalued, unappreciated, resentful, and ill with exhaustion.

You are here to develop your social skills and be a team player. You must break through low self-esteem to be talkative, fun loving and relaxed around others

You are here to create a stable, nurturing, tranquil home to maintain your security and well-being. Then nurture a family in an environment of stability and love

You are here to learn to be responsible and do good for those you care for. People naturally put you in positions of responsibility, but you often resent always being the 'responsible one.'

You are here to develop your musical creative artistry and/or your artistic and aesthetic potential. You could nurture others with your musical potential and your eye for colour and aesthetics.

Life Path Master 33/6 with Birthday Number 4

Life Path Master 33/6 (90% Focus)	Birthday Number 4 (10% Focus)
You are an old soul, here to spiritually channel, communicate & manifest ideas to raise the world's vibration. You are here to learn to be a master communicator, to teach and/or entertain, to emotionally nurture and heal others in a big way. You must learn to handle the energy of this big responsibility to your audience. You can be too responsible and do too much.	You are here to learn to commit to a person and/or place, so that you can put down roots and dig the foundations for security. You can be uncommitted and therefore unable to build stability and security.
You are here to learn to express yourself verbally to inspire, inform and delight. You may struggle in some way verbally, chronic shyness, speech delay, stutter, language barriers or struggling to find the words	You are here to learn to set and achieve goals to take you on your journey towards inner and outer stability and security. Foundations, structures, families, and business empires are built 1 goal at a time.
You are here to learn to express yourself creatively to inspire, inform and delight. You may procrastinate and thus struggle to finish creative projects, due to lack of self-belief	You are here to learn to plan, create a process and/or procedure to ensure the achievement of your goals. You can be directionless, lazy and block your own progression
You must learn to be dynamic, take risks and be confident to enjoy the attention and limelight of an audience. You can be shy, under confident and feel unable to take risks.	You are here to develop deep meticulous focus on achieving stability, like a stable home, business or income and building your inner security. You can be scattered
You need to develop as an entrepreneur who is able to promote, network and make money creatively.	You are here to learn to be detail orientated, analytical, organised, and accurate to ensure your plans and processes are watertight. You can be

disorganised and miss steps in the plan

You are here to learn to express your emotions positively. You can be extremely sensitive to criticism and a sponge for other people's emotions, causing you to express emotions negatively

You are here to develop a work ethic, to work hard and develop enjoyment of routine work and tasks. When low you can be lazy and stuck in 1 place, without progression

You are here to develop the habit of acting, be a doer and executer of ideas. When low, you can struggle with apathy, laziness and lack of focus and direction

You are here to develop patient perseverance, so that every step in the process towards your goals for your stable foundation are taken. You are prone to impatience and missing steps

You are here to learn to be social, talkative, the life of the party and bringer of fun & positivity. You need to be the networker, communicating an emotional message. You can be quiet and struggle to speak

You are here to learn to come to terms with limitation — both the limitations that are externally imposed on you and the limitations that you impose upon yourself.

You must develop independence; that becomes interdependence.

the 3 energy likes to be looked after and can be prone to avoiding work or anything needing routine and commitment.

You are here to look at your wounded or problematic relationships and work through the feelings of lack and pain they have brought to you.

You are here to be opportunistic, to network and make useful connections. Confidently snap up opportunities to spread the word, progress ideas and projects. You are extremely shy, and you may even avoid social contact at all.

You are prone to choosing social isolation, avoiding social situations due to social anxiety. It is important that you socialise regularly in familiar groups and with likeminded friends.

You must learn to take responsibility and listen to guidance; you can be irresponsible. You must think before you act, and take full responsibility

for what you do	
You are here to be a visionary of the ideal, the dreamer of a utopian world. You want to create a better world with your ideals. You may be judgemental of yourself, other people, and the world for not meeting your unreachable ideals causing disappointment and nefarious counterintuitive actions.	
You are here to learn to not use your ideals as a benchmark for your happiness. You often judge yourself and others for not hitting perfection, causing you great unhappiness	
You are here to learn to reconcile your ideals with practical reality. You must accept that the universe or source energy is everything existing in perfect balance, to fully experience love, you must fully experience hate	
Your perfectionism can make you an over achiever due to self-judgement. You never meet your own standards. You must see the big picture and not get stuck in petty detail. You can often judge small imperfections and ruin or miss your successes.	
You are here to learn to be a nurturer, compassionate caring and giving, especially to those that are vulnerable or struggling within your close relationships, your community, and the wider world. When low, you can be incredibly neglectful.	
You are here to develop boundaries	

to ensure your mental and physical health. You do a lot for others, sometimes too much, which can make you feel undervalued, unappreciated, resentful, and ill with exhaustion.	
You are here to develop your social skills and be a team player. You must break through low self-esteem to be talkative, fun loving and relaxed around others	
You are here to create a stable, nurturing, tranquil home to maintain your security and well-being. Then nurture a family in an environment of stability and love	
You are here to learn to be responsible and do good for those you care for. People naturally put you in positions of responsibility, but you often resent always being the 'responsible one.'	
You are here to develop your musical creative artistry and/or your artistic and aesthetic potential. You could nurture others with your musical potential and your eye for colour and aesthetics.	

Life Path Master 33/6 with Birthday Number 5

Life Path Master 33/6 (90% Focus)	Birthday Number 5 (10% Focus)
You are an old soul, here to spiritually channel, communicate & manifest ideas to raise the world's vibration. You are here to learn to be a master communicator, to teach and/or entertain, to emotionally nurture and heal others in a big way. You must learn to handle the energy of this big responsibility to your audience. You can be too responsible and do too much.	You are easily bored and want to look at or study lots of topics. Initial varied experience is needed in order to choose a specialism, you are here to learn to be disciplined, to continue with a topic or activity beyond the boredom of the detail, towards mastery and specialism.
You are here to learn to express yourself verbally to inspire, inform and delight. You may struggle in some way verbally, chronic shyness, speech delay, stutter, language barriers or struggling to find the words	You are here to develop the ability to balance variety, change and adventure with the stability of family and skill mastery. You can be totally spontaneous and take risks, jumping from one experience to another, but never settling or progressing
You are here to learn to express yourself creatively to inspire, inform and delight. You may procrastinate and thus struggle to finish creative projects, due to lack of self-belief	You need to learn to be extremely intuitive and access your intuitive wisdom when making decisions, assessing people and situations.
You must learn to be dynamic, take risks and be confident to enjoy the attention and limelight of an audience. You can be shy, under confident and feel unable to take risks.	You are here to develop your ability to attain inner freedom and outer freedom by doing things you might not want to do. Doing what you want is not necessarily freedom, you can become a slave to your desires. Freedom and discipline are inherently linked.
You need to develop as an entrepreneur who is able to	You are here to learn to develop your verbal and written

promote, network and make money creatively.

communication skills towards charismatic sharing of ideas and stories related to your specialism. You have the potential to be a great communicator

You are here to learn to express your emotions positively. You can be extremely sensitive to criticism and a sponge for other people's emotions, causing you to express emotions negatively

You are here to learn to be committed, dependable, to do what you say you are going to do. You often forget what you promise because you are so chaotic, scattered, and changeable, looking for the next new experience

You are here to develop the habit of acting, be a doer and executer of ideas. When low, you can struggle with apathy, laziness and lack of focus and direction

You are here to develop your social skills and charisma, to have the potential to be fun loving, positive, and optimistic. You can be uptight and argumentative

You are here to learn to be social, talkative, the life of the party and bringer of fun & positivity. You need to be the networker, communicating an emotional message. You can be quiet and struggle to speak

You are here to develop consistent independence. You can swing from independence to dependence and back again. Risky behaviour and 'get rich quick' schemes can bring on dependence

You must develop independence; that becomes interdependence.

the 3 energy likes to be looked after and can be prone to avoiding work or anything needing routine and commitment.

You are here to learn to develop fearlessness and help others to live fearlessly. You can be fearful of many things, restriction, and boredom, to name but a few. You need to challenge yourself and others past your own comfort zone

You are here to be opportunistic, to network and make useful connections. Confidently snap up opportunities to spread the word, progress ideas and projects. You are extremely shy, and you may even avoid social contact at all.

You are here to learn to make good use of your energy and drive, if you feel restricted and under confident, you will be restless, and you may turn into a drama queen. Use your energy for experience and adventure, be courageous

You must learn to take responsibility and listen to guidance; you can be irresponsible. You must think before you act, and take full responsibility for what you do	
You are here to be a visionary of the ideal, the dreamer of a utopian world. You want to create a better world with your ideals. You may be judgemental of yourself, other people, and the world for not meeting your unreachable ideals causing disappointment and nefarious counterintuitive actions.	
You are here to learn to not use your ideals as a benchmark for your happiness. You often judge yourself and others for not hitting perfection, causing you great unhappiness	
You are here to learn to reconcile your ideals with practical reality. You must accept that the universe or source energy is everything existing in perfect balance, to fully experience love, you must fully experience hate	
Your perfectionism can make you an over achiever due to self-judgement. You never meet your own standards. You must see the big picture and not get stuck in petty detail. You can often judge small imperfections and ruin or miss your successes.	
You are here to learn to be a nurturer, compassionate caring and giving, especially to those that are vulnerable or struggling within your	

close relationships, your community, and the wider world. When low, you can be incredibly neglectful.

You are here to develop boundaries to ensure your mental and physical health. You do a lot for others, sometimes too much, which can make you feel undervalued, unappreciated, resentful, and ill with exhaustion.

You are here to develop your social skills and be a team player. You must break through low self-esteem to be talkative, fun loving and relaxed around others

You are here to create a stable, nurturing, tranquil home to maintain your security and well-being. Then nurture a family in an environment of stability and love

You are here to learn to be responsible and do good for those you care for. People naturally put you in positions of responsibility, but you often resent always being the 'responsible one.'

You are here to develop your musical creative artistry and/or your artistic and aesthetic potential. You could nurture others with your musical potential and your eye for colour and aesthetics.

Life Path Master 33/6 with Birthday Number 6

Life Path Master 33/6 (90% Focus)	Birthday Number 6 (10% Focus)
You are an old soul, here to spiritually channel, communicate & manifest ideas to raise the world's vibration. You are here to learn to be a master communicator, to teach and/or entertain, to emotionally nurture and heal others in a big way. You must learn to handle the energy of this big responsibility to your audience. You can be too responsible and do too much.	You are here to be a visionary of the ideal, the dreamer of a utopian world. You must act to create a better world with your ideals.
You are here to learn to express yourself verbally to inspire, inform and delight. You may struggle in some way verbally, chronic shyness, speech delay, stutter, language barriers or struggling to find the words	You are here to learn to not use your ideals as a benchmark for your happiness. You must not base your emotional wellbeing on the achievement of your ideals. You often judge yourself and others for not hitting perfection, causing you great unhappiness
You are here to learn to express yourself creatively to inspire, inform and delight. You may procrastinate and thus struggle to finish creative projects, due to lack of self-belief	Your perfectionism can make you an over achiever due to your constant self-judgement. You never meet your own standards. You must keep your big picture in mind and not get stuck in petty detail. You can often judge small imperfections and ruin or miss your successes.
You must learn to be dynamic, take risks and be confident to enjoy the attention and limelight of an audience. You can be shy, under confident and feel unable to take	You are here to learn to be a nurturer, compassionate caring and giving, especially to those that are vulnerable or struggling within your close relationships, your community, and the wider world. Your

risks.

judgemental nature can make you cruel and neglectful.

You need to develop as an entrepreneur who is able to promote, network and make money creatively.

You are here to develop boundaries to ensure your mental and physical health. You do a lot for others, sometimes too much, which can make you feel undervalued, unappreciated, and ill with exhaustion. You may force unsolicited advice and meddle in other people's affairs.

You are here to learn to express your emotions positively. You can be extremely sensitive to criticism and a sponge for other people's emotions, causing you to express emotions negatively

You are here to develop your social skills and be a team player. You must break through low self-esteem to be talkative, fun loving and relaxed around others. You can be shy and hide in the background.

You are here to develop the habit of acting, be a doer and executer of ideas. When low, you can struggle with apathy, laziness and lack of focus and direction

You are here to create a stable, nurturing, tranquil home to maintain your security and well-being. Then nurture a family in an environment of stability and love. When low you can be a selfish, neglectful drama queen.

You are here to learn to be social, talkative, the life of the party and bringer of fun & positivity. You need to be the networker, communicating an emotional message. You can be quiet and struggle to speak

You are here to learn to be responsible and do good for those you care for. People naturally put you in positions of responsibility, but you often resent always being the 'responsible one.' Have boundaries on your responsibility so that you do not do too much.

You must develop independence; that becomes interdependence.

the 3 energy likes to be looked after and can be prone to avoiding work or anything needing routine and

You are here to learn to develop and use your artistic and aesthetic potential. Artistic, enhancing make up, great art and home designs. You have great musical potential that

commitment.	you may not develop.
You are here to be opportunistic, to network and make useful connections. Confidently snap up opportunities to spread the word, progress ideas and projects. You are extremely shy, and you may even avoid social contact at all.	
You must learn to take responsibility and listen to guidance; you can be irresponsible. You must think before you act, and take full responsibility for what you do	
You are here to be a visionary of the ideal, the dreamer of a utopian world. You want to create a better world with your ideals. You may be judgemental of yourself, other people, and the world for not meeting your unreachable ideals causing disappointment and nefarious counterintuitive actions.	
You are here to learn to not use your ideals as a benchmark for your happiness. You often judge yourself and others for not hitting perfection, causing you great unhappiness	
You are here to learn to reconcile your ideals with practical reality. You must accept that the universe or source energy is everything existing in perfect balance, to fully experience love, you must fully experience hate	
Your perfectionism can make you an over achiever due to self-judgement. You never meet your own standards.	

You must see the big picture and not get stuck in petty detail. You can often judge small imperfections and ruin or miss your successes.

You are here to learn to be a nurturer, compassionate caring and giving, especially to those that are vulnerable or struggling within your close relationships, your community, and the wider world. When low, you can be incredibly neglectful.

You are here to develop boundaries to ensure your mental and physical health. You do a lot for others, sometimes too much, which can make you feel undervalued, unappreciated, resentful, and ill with exhaustion.

You are here to develop your social skills and be a team player. You must break through low self-esteem to be talkative, fun loving and relaxed around others

You are here to create a stable, nurturing, tranquil home to maintain your security and well-being. Then nurture a family in an environment of stability and love

You are here to learn to be responsible and do good for those you care for. People naturally put you in positions of responsibility, but you often resent always being the 'responsible one.'

You are here to develop your musical creative artistry and/or your artistic and aesthetic potential. You

could nurture others with your musical potential and your eye for colour and aesthetics.	

Life Path Master 33/6 with Birthday Number 7

Life Path Master 33/6 (90% Focus)	Birthday Number 7 (10% Focus)
You are an old soul, here to spiritually channel, communicate & manifest ideas to raise the world's vibration. You are here to learn to be a master communicator, to teach and/or entertain, to emotionally nurture and heal others in a big way. You must learn to handle the energy of this big responsibility to your audience. You can be too responsible and do too much.	You are here to learn to have faith that you are an immortal soul that has experience from previous lives. You must trust the soul within you by listening to and following your intuition without over thinking and applying logic. Listen to and follow your inner voice and feel safe enough to communicate your soul wisdom to the world without fear of ridicule.
You are here to learn to express yourself verbally to inspire, inform and delight. You may struggle in some way verbally, chronic shyness, speech delay, stutter, language barriers or struggling to find the words	You are here to trust that the world is not against you. The universe is everything existing in perfect balance, it is like a cosmic library of all knowledge and experience. We must experience it all to learn and evolve
You are here to learn to express yourself creatively to inspire, inform and delight. You may procrastinate and thus struggle to finish creative projects, due to lack of self-belief	Your focus for this lifetime must be Inner development rather than outer development and success. You must develop yourself constantly with self-discovery and spiritual wisdom. Meditation and time in nature is imperative for you
You must learn to be dynamic, take risks and be confident to enjoy the attention and limelight of an audience. You can be shy, under confident and feel unable to take risks.	You are here to learn to be a problem solver, thinker, a studier of the metaphysical and the big questions. You need to research, learn, and analyse theories to accrue wisdom.
You need to develop as an entrepreneur who is able to	You are here to learn to filter your research through your intuition and

promote, network and make money creatively.	use your research of other people's theories for your own needs. You can be too analytical and ignore your intuition. Or totally spiritual and ignore other theories. You must balance the two.
You are here to learn to express your emotions positively. You can be extremely sensitive to criticism and a sponge for other people's emotions, causing you to express emotions negatively	You are here to be a free thinker, to be less interested in popular culture and following norms of fashion and appearance. This can make you feel different and out of place and lonely
You are here to develop the habit of acting, be a doer and executer of ideas. When low, you can struggle with apathy, laziness and lack of focus and direction	You are here to develop the ability to focus on something long enough to develop it into something useful. You can be a little scattered and struggle to focus
You are here to learn to be social, talkative, the life of the party and bringer of fun & positivity. You need to be the networker, communicating an emotional message. You can be quiet and struggle to speak	You are here to develop interdependence, self-sufficiency but also a healthy dependence on other people. You like to do things for yourself but take care not to push others away
You must develop independence; that becomes interdependence. the 3 energy likes to be looked after and can be prone to avoiding work or anything needing routine and commitment.	You are here to learn to deal with and reconcile your sensitive emotions. Others often think you are aloof, but you are a well of deep emotions. You need to connect emotionally, both to yourself and to other people
You are here to be opportunistic, to network and make useful connections. Confidently snap up opportunities to spread the word, progress ideas and projects. You are extremely shy, and you may even avoid social contact at all.	You are here to learn to balance your need to be alone and work alone with social contact. You love to be alone, but you must ensure that you do not isolate yourself beyond what is healthy

You must learn to take responsibility and listen to guidance; you can be irresponsible. You must think before you act, and take full responsibility for what you do	
You are here to be a visionary of the ideal, the dreamer of a utopian world. You want to create a better world with your ideals. You may be judgemental of yourself, other people, and the world for not meeting your unreachable ideals causing disappointment and nefarious counterintuitive actions.	
You are here to learn to not use your ideals as a benchmark for your happiness. You often judge yourself and others for not hitting perfection, causing you great unhappiness	
You are here to learn to reconcile your ideals with practical reality. You must accept that the universe or source energy is everything existing in perfect balance, to fully experience love, you must fully experience hate	
Your perfectionism can make you an over achiever due to self-judgement. You never meet your own standards. You must see the big picture and not get stuck in petty detail. You can often judge small imperfections and ruin or miss your successes.	
You are here to learn to be a nurturer, compassionate caring and giving, especially to those that are vulnerable or struggling within your	

close relationships, your community, and the wider world. When low, you can be incredibly neglectful.	
You are here to develop boundaries to ensure your mental and physical health. You do a lot for others, sometimes too much, which can make you feel undervalued, unappreciated, resentful, and ill with exhaustion.	
You are here to develop your social skills and be a team player. You must break through low self-esteem to be talkative, fun loving and relaxed around others	
You are here to create a stable, nurturing, tranquil home to maintain your security and well-being. Then nurture a family in an environment of stability and love	
You are here to learn to be responsible and do good for those you care for. People naturally put you in positions of responsibility, but you often resent always being the 'responsible one.'	
You are here to develop your musical creative artistry and/or your artistic and aesthetic potential. You could nurture others with your musical potential and your eye for colour and aesthetics.	

Life Path Master 33/6 with Birthday Number 8

Life Path Master 33/6 (90% Focus)	Birthday Number 8 (10% Focus)
You are an old soul, here to spiritually channel, communicate & manifest ideas to raise the world's vibration. You are here to learn to be a master communicator, to teach and/or entertain, to emotionally nurture and heal others in a big way. You must learn to handle the energy of this big responsibility to your audience. You can be too responsible and do too much.	You are both spiritual and worldly. But you are here to learn the secrets of worldly financial success. You seek the freedom that comes from financial success. But freedom brings responsibility, your ethics will be tested multiple times
You are here to learn to express yourself verbally to inspire, inform and delight. You may struggle in some way verbally, chronic shyness, speech delay, stutter, language barriers or struggling to find the words	You are here to learn to use your financial success as a tool to help others achieve the same financial success. You often spend your abundance on materialistic status symbols rather than helping others
You are here to learn to express yourself creatively to inspire, inform and delight. You may procrastinate and thus struggle to finish creative projects, due to lack of self-belief	You are here to develop a healthy attitude towards money. You may resent or hate wealthy people, or you may feel guilty about your own wealth. You must understand that financial wealth does not equate to poor ethics
You must learn to be dynamic, take risks and be confident to enjoy the attention and limelight of an audience. You can be shy, under confident and feel unable to take risks.	You are here to develop balanced determination for achievement but with integrity and for the good of others. You can be either obsessed with achievement or fearful of achievement from low self-esteem. It is important that you develop a positive mindset because you attract what you think about.
You need to develop as an entrepreneur who is able to promote,	You are here to develop inner confidence and balanced personal

network and make money creatively.	power. You can swing from over dominance or misuse of power to hiding away or submission to others
You are here to learn to express your emotions positively. You can be extremely sensitive to criticism and a sponge for other people's emotions, causing you to express emotions negatively	You are here to develop skilled leadership, which consists of subject competence coupled with excellent social skills and charisma
You are here to develop the habit of acting, be a doer and executer of ideas. When low, you can struggle with apathy, laziness and lack of focus and direction	You are here to work hard as an excellent practical businessperson, but you must ensure that you do not work too hard, you need time out and time for your family
You are here to learn to be social, talkative, the life of the party and bringer of fun & positivity. You need to be the networker, communicating an emotional message. You can be quiet and struggle to speak	You are here to be worldly, strong, resilient, disciplined, and realistic. To be successful you need to be strong, tough, and able to cope with The ups and downs of the world
You must develop independence; that becomes interdependence. the 3 energy likes to be looked after and can be prone to avoiding work or anything needing routine and commitment.	You are here to develop bravery and the courage to take risks to progress. Success comes from having the bravery to take risks
You are here to be opportunistic, to network and make useful connections. Confidently snap up opportunities to spread the word, progress ideas and projects. You are extremely shy, and you may even avoid social contact at all.	You are here to develop organisation and management skills, resolve to making things happen and to define and meet your goals.
You must learn to take responsibility and listen to guidance; you can be	

irresponsible. You must think before you act, and take full responsibility for what you do

You are here to be a visionary of the ideal, the dreamer of a utopian world. You want to create a better world with your ideals. You may be judgemental of yourself, other people, and the world for not meeting your unreachable ideals causing disappointment and nefarious counterintuitive actions.

You are here to learn to not use your ideals as a benchmark for your happiness. You often judge yourself and others for not hitting perfection, causing you great unhappiness

You are here to learn to reconcile your ideals with practical reality. You must accept that the universe or source energy is everything existing in perfect balance, to fully experience love, you must fully experience hate

Your perfectionism can make you an over achiever due to self-judgement. You never meet your own standards. You must see the big picture and not get stuck in petty detail. You can often judge small imperfections and ruin or miss your successes.

You are here to learn to be a nurturer, compassionate caring and giving, especially to those that are vulnerable or struggling within your close relationships, your community, and the wider world. When low, you can be incredibly neglectful.

You are here to develop boundaries to ensure your mental and physical health. You do a lot for others, sometimes too much, which can make you feel undervalued, unappreciated, resentful, and ill with exhaustion.	
You are here to develop your social skills and be a team player. You must break through low self-esteem to be talkative, fun loving and relaxed around others	
You are here to create a stable, nurturing, tranquil home to maintain your security and well-being. Then nurture a family in an environment of stability and love	
You are here to learn to be responsible and do good for those you care for. People naturally put you in positions of responsibility, but you often resent always being the 'responsible one.'	
You are here to develop your musical creative artistry and/or your artistic and aesthetic potential. You could nurture others with your musical potential and your eye for colour and aesthetics.	

Life Path Master 33/6 with Birthday Number 9

Life Path Master 33/6 (90% Focus)	Birthday Number 9 (10% Focus)
You are an old soul, here to spiritually channel, communicate & manifest ideas to raise the world's vibration. You are here to learn to be a master communicator, to teach and/or entertain, to emotionally nurture and heal others in a big way. You must learn to handle the energy of this big responsibility to your audience. You can be too responsible and do too much.	You are here to learn to follow your intuitive wisdom and live to spiritual laws, rather than worldly laws, conventions, and ideals. You tend to follow worldly laws and prejudices as an excuse for your actions. But if you had followed your intuitive spiritual wisdom, you would not have acted that way. Focus on faith over logic
You are here to learn to express yourself verbally to inspire, inform and delight. You may struggle in some way verbally, chronic shyness, speech delay, stutter, language barriers or struggling to find the words	You are here to learn to act with integrity for the benefit of others. You are powerful and you must use your power for the benefit of others. You can act for selfish or nefarious reasons
You are here to learn to express yourself creatively to inspire, inform and delight. You may procrastinate and thus struggle to finish creative projects, due to lack of self-belief	You are here to learn to lead by example, do you practise what you preach? You can be quite domineering, an adviser with all the answers. But you must let others make their own mistakes
You must learn to be dynamic, take risks and be confident to enjoy the attention and limelight of an audience. You can be shy, under confident and feel unable to take risks.	You are here to make your life your teaching, you need to counsel with wisdom. You are a developed soul, the totality of all the numbers, full of cellular experience and higher knowledge
You need to develop as an entrepreneur who is able to promote, network and make money	You are here to develop broad mindedness, meet and accept diverse people. You must learn to be

creatively.	a humanitarian and make the world a better place. You need a global consciousness, as you can be narrow minded, judgemental, and even bigoted.
You are here to learn to express your emotions positively. You can be extremely sensitive to criticism and a sponge for other people's emotions, causing you to express emotions negatively	You are here to learn to take responsibility for your powerful choices. You sometimes run away from the consequences of your actions
You are here to develop the habit of acting, be a doer and executer of ideas. When low, you can struggle with apathy, laziness and lack of focus and direction	You need to develop towards being a successful entrepreneur or businessperson if it is with something you feel passionate about. You must choose work that has meaning for you. You are a powerful force for change
You are here to learn to be social, talkative, the life of the party and bringer of fun & positivity. You need to be the networker, communicating an emotional message. You can be quiet and struggle to speak	You are here to develop excellent social skills and charisma. You could develop the skills of a powerful speaker and influencer of others. People will hang on your every word
You must develop independence; that becomes interdependence. the 3 energy likes to be looked after and can be prone to avoiding work or anything needing routine and commitment.	You are here to look after the wellbeing of others. But when you are in trouble or need support, people do not notice. You must ask for what you need, you must ask for help
You are here to be opportunistic, to network and make useful connections. Confidently snap up opportunities to spread the word, progress ideas and projects. You are extremely shy, and you may even avoid social contact at all.	You are here to wrap things up, let go and surrender. You can have a victim mentality, holding onto feelings that no longer serve you, unable to move on from perceived injustice, normally rooted in family issues.

You must learn to take responsibility and listen to guidance; you can be irresponsible. You must think before you act, and take full responsibility for what you do

You are here to be a visionary of the ideal, the dreamer of a utopian world. You want to create a better world with your ideals. You may be judgemental of yourself, other people, and the world for not meeting your unreachable ideals causing disappointment and nefarious counterintuitive actions.

You are here to learn to not use your ideals as a benchmark for your happiness. You often judge yourself and others for not hitting perfection, causing you great unhappiness

You are here to learn to reconcile your ideals with practical reality. You must accept that the universe or source energy is everything existing in perfect balance, to fully experience love, you must fully experience hate

Your perfectionism can make you an over achiever due to self-judgement. You never meet your own standards. You must see the big picture and not get stuck in petty detail. You can often judge small imperfections and ruin or miss your successes.

You are here to learn to be a nurturer, compassionate caring and giving, especially to those that are vulnerable or struggling within your

close relationships, your community, and the wider world. When low, you can be incredibly neglectful.	
You are here to develop boundaries to ensure your mental and physical health. You do a lot for others, sometimes too much, which can make you feel undervalued, unappreciated, resentful, and ill with exhaustion.	
You are here to develop your social skills and be a team player. You must break through low self-esteem to be talkative, fun loving and relaxed around others	
You are here to create a stable, nurturing, tranquil home to maintain your security and well-being. Then nurture a family in an environment of stability and love	
You are here to learn to be responsible and do good for those you care for. People naturally put you in positions of responsibility, but you often resent always being the 'responsible one.'	
You are here to develop your musical creative artistry and/or your artistic and aesthetic potential. You could nurture others with your musical potential and your eye for colour and aesthetics.	

Life Path Master 33/6 with Birthday Master 11

Life Path Master 33/6 (90% Focus)	Birthday Master 11 (10% Focus)
You are an old soul, here to spiritually channel, communicate & manifest ideas to raise the world's vibration. You are here to learn to be a master communicator, to teach and/or entertain, to emotionally nurture and heal others in a big way. You must learn to handle the energy of this big responsibility to your audience. You can be too responsible and do too much.	You are an old soul, with higher potential and higher responsibility to improve the world. You are here to learn to connect to source energy to channel unique new ideas and messages to change the world. You are here to learn to be happy in the limelight expressing new ideas for an audience. You need to develop and trust your massive intuitive potential. You often hide your ideas due to low confidence
You are here to learn to express yourself verbally to inspire, inform and delight. You may struggle in some way verbally, chronic shyness, speech delay, stutter, language barriers or struggling to find the words	You are here to learn to be the ideas person, but you struggle to bring your unique ideas to reality because you lose interest quickly after the initial idea of sabotage yourself due to crippling low confidence. You are an idealistic dreamer whose ideas are often not grounded in reality
You are here to learn to express yourself creatively to inspire, inform and delight. You may procrastinate and thus struggle to finish creative projects, due to lack of self-belief	You are here to learn to be confident in your uniqueness because unique people have unique ground-breaking ideas. It is important that you are not craving validation from others. Your validation should come from your intuition.
You must learn to be dynamic, take risks and be confident to enjoy the attention and limelight of an audience. You can be shy, under confident and feel unable to take risks.	You need to bring unique, new ideas that break barriers, or challenge others comfort zone. You must learn to be brave, confident and be willing to take risks

You need to develop as an entrepreneur who is able to promote, network and make money creatively.	You need to be a practical initiator, a doer, action orientated that learns by experience. Ideas will stay unmanifested until you act! Only action brings change
You are here to learn to express your emotions positively. You can be extremely sensitive to criticism and a sponge for other people's emotions, causing you to express emotions negatively	You need to set intentions then use spiritual practice and visualisation to channel your advanced, intense master energy into initiation and action. Unchanneled or mismanaged energy can cause intense nervous energy and anxiety. You may medicate these with unhealthy substances.
You are here to develop the habit of acting, be a doer and executer of ideas. When low, you can struggle with apathy, laziness and lack of focus and direction	You are here to learn to be interdependent, not so independent that you push others away and refuse to delegate. You cannot do everything alone. Independence is an illusion; we are all interconnected
You are here to learn to be social, talkative, the life of the party and bringer of fun & positivity. You need to be the networker, communicating an emotional message. You can be quiet and struggle to speak	You need to be determined to succeed. Constant self-discovery and intuitive spiritual development is key for you to develop complete trust in the skills you have learned and mastered to serve as a kind of "security blanket" for you when you are feeling insecure
You must develop independence; that becomes interdependence. the 3 energy likes to be looked after and can be prone to avoiding work or anything needing routine and commitment.	You need to learn to be a supportive, nurturing leader, be firm and assertive but also empathic and supportive. You must lead others to the fruition of your ideas, but with balanced personal power
You are here to be opportunistic, to network and make useful connections. Confidently snap up	Your power causes ripples, both positive and negative, you must remember that great power brings

opportunities to spread the word, progress ideas and projects. You are extremely shy, and you may even avoid social contact at all.

great responsibility. You must ensure that your intentions are good

You must learn to take responsibility and listen to guidance; you can be irresponsible. You must think before you act, and take full responsibility for what you do

You are here to learn to be responsible to others, your family, team, or group but in a balanced way. You can be too responsible and do too much. You are irresponsible if you feel undervalued, resentful, and exhausted.

You are here to be a visionary of the ideal, the dreamer of a utopian world. You want to create a better world with your ideals. You may be judgemental of yourself, other people, and the world for not meeting your unreachable ideals causing disappointment and nefarious counterintuitive actions.

You must develop and improve your social skills, focus on widening and deepening your relationships and make decisions subjectively. It is important that you deepen your relationships and connect 121

You may struggle to maintain long term close and romantic relationships.

You are here to learn to not use your ideals as a benchmark for your happiness. You often judge yourself and others for not hitting perfection, causing you great unhappiness

You must learn not to smother your loved ones or have expectations that can never be met. OR back away from wanting love because it hurts too badly. You need to balance your intense need for love for healthy relationships.

You are here to learn to reconcile your ideals with practical reality. You must accept that the universe or source energy is everything existing in perfect balance, to fully experience love, you must fully experience hate

You are here to learn to be intuitive and sensitive to the needs of others. You are here to be of service to others, the development of intuition will aid you in this journey

Your perfectionism can make you an over achiever due to self-judgement. You never meet your own standards.

You are here to learn to be a cooperative team player to get the job done as part of a cohesive team.

You must see the big picture and not get stuck in petty detail. You can often judge small imperfections and ruin or miss your successes.	You can be a disruptive, uncooperative drama queen.
You are here to learn to be a nurturer, compassionate caring and giving, especially to those that are vulnerable or struggling within your close relationships, your community, and the wider world. When low, you can be incredibly neglectful.	You must develop the assertiveness to demand boundaries to being overworked, walked all over, taken advantage of, and/or taken for granted. You must not be a "shape shifter" who changes who you are in order to please others or keep the peace. Be you and consider yourself too.
You are here to develop boundaries to ensure your mental and physical health. You do a lot for others, sometimes too much, which can make you feel undervalued, unappreciated, resentful, and ill with exhaustion.	You are here to serve the world, help the team, the task and be dependable. You can always be relied upon to keep the cogs turning behind the scenes
You are here to develop your social skills and be a team player. You must break through low self-esteem to be talkative, fun loving and relaxed around others	You are here to be the tactful mediator of the team/group/family, helping to resolve conflicts fairly and for the good of everyone involved. You hate conflict and often run and hide until it is over
You are here to create a stable, nurturing, tranquil home to maintain your security and well-being. Then nurture a family in an environment of stability and love	You are here to learn to plan the next steps after channelling your message or idea & build a team to achieve it. The energy of the 11/2 needs to be the nurturer of ideas and a builder of teams
You are here to learn to be responsible and do good for those you care for. People naturally put you in positions of responsibility, but you often resent always being the	You must learn to give yourself your own kudos. Oftentimes you judge yourself on what everyone else says or thinks about you. You need to develop your internal compass and turn inward for validation, do what

'responsible one.'	YOU think you should do
You are here to develop your musical creative artistry and/or your artistic and aesthetic potential. You could nurture others with your musical potential and your eye for colour and aesthetics.	

Life Path Master 33/6 with Birthday Master 22/4

Life Path Master 33/6 (90% Focus)	Birthday Master 22/4 (10% Focus)
You are an old soul, here to spiritually channel, communicate & manifest ideas to raise the world's vibration. You are here to learn to be a master communicator, to teach and/or entertain, to emotionally nurture and heal others in a big way. You must learn to handle the energy of this big responsibility to your audience. You can be too responsible and do too much.	You are an old soul, as spiritual as you are practical, here to channel and then manifest ideas in reality to build world safety, stability, and security. You must learn to handle the master builder energy and focus it to manifestation. You have a big responsibility to the team and the world to build structures (buildings, concepts, body, mind, spirit, businesses, organisations, even an empire for the purpose of world stability and security
You are here to learn to express yourself verbally to inspire, inform and delight. You may struggle in some way verbally, chronic shyness, speech delay, stutter, language barriers or struggling to find the words	You must develop and improve your social skills, focus on widening and deepening your relationships to assist you to manifest your big ideas. It is important that you learn to deepen your relationships and connect 121, you cannot do this alone!
You are here to learn to express yourself creatively to inspire, inform and delight. You may procrastinate and thus struggle to finish creative projects, due to lack of self-belief	You must learn to have balanced, healthy relationships with others that are part of your sense of security. You must learn not to smother your loved ones and your team or have expectations that can never be met. OR Your big task in this lifetime may disrupt your love relationships. You may back away from wanting love because it hurts too badly or attacks

	your sense of security
You must learn to be dynamic, take risks and be confident to enjoy the attention and limelight of an audience. You can be shy, under confident and feel unable to take risks.	You are here to learn to listen to and follow your intuition. Intuition is needed for you to be sensitive to the needs of others. You are here to be of service to change the world, the development of intuition will aid you in this journey
You need to develop as an entrepreneur who is able to promote, network and make money creatively.	You are here to learn to be a cooperative team player to get the job done as part of a cohesive team. You may fail to communicate effectively with others. You can be a hard-headed and high handed at times.
You are here to learn to express your emotions positively. You can be extremely sensitive to criticism and a sponge for other people's emotions, causing you to express emotions negatively	You must develop the assertiveness to demand boundaries to being overworked, walked all over, taken advantage of, and/or taken for granted. You must also develop your ability to respect other people's boundaries and not be high handed.
You are here to develop the habit of acting, be a doer and executer of ideas. When low, you can struggle with apathy, laziness and lack of focus and direction	You are here to be of service to the world, the leader, the team, the task and be dependable. You can always be counted upon to keep the cogs turning behind the scenes
You are here to learn to be social, talkative, the life of the party and bringer of fun & positivity. You need to be the networker, communicating an emotional message. You can be quiet and struggle to speak	You are extremely sensitive, and you hate and run away from conflict. But you are here to learn to be a tactful mediator, helping to resolve conflicts fairly and for the good of the team/family/group

You must develop independence; that becomes interdependence. the 3 energy likes to be looked after and can be prone to avoiding work or anything needing routine and commitment.	You are here to learn to stay focused and plan the next steps after you have channelled a new idea & build a team to achieve it. The energy of the 22 needs to be the nurturer, the builder of ideas and teams.
You are here to be opportunistic, to network and make useful connections. Confidently snap up opportunities to spread the word, progress ideas and projects. You are extremely shy, and you may even avoid social contact at all.	You must learn to give yourself your own kudos. Oftentimes you judge yourself on what everyone else says or thinks about you. You need to develop your internal compass and turn inward for validation, do what you think you should do
You must learn to take responsibility and listen to guidance; you can be irresponsible. You must think before you act, and take full responsibility for what you do	You are here to learn to commit to a person and/or place, so that you can put down roots and dig the foundations for security. You can be uncommitted and therefore unable to build stability and security
You are here to be a visionary of the ideal, the dreamer of a utopian world. You want to create a better world with your ideals. You may be judgemental of yourself, other people, and the world for not meeting your unreachable ideals causing disappointment and nefarious counterintuitive actions.	You are here to learn to set and achieve goals to take you on your journey towards inner and outer stability and security. Foundations, structures, families, and business empires are built 1 goal at a time.
You are here to learn to not use your ideals as a benchmark for your happiness. You often judge yourself and others for not hitting perfection, causing you great unhappiness	You are here to learn to plan, create a process and/or procedure to ensure the achievement of your goals and bring strength and stability to dynamic ideas. You can be directionless, lazy and block your own progression.
You are here to learn to reconcile your ideals with practical reality.	You are here to develop deep meticulous focus on achieving

You must accept that the universe or source energy is everything existing in perfect balance, to fully experience love, you must fully experience hate

stability, like a stable home, business or income and building your inner security. You can be scattered and miss steps in your impatience.

Your perfectionism can make you an over achiever due to self-judgement. You never meet your own standards. You must see the big picture and not get stuck in petty detail. You can often judge small imperfections and ruin or miss your successes.

You are here to learn to be detail orientated, analytical, organised, and accurate to ensure your plans and processes are watertight. You can be disorganised, flaky and miss steps in your plan

You are here to learn to be a nurturer, compassionate caring and giving, especially to those that are vulnerable or struggling within your close relationships, your community, and the wider world. When low, you can be incredibly neglectful.

Your master 22/4 Birthday means that you are an old soul and you have agreed to bring safety, stability, and security to the world. You innovate and build empires, organisations, and businesses. This involves hard work, detail focus, routine work, and tasks. You are here to develop a work ethic, to work hard and develop enjoyment of routine work and tasks

You are here to develop boundaries to ensure your mental and physical health. You do a lot for others, sometimes too much, which can make you feel undervalued, unappreciated, resentful, and ill with exhaustion.

You are here to develop patient perseverance, so that every step in the process towards your goals for your stable foundation are taken. You are prone to impatience and corner cutting.

You are here to develop your social skills and be a team player. You must break through low self-esteem to be talkative, fun loving and relaxed around others

You are here to develop determination and the perseverance to keep going past obstacles to achieve your goals. You are prone to giving up at the first hurdle.

You are here to create a stable, nurturing, tranquil home to

You are here to learn to come to terms with limitation — both the

maintain your security and well-being. Then nurture a family in an environment of stability and love	limitations that are externally imposed on you and the limitations that you impose upon yourself.
You are here to learn to be responsible and do good for those you care for. People naturally put you in positions of responsibility, but you often resent always being the 'responsible one.'	You are here to look at your wounded or problematic relationships and work through the feelings of lack and pain they have brought to you. All experiences have lessons embedded within them
You are here to develop your musical creative artistry and/or your artistic and aesthetic potential. You could nurture others with your musical potential and your eye for colour and aesthetics.	Avoid social isolation by socialising regularly in familiar groups and with likeminded friends.

This book covers the first and most important part of any Numerology reading, it clarifies a person's all important Life Purpose, why they are here, the tasks and challenges they need to develop and improve in this life time. My 2nd book will cover how a person's Life Purpose will be helped or hindered by their main talents. A person's main talents are in their 'Expression Number,' or some call it their 'Destiny Number.' The Expression number is calculated from a person's Birth Song, their FULL birth name, this encompasses a person's strongest innate talents and abilities in this incarnation. The task is to figure out how to use your Expression Number talent and other numbers in your 'Tool Box' to help you to achieve the tasks and difficulties in your Life Purpose.

Printed in Great Britain
by Amazon